JOKING ABOUT JIHAD

GILBERT RAMSAY
MOUTAZ ALKHEDER

Joking About Jihad

Comedy and Terror in the Arab World

HURST & COMPANY, LONDON

First published in the United Kingdom in 2020 by
C. Hurst & Co. (Publishers) Ltd.,
41 Great Russell Street, London, WC1B 3PL
© Gilbert Ramsay and Moutaz Alkheder, 2020
All rights reserved.
Printed in India.

The right of Gilbert Ramsay and Moutaz Alkheder to be identified as the
authors of this publication is asserted by them in accordance with the
Copyright, Designs and Patents Act, 1988.

Distributed in the United States, Canada and Latin America by
Oxford University Press, 198 Madison Avenue, New York, NY 10016,
United States of America.

A Cataloguing-in-Publication data record for this book
is available from the British Library.

ISBN: 9781787383166

www.hurstpublishers.com

CONTENTS

v

INTRODUCTION

As the title suggests, this book concerns 'joking about jihad'. To be specific, we do not mean jokes about jihad in the general Islamic sense,[1] but rather jokes about jihadi groups and the ideologies and movements they represent. Even more specifically, we are primarily concerned with all this in relation to the Arab world.

'Arab world' and 'Arab' are contested terms, however, we will not get embroiled in the complex and important debates around what they mean and whether they should be used at all. Our research was initially bounded more by language than by political or cultural geography. We started out writing a book primarily about material in the Arabic language. Since language is intrinsically intertwined with culture and identity, by extension, we ended up writing about the cultural zone in which that language predominates. We refer to this as the Arab world, though we do so without meaning to imply a monolithic Arab identity, or deny the distinct identities of minorities subsumed within it. Sometimes, when we wish to suggest that our observations might also apply to countries beyond this linguistic zone, we use another contested term: 'Middle East'. We use this in a colloquial sense, as it is in common usage in Arabic and English; it is an imperfect term, though, and we do not propose to defend it.

For many, Arabs and non-Arabs alike, jihadis are a controversial subject for humour—people would rarely hesitate to say as much when we told them the subject of the book we were working on. The reasons for this opinion, however, tended to vary. People in the United Kingdom, where we both live, who do not have a close connection to

1

Islam or the Arab world, seem to view the topic as unacceptably sick. The mention of groups like the Islamic State or Al Qaeda, for example, immediately brings to mind beheading videos, the burning or drowning of people in cages, militants throwing queer people from buildings and, perhaps most insidiously, the systematic genocide and enslavement of the Yazidi people. It hardly seems like a viable topic for joking—certainly not so close to the events themselves.

Arabs—including those we spoke to or whose opinions we solicited in researching this book—share these misgivings to an extent. However, at the risk of a huge generalisation, many of them have been forced to develop thick skins. They have grown inured to news of atrocities and developed a black sense of humour accordingly. Their objections to a text on 'joking about jihad', therefore, tended to be different. Why, of all the brutal actors one might focus on, are we interested in singling out Sunni extremists who—appalling though they might be—are hardly alone in their crimes? What about the Shia and radical pro-regime death squads of the Syrian and Iraqi governments? What about the Saudi Arabian and Emirati regimes and their bombardment of Yemen? What about the Sisi regime's savage repression of domestic opponents in Egypt, including the non-violent, democratically elected Islamist opposition in 2013. What about Iran and its proxy fighters? What about the civilian casualties of Western bombs? Or Russian bombs? What about Israel?

These points have a disquieting force. The singling out of Sunni extremist groups as the global terrorism threat derives from the narrow concerns of the West's War on Terror. Arguably rooted in the perception of Islam and Muslims as a savage people in need of civilising at gunpoint, it has produced a discourse eagerly seized upon by Islamophobic extremists, as well as by states like Russia, China and Myanmar, which have used the language of counterterrorism as a cover for the systematic persecution of Muslim minorities.

However, the objection that satire should not focus exclusively on Sunni jihadis could be seen as an example of 'whataboutery'—the attempt not to broaden debate, but simply avoid it. The fact of the matter is that while there has always been plenty of Arabic satire directed against corrupt authoritarian regimes, Western imperialists and the Zionist enemy, until relatively recently, the subject of militant

INTRODUCTION

Islamism has been a no-go area for humourists. One reason for this is, on the face of it, fairly obvious. In all Arabic-speaking countries, presenting the rituals, practices and beliefs related to Islam in a humorous light—even when the fun is being poked at the actors politicising and manipulating them—is extremely difficult. And yet, cultural objections to the comedic treatment of religion, though real and important, are, as we shall show, more complex than they appear at first glance. On the other hand, there is the less obvious, but perhaps more formidable difficulty: the reluctance of Arab intellectuals, many of whom see themselves as the undisputed champions of modernity, to recognise that Islamists can represent anything other than an unsophisticated rabble.

While this book will look at some earlier examples, it was not until the advances made by Islamists following the Arab Spring, and especially the Syrian Civil War and the rise of the Islamic State, that it become routine for comedy across the Arab world to feature material focusing on the subject matter of so-called Daeshis and other jihadis. Though reluctantly and tentatively, this material, and the comedians and comedy writers responsible for creating it, crossed a cultural rubicon, exposing Arabic-speaking media audiences to the possibility that things hitherto regarded as unspeakable or even sacrosanct could, at least under certain circumstances, be the object of mirth.

In this book, we have two main aims. Our larger task is to examine the emergence of 'joking about jihad' in Arabic-language comedy. We will try to situate this within the broader theoretical context of humour as it relates to violence and political change, and the cultural context of the jokes and joking practices not only of the secularist opponents of militant Islamism, but also of jihadis and other Islamists. In the tradition of sociological and folkloric research into the subject of humour, we will be concerned with how comedies and more informal jokes— those associated with struggles between Islamists and their opponents—can be held up to illuminate underlying fears and tensions experienced by the people living through these upheavals.

At the same time, we also maintain a narrower purpose; one which reflects our intentions when we set out to research and write this book. While we did not formally begin writing this text until mid-2017, with hindsight, its genesis dates back to a chance conversation we had almost exactly two years earlier. Some interviews conducted in connection with Gilbert's research in Jordan in 2016 also have gone into the book. The significance here being that the initial impetus came when IS and its self-declared caliphate was very much at the height of its power and when anti-IS satire was also, accordingly, at its high-water mark. At this point, finding appropriate scholarly distance was not always easy, and fighting the movement's ideological appeal seemed like a noble cause.

When we found that we shared an interest in contemporary Arabic humour and satire, the idea of researching the capacity of humour to combat IS seemed to have a simple and immediate force. Both of us, of course, should have known better than to imagine that humour could be a panacea against radicalisation. And yet, it is in the nature of humour itself to make at least a temporary optimist of even the most hardened cynic. For all our acute awareness of the horrors unfolding in the Arab world in general, particularly in Moutaz's homeland of Syria, and as much as we appreciated the profound complexity of the political currents that had led to this point, we still felt that humour, deployed in the right way, might have the ability to cut through the bombastic posturing of the warring parties, among them IS, whose overblown self-image and distinctive iconography seemed to be an irresistible target for humorous subversion.

At this time, policymakers worldwide were scrambling to find effective approaches for countering the appeal of the IS brand of Islamist extremism. Where, we wondered, were the in-depth studies examining the existing attempts of Arabs and Muslims to do just this? Surely if anyone knew how to mount a really effective critique of these movements, it would be the writers and creatives who were themselves immersed in the culture that these Islamists claimed to represent. By identifying the outstanding examples of Arabic comedy aimed at Islamist extremists, and scrutinising them to ascertain the root of their effectiveness, we imagined that we might hit upon some sort of magical formula for the perfect anti-jihadi joke. The joke that would somehow bring home to one and all the absurdity already inherent in these groups' juxtaposition of violent excess and small-minded puritanism.

What we imagined, then, was that our book would celebrate the bold humourists in the Muslim and, specifically, in the Arab world who

INTRODUCTION

were fighting jihadis, not in the way they want to be fought—the way they literally *dream* about being fought—with guns and bombs, with elite special forces and gleaming high-tech munitions, but with cleverly honed punch lines and perfectly timed slapstick. We wanted to find these brilliant pioneers of comedy, celebrate them and explain exactly why what they were doing was so brilliant.

While times have changed and we have become disabused of some of our initial idealism, the quest for the perfect anti-jihadi joke remains present within the pages of this book, partly as a serious research question, but also as a framing device. What is the present-day doctrine on how to 'deploy' humour against militant extremists? What can the findings of decades of scholarly humour research tell us about what is and isn't likely to be effective? What can we learn from Arab comedians' first approaches to the cultural challenge of making Islamist extremism funny? Is there anything that ought to be learned from the example of humour, as used by fundamentalist Muslims and, in particular, by jihadis themselves? What can we take from the folk humour of ordinary people as it concerns the subject of jihadism and Islamist militancy?

In short, two key sets of research questions intertwine, dialogue and, occasionally, jostle within the pages of this book. On the one hand, we want to know: *What is an effective way of joking about jihadis? What are the key pitfalls and sensitivities? What can we learn about this from a close reading of actual jokes on the subject by comedians and ordinary speakers of Arabic?*

At the same time, we are concerned with exploring: *How are the subjects of jihadism and Islamism treated humorously in the contemporary Arab world—including by jihadis and Islamists themselves? And in what ways does joking in this domain appear to illustrate the underlying beliefs and concerns of those making the jokes?*

Our exploration of these two themes unfolds as follows. In chapter 1, 'Bono Loses the Plot', we explore the possibilities of joking about jihad primarily from the point of view of global counterextremism practitioners, for whom humour represents a subset of what is now often called the 'counternarrative' (a euphemism for a subset of propaganda). As we shall see, the idea of undermining the appeal of terrorist groups by means of laughter, mockery and comedy is actually taken seriously by governments and other interested parties in the present day, and the merits and demerits of the approach have been debated by strategic analysts, specialist think tanks and, to a more limited extent, scholars. Comedy has some obvious apparent merits: it avoids glorifying terrorists and stirring up unhelpful moral panics since, by definition, it refuses to take them seriously. It offers a way to present important information in an attractive form that may be more likely to win attention, and, for that reason, is also more likely to seep into culture, becoming 'viral' content that people share and make their own. And yet it has its downsides as well—many of which are simply the obverse of these presumed advantages: it risks creating humiliation and offence, something that is exacerbated by the tendency of jokes to acquire a life of their own and spiral out of control.

Chapter 2, 'Laughter and Slaughter', aims to add theoretical depth to these ideas by drawing on the scholarly literature on humour as it relates to persuasion, political change and political violence. Despite the confidence placed in it by commercial advertisers and, it seems, strategic communications specialists, the scientific evidence for the persuasive power of humour seems to be surprisingly equivocal and elusive. But the reasons for the faith many place in the power of humour run deeper than instrumental factors. Humour—especially, it could be argued, in the post-Enlightenment West—has acquired positive associations with liberty, civility and equality. In the present day, such convictions have been given expression in phenomena such as 'laughtivism'—civil resistance by means of humorous stunts. But is this vision of humour really justified? And can it be reconciled with much darker manifestations of laughter and merriment which, though often overlooked, cannot be ignored? We argue that only by staring the uncomfortable relationship between laughter and slaughter full in the face is it possible to begin to identify and disentangle the mechanisms that could make humour an effective tool for countering violence, hatred and oppression. Ultimately, by tracing the roots of humour, we isolate four ideal type mechanisms that are relevant to the intersection of humour and conflict which we term: *pillory*, *travesty, raillery* and *coxcombry*.

Chapter 3, 'Let Him Wear it Himself', examines the first Arabic comedies to specifically lampoon Islamists. Arabs and Muslims have been joking at the expense of the more puritanical strains within their religion since the earliest days of Islam; and yet modern political Islam, despite being a significant political force since the 1930s, was for decades largely ignored by creative media in the Arab world. Things first began to change in Egypt in the 1990s, after a decade in which Islamism began to represent an increasingly educated, middle-class phenomenon, posing a cultural and even physical threat to the existing intelligentsia. Then, a decade later, Saudi media would take a leading role, especially with the comedy series *Tash Ma Tash*. Focusing on detailed analyses of the important Egyptian film *The Terrorist* (1994) and on *Tash Ma Tash* (*You Either Get it or You Don't*), we examine how writers working within the constraints of traditional comedy forms set about the task of making Islamist militancy laughable. Despite being innovative in their subject matter, we note that both works—operating within the constraints of authoritarian political cultures—struggled to portray Islamists in a comic way, while upholding essentially conservative visions of society as the only real alternative to radicalisation.

Arab comedians who take on Islamists constantly risk falling foul of deep-seated taboos about mixing comedy and religion. But where do these taboos come from? Who are the clerics who help to enforce them? And is fundamentalist Islam really as implacably hostile to laughter as it seems? In chapter 4, we set out to provide a brief overview of attitudes to humour in Islam, focusing intentionally on the relatively conservative views put forward by popular Islamic scholars, often by means of the mass media or the internet. We find these are more nuanced than one might expect, with even the theologians who seem the dourest and the most hard-line often turning out to be adept comics in their own right—they do not always steer clear of the sacrosanct topics they may condemn others for poking fun at.

In chapter 5, we get to the heart of our subject, examining the proliferation of comedy aimed at jihadis that emerged in response to the shocking rise of IS. This diversity of material, coming from across the Middle East and involving a variety of old and new media, clearly established that, however sensitive the topic might be, jihadis were fair game for comic treatment. And yet, as we argue, much of the material itself fell back on relatively unimaginative and simplistic stereotypes. Only a handful of examples moved beyond the notion of them as uneducated buffoons or dim-witted ogres, offering a more nuanced satire of the chaos that seemed poised to consume the region.

JOKING ABOUT JIHAD

In chapter 6, we move beyond the cartoonish image of jihadi Salafis by focusing on their own traditions of joking and laughter. Jihadi joking does little to soften their image as savage militants—if anything, it underscores their callous disregard for anyone who does not share their beliefs. But is does also show a capacity for joy, exuberance and, perhaps most importantly, self-awareness. By showing how jihadis in the Syrian conflict and beyond made active use of humorous anecdotes and jokes (so-called *tara'if*) to increase the attractiveness of their way of life and ridicule their sectarian opponents, we demonstrate that any humour intended to undercut this movement will have to take into account that their opponent has more sophistication and capacity for self-reflection than is often admitted. At the same time, jihadi jokes, when carefully read, may also reveal the subtle fracture lines of self-doubt.

Chapter 7 moves beyond the realm of professional comedians to consider popular attitudes to joking about jihad. Drawing on existing data and our own survey of attitudes regarding the acceptability of joking about jihadi groups, we consider the complex and evolving attitudes to this question. We also examine the modern-day folk humour represented by memes and jokes shared online. What we find is further evidence of an Arab world deeply polarised between liberal and conservative, secularist and Islamist, Sunni and Shia, in which humour often serves more to reinforce group boundaries than to actively probe the others' beliefs and attitudes.

Despite this seemingly dispiriting picture, there are some rays of hope. Recognising the polarised nature of the Arab world, some satirists have begun to make deliberate efforts to cut through this, striving to create more inclusive ways of using humour as a meeting point for angry people with very different viewpoints. Others have created material which draws on subtler and more complex readings of jihadis, even while lampooning them. Meanwhile, the emergence of humour by Islamist or formerly Islamist voices has created new juxtapositions and, paradoxically, new critiques of religious conservatism. The idea of precision-tooled joking as a perfect munition of the mind is—perhaps thankfully—probably not realistic. And yet even in an age in which polarisation seems to be increasingly entrenched and widespread, there are creative comedians in the Arab world who may be showing a way forward.

8

INTRODUCTION

A final word is also due about the process of researching this book. *Joking about Jihad* is unapologetically interdisciplinary. By professional affiliation, we are scholars of terrorism and political violence, within the wider context of the discipline of international relations. However, in researching this book, we took great pleasure in delving into the literatures of Arabic popular cultural studies, Islamic studies and humour studies—which is itself an inherently interdisciplinary field, incorporating insights from psychology, philosophy, history, linguistics, folklore, comparative literature and even evolutionary biology. Some may feel that we have been too broad in our approach, and naturally we have been forced by space constraints to omit or touch only fleetingly on enormous literatures and well-developed scholarly debates. We hope that our enthusiasm for the wealth of material we encountered comes across nonetheless.

Befitting the diversity of our approach, we also deployed a broad range of research methods. Interviews with around two dozen individuals, including comedians, policymakers, Arabic cultural critics and eyewitnesses to jihadi activities were an important source of information for this book. As noted above, some of these were conducted in 2016, when Gilbert was in Jordan researching counterextremism initiatives. Others took place in the UK, typically via Skype or its end-to-end encrypted equivalents, involving both the authors. A small number of further interviews were conducted on a brief trip to Egypt undertaken by Gilbert (and Shabana, his very patient wife) in 2018. Some interviewees were happy to be named while others preferred to remain anonymous, and several agreed to be interviewed only as general background. Interviews with comedians were semi-structured in nature. All were asked the same basic questions about how they began in comedy, about why they chose to make jokes about jihadis, about what they perceived to be the key obstacles and difficulties in doing so, about how they attempted to overcome these, about the limits they set for themselves, about their opinion of other Arab comedians engaging with the same topic and about what they believed the impact of their work to be. Where—as they inevitably did—conversations naturally moved in particular directions, we did not prevent them from doing so. Other interviews were more variable, depending on the specific expertise of the individual concerned. In the interviews with comedians, we were, in the first instance, interested in understanding the individual's subjective opinions about their work. However, in practice we often learned biographical or circumstantial information which was at least as interesting. Conversely, interviews with policymakers were typically focused in the first instance on gathering data. We recognise that not all the information given in this way, due to its sensitivity, can be fully verified via other sources, and therefore ask the reader to exercise discretion.

We also rely heavily on critical analysis of media texts. To this end, Moutaz compiled what we believe to be (at the time of writing) an exhaustive collection of video material in Arabic which satirises jihadis. While some of this is the work of amateurs or internet-only creators, much of it turned out to be derived originally from commercial Arabic television and film. He also compiled large collections of visual and textual material from platforms such as Facebook, Twitter, Pastebin and various blogs and forums, and carried out an extensive search for examples of Arabic films—particularly but not exclusively Egyptian— and television series from around the Arab world that address themes relevant to our subject of research. He identified forty-two Arabic films and twenty-nine television series from between 1945 and 2017 that address themes either of Islamic religiosity or of terrorism. This is in addition to other media, including novels and plays, on which we also gathered data, albeit less comprehensively. Gilbert also attended a performance of the Jordanian counterextremist play *Terrorism at the Door*, and the question and answer session that followed.

Finally, in an attempt to gain some insight into what Arab audiences think about the acceptability of joking about jihad, we created an online survey, for which we gathered over six hundred responses. We discuss our findings from this in chapter 7.

We would like to extend our heartfelt thanks to all the people who trusted us with their knowledge, experience, insight and their time in helping us to make this book.

1

BONO LOSES THE PLOT

COMEDY AND COUNTERTERRORISM

> Don't laugh, but I think comedy should be deployed. Because if you look at National Socialism and Daesh, we've seen this before. They've got all the signs. It's show business. The first people that Adolf Hitler threw out of Germany were the Dadaists and the Surrealists. It's like, you speak violence. You speak their language. But you laugh at them when they're goose-stepping down the street. And it takes away their power. So I'm suggesting that the Senate send in Amy Schumer and Chris Rock and Sacha Baron-Cohen.[1]

When Bono offered this advice to the United States Senate's Appropriations Committee on how best to fight terrorism during a lengthy, videoed, discussion to which he had been originally invited to talk about his philanthropic work with refugees, his comments promptly went viral. If the singer hoped to inspire ridicule, he succeeded. Unfortunately, most of this was directed not at Daesh, but at him. The onslaught did, at least, come from an admirably balanced cross section of the media. In a session of *Red Eye*, Fox News' Stewart Varney seized on it as a typical example of clueless, wishy-washy liberalism,[2] while comedian Rob LeDonne, writing in British left-leaning newspaper the *Guardian*, said that he had 'lost the plot'.[3]

Whether or not Bono's idea was really as terrible as it seemed, it was, at the very least, not as original as he apparently thought. In fact, as Senator Jeanne Shaheen, who was chairing the House committee, was swift to point out (so swift that she makes it into the clip itself), far from being a crazy, far-out fantasy, the use of comedy to fight the Islamic State was 'one of things we're looking at'. Unbeknownst to both Bono and, apparently, his detractors, 'weaponised' humour was already an established part of a secret, and sometimes not-so-secret, war being conducted against the group, as it had been against other jihadi groups before it.

Could it be, then, that the U2 frontman was onto something after all? Is laughing at jihadis really a viable counterterrorism policy? And what can we learn from the attempts that have so far been made to 'deploy' comedy to this purpose?

When, in response to the 9/11 attacks, then President George W. Bush declared a 'War on Terror', strategists were quick to argue that one important dimension of this new war was what was often referred to as a 'war of ideas'.[4] The situation, as these analysts saw it, was para-doxical. The United States was the richest, the most militarily powerful and, one could convincingly argue, the most culturally influential coun-try that had ever existed.[5] All over the world people watched its films and television programmes. All over the world, people dressed like Americans, in American brands, or imitations of it. Its news media set the template for what news ought to look like. Its computer program-mers ensured that the underlying code of the internet was written in what was, essentially, English. In places thousands of miles from Washington or New York or Los Angeles, people dreamed of changing their lives by acquiring the gloss of American-ness that would come with attending an American educational institution. Indeed, it was the commonality of this very practice that had made the attacks on the World Trade Centre possible in the first place.[6]

And yet, when it came to Al Qaeda's apparently compelling and increasingly well-executed media content, it seemed to those charged with tackling the organisation cum network cum movement cum ideol-ogy (its classification is another area of lively debate),[7] that they found themselves in the unfamiliar and uncomfortable position of being behind the curve. As Richard Holbrooke, then US ambassador to the United Nations wanted to know, 'how can a man in a cave out-commu-nicate the world's leading communications society?'[8] Over time, the soldiers and civil servants charged with counteracting jihadi propaganda developed the self-perception that they were fighting a 'guerrilla war'[9] against an opponent who, as the perennial complaint ran, was 'beating us at our own game'.[10]

One such complainant was J. Michael Waller. Describing himself as a 'scholar-practitioner in public diplomacy, political warfare, psychological operations and information operations in support of US foreign and military policy',[11] Waller's CV, which includes undercover stints helping to train the controversial right-wing Contras militia in Nicaragua as well as 'Afghan resistance fighters against the Soviet Army', might belong to a character in a Tom Clancy novel. Convinced that his experience in political subversion could be used to powerful effect in America's new conflict, in 2007 he published a work of information warfare strategy with the seemingly paradoxical title: *Fighting the War of Ideas Like a Real War*.[12]

Essentially, Waller's view was that the US wasn't selling itself hard enough. He called for an 'unashamedly offensive strategy' that would aim to act as an 'accelerant' to the glacial efforts of public diplomacy.[13] Like a platoon of marines on a search and destroy mission in some hostile third-world jungle, his strategy proposed to 'isolate and marginalize the enemy and its allies', then to 'confront their ideology of tyranny and hate'. Meanwhile, the silent majority of ordinary decent 'moderates' would be seduced by the irresistible charm of 'America's belief in freedom, justice, opportunity and respect for all'.

Humour, as a chapter of Waller's monograph insists, had a crucial role to play in all this. Among its many virtues, he argued that it had the capacity to 'raise morale at home', 'strip the enemy of his mystique', 'erode the enemy's claim to justice', deprive him of 'his ability to terrorize' and eliminate 'his image of invincibility'.[14] Most fundamentally, however, ridicule was to be regarded as a 'secret weapon that's worse than death'—a quotation he claimed to have drawn from a speech by Osama bin Laden.[15] The terrorists, Waller insisted, craved one thing more than anything—literally more than life itself: to be taken seriously. By excessively 'demonizing' them, US rhetoric was, ironically, doing just this. It gave them the notoriety that they craved. Ridicule, or refusing to take them seriously, was seen as the answer to this problem.

While his argument was developed in unusual detail, Waller was not alone in making this point. In July 2010, political scientist Daniel Byman, the co-author of the 9/11 Commission Report, among other achievements, and Christine Fair, another leading security scholar, published an article in *Atlantic* magazine under the title 'The Case for Calling them Nitwits'. Here, they opined: 'Our terrorist enemies trade on the perception that they're well trained and religiously devout, but in fact, many are fools and perverts who are far less organized and sophisticated than we imagine'.[16]

In contrast to their formidable image, Byman and Fair noted that there were numerous examples of incompetent terrorists who bungled their operations, sometimes with fatal consequences for themselves. They also pointed out that 'many laptops seized from the Taliban and Al-Qaeda are loaded with smut'. While US intelligence analysts, selflessly responding to the call of duty, had 'devoted considerable time to poring over the terrorists' favoured websites, searching for hidden messages', they had been forced to come to the conclusion that 'some of these guys are just perverts'.

In the same year, Jarret Brachman, the director of research at Westpoint training college at the time and renowned for his enthusiastic online pursuit of jihadis, was surprised to encounter a video message from Al Qaeda's then second in command, Ayman al-Zawahiri, in which his own work was specifically singled out for ridicule. As Brachman recalled the event:

It wasn't the first time one of our West Point reports—a series of publicly available papers on Al Qaeda's strategy and ideology—was referenced in an official Al Qaeda video. It was, however, the first time the video was *funny*. 'Do they think they can have enormous budgets', Zawahiri deadpanned, 'then have me come along and correct their mistakes for free?'[17]

Deadpan is the right word. Zawahiri's delivery in the interview in question is decidedly straight-faced, even grumpy, as he works through study after study by the US military academy, pointing out what are (to him, at least) schoolboy errors in Islamic history and theology, as well as in his own personal biography. But it is hard to disagree with Brachman's overall assessment. In the repartee between Zawahiri, in the role of the curmudgeonly scholar, and his interviewer for Al Qaeda media outlet *Al-Sahab*, who doled out his own sarcastic assessments, there is more than a touch of sarcasm.[18]

In any case, whether sarcasm was intended or not, the video was, on Brachman's account, a wake-up call to the potential value of humour. Online, he took to baiting the armchair jihad enthusiasts he henceforth dubbed 'jihobbyists', referring to them as 'orcs' and claiming that a particular jihadi writer lived in his mother's basement.[19] (Fighting fire with fire in this war of words, jihobbyist trolls—to the authors' recollection, since this moment of counterterrorism history has sadly disappeared from the internet—edited Brachman's head into a Lord of the Rings video, dubbing him 'Ferret Crotchman'.)

Two years on, the military value of humour was explored once again, this time by a team of authors writing in the journal *Perspectives on Terrorism*. Drawing, in part, on work done for the US Navy-funded research project 'Identifying and Countering Extremist Narratives', Goodall, Cheong, Fleischer and Corman reiterated the idea that the US was engaged on the losing side in a 'war of narratives'. As the authors argued:

> Efforts at countering that narrative [i.e. of jihadi-Salafism] have been met with mixed success. One tool of countering these narratives … is that of employing ridicule in an offensive capacity (no pun intended).[20]

Differing somewhat from the approach of the other authors just mentioned, the overall thrust of the argument in this paper depends less on the power of humour to trivialise and belittle, and more on its presumed ability to 'disrupt the narrative landscape'. Drawing on the analogy of wartime rumours as 'narrative IEDs', whose tendency to spread and cause reputational damage to one actor or another is highly unpredictable and has nothing to do with their objective reliability, it reasoned that ridicule might be able to reach where more serious and fact-based communications could not.

All of the examples cited thus far are from American analysts, speaking primarily about things the US might do. Increasingly, however, counter violent extremism has become a global affair, taken over by an alliance of states together with powerful private concerns and a complex thicket of NGOs, think tanks and small, specialist start-ups. These seek to apply expertise in creative media, communications and information technology to the problem of how best to undermine the appeal of jihadi groups in the Islamic world and beyond. This process has been further accelerated in recent years with the 2014 formation of the Global Coalition Against Daesh, which, at the time of writing, comprises seventy nine countries aiming, among other things, to 'coalesce strategic communications' in order (using a characteristically spatial metaphor) to 'contest the information space in which Daesh operates'.[21]

With the globalisation and professionalisation of what is commonly shortened to CVE, the place of humour within the arsenal of influence operations seemed to have become solidified. For example, Quilliam, a prominent British think tank founded by former members of the Islamist group *Hizb al-Tahrir*, insisted in its report *Jihad Trending* that 'humour can also be a powerful tool and comic ridicule, within limits can be used to focus attention on the absurd and anachronistic nature of extremist discourse and activity'.[22] Meanwhile the Hedayah Institute, an Abu Dhabi-based think tank, classified 'humorous and sarcastic narratives' as one of its key varieties of 'resonant content'.[23]

The Institute for Strategic Dialogue—a major player due to its status as curator of the Google-backed 'Against Violent Extremism' network, among other things—goes further, offering specific insights into what it sees as humour's role. In its official recommendations to the European Commission, the institute suggests that; 'humour and satire can be effective' when used to 'de-glamourise the rebellious appeal of extremist groups' or 'demystify extremist narratives subtly. Its views do, however, contain a note of ambivalence. It warns that 'not everyone will find the same things funny'.[24] Moreover, in seemingly direct contradiction to those who might celebrate humour's ability to spread organically, it also insists (in a different recommendation) that 'going viral is not the aim. Going viral implies untargeted and unpredictable.' Clearly 'narrative IEDs' are not something the ISD would endorse.

Other experts operating in the same policy space would not necessarily agree, however, with this suspicion of virality. An often-referenced study by British think tank Demos set out to examine actual examples of anti-jihadi 'counterspeech' which were being spontaneously shared by Facebook users in six countries: the UK, France, Morocco, Tunisia, Indonesia and India. The report found that: 'Humorous counterspeech pages and content received consistently high levels of engagement from Facebook users across each of the countries', a finding which was prominently reported in the media. Less attention, we should perhaps point out, was given to the fact that comedy was dominant only in the UK, France and India. In the Muslim-majority countries, people seemingly preferred counterspeech based on religious arguments.[25]

With the partial exception of scholars specialising in counterterrorism and US national security, it may be observed that much of the discussion on the role of humour in counterextremism has taken place outside of strictly academic contexts. It is probably fair to say that mainstream scholarship in the social sciences and humanities has tended to see the area as suspect—haunted by fears of being seen as 'embedded' in militaristic projects and of the US military's attempts to use anthropological and other cultural expertise for the purpose of 'human terrain mapping'. With the emergence of IS between 2014 and 2016, however, this began to change, albeit modestly, as a small but diverse group of scholars began to add their voices to the discussion.

Media scholar Ahmed al-Rawi, for example, has published an academic paper surveying anti-IS humour in Arabic, which, he argues, should be understood through the framework of 'cultural resistance'. Anna Johansson (whose work we shall consider below) has analysed the quirky ISISchan meme as 'challenging stereotypical representations of femininity in the War on Terror'. In 2017, two particularly relevant and thought-provoking papers were published by Arabist Nathaniel Greenberg[26] and Arabic media specialist Marwan Kraidy.[27] The papers resemble one another quite closely both in content and in their essential arguments. Both devote particular attention to the Iraqi series *Dawlat al-Khurafa* (The Mythical State—Kraidy translates this as Apocryphal State). Both seek to juxtapose their discussion of the potential of anti-IS humour in an analysis of the aesthetics of IS terror. The two papers do, however, draw on different theoretical and conceptual reference points. Greenberg favours Roland Barthes and Gilles Deleuze in arguing that the key to understanding IS is in the way it uses the infinitely reproducible properties of digital media to sustain the promulgation of factually irrefutable myths. Kraidy, on the other hand, draws on Guy Debord's notion of the society of the spectacle, insisting that IS functions propagandistically by creating, through media saturation, a surrogate reality in the minds of its viewers. For Greenberg, the potential power of satire against this arises precisely from the fact that, like the IS promulgated myths themselves, it does not rely on factual truth, but instead tackles IS myths at the level of their real power-source: aesthetics. Kraidy, on the other hand, tenuously expresses the hope that shows like *Dawlat al-Khurafa*, through the satirical device of 'doubling', or holding up a mirror to truth, may be able to create a 'counter-spectacle' capable of fracturing and dispersing the great media illusion.

But if comedy now seems to be accepted, though often with some reservations, as a regular part of the tool kit by global counterextrem-ism practitioners and some less predictable voices, how does this trans-late in actual practice? Anti-IS comedy, Greenberg observes, has been 'seemingly spontaneous in some instances and tightly measured in others'. While detailed examination of specific examples of Arabic comedy belong to a later chapter, it is useful at this point to identify a number of different modes by which comic material is apparently pro-duced and promoted by Western-backed networks specifically for counterextremist purposes.

The most direct, most obvious and almost certainly least usual way in which counterextremism specialists use comedy and ridicule is by openly creating and disseminating their own material. Occasionally, this is actually done in-house, although the prevailing view seems to suggest that this is not advisable. Waller refers, tantalisingly, to a car-toon about inept jihadis created by the US military, which he describes as 'a cross between *Road Runner* and *The Three Stooges*'. Although the cartoon apparently 'tested well with Muslim audiences', it was ulti-mately spiked for reasons of 'political correctness'.[28]

A much better example—one which saw the light of day—was the US State Department's *Think Again Turn Away* campaign against IS recruitment. The campaign's flagship video, described as a 'parody' by the website News.au, relies on a sarcastic tone, spoofing the style of an IS recruitment video in order to present the organisation.[29] 'Come over', says the video, using a characteristically jihadi style of Arabic, 'for Syria is not for the Syrians, nor is Iraq for the Iraqis'. Meanwhile, English text 'advertises' the advantages of joining: 'You can learn useful new skills for the *Ummah*: blowing up mosques, crucifying and executing Muslims, plundering public resources … travel is inexpensive … because you won't need a return ticket!'

As various commentators pointed out at the time,[30] a major flaw of the 'bizarre' video was that, aside from its sarcastic spin, what it said diverged very little from what IS was already saying itself, quite openly. The shocking depictions of violence presented in the video were no different from the scenes already on proud display in IS propaganda, which was full of footage of blowing up (Shia) mosques and crucifying ('treacherous') Muslims.[31] The tag line 'Syria is not for the Syrians, nor is Iraq for the Iraqis' was pretty much the unique selling point of the IS caliphate, which purported to be a cosmopolitan society welcoming of all Muslims, whatever their origin. As for the final line—given that IS specifically promised that its recruits would either make new lives for themselves in an Islamic utopia or gain glorious martyrdom in the attempt, the video was practically doing IS's propaganda work for it. In other words, the video was explicitly premised on appealing to those who already rejected IS's core precepts, people who in no way needed to 'think again' and 'turn away'.

Ridicule is also, at times, used opportunistically by the Digital Outreach Team, a small organisation within the US State Department tasked with engaging with social media and internet forums using languages widely spoken in the Muslim world—primarily Arabic. The Digital Outreach Team jumps on stories that seem embarrassing to jihadis. At the time of writing, for example, they had recently publicised the defacement of an IS website by hackers, who replaced it with a picture of IS leader and self-proclaimed caliph Abu Bakr al-Baghdadi surrounded by scantily clad dancers.[32] Previously, during the revolution in Egypt, the team published a video that juxtaposed footage of peaceful demonstrators with speeches by Al Qaeda leader Ayman al-Zawahiri, insisting that political change would never come to Egypt except by violence. Short gifs and videos created and shared by the team sometimes involve comical, or at least satirical, cartoon images, though by and large it seems to be relatively cautious in its use of comic material.[33]

Other examples seem more opportunistic. Waller is particularly enamoured of a well-known episode in which US forces in Iraq got hold of the unedited footage from a propaganda video made by Al

Qaeda in the Arabian Peninsula. The version of the video distributed by the organisation showed its then leader, Abu Mus'ab al-Zarqawi, firing a Kalashnikov in a display of machismo. In the unedited version, however, Zarqawi seems to lack even basic knowledge about how to use the weapon. He holds it up and squeezes the trigger, expecting to produce an impressive burst of machine gun fire. Disappointingly, the gun fires a single shot. After fiddling with the weapon in vain, like a grandparent trying to turn their smartphone's speaker mode off, a nearby foot soldier is forced to come to his assistance. Later on, we see another Al Qaeda member take hold of the gun by its barrel and immediately pull his hand away, apparently unaware that it would be hot.[34] All in all, it was an irresistibly comical display of incompetence, and the US army accordingly called a press conference in the hope of bringing this supposed paragon of Sunni Arab resistance down a notch or two. As Waller observes, though, all didn't go entirely to plan. The Arab press fired back, asking if Zarqawi was really so useless, what did it say about the US military that they were unable to apprehend him?

Examples like this, in which agents of a state seek to destroy an enemy's credibility by revealing compromising material seem, at the very least, to blur the line between comedy and the less amusing practice of 'dirty tricks', which propagandists and intelligence services have long used to discredit opponents. Indeed, Byman and Fair's recommendation that jihadis' alleged predilection for pornography be incorporated into official messaging has since been realised in official propaganda created by the Global Coalition Against Daesh. At least in this instance, however, the information is delivered with a very straight face.[35]

And there are considerably darker examples than this. Goodall, Cheong, Fleischer and Corman point to the case of Noordin Mohammed Top, an alleged bomb maker for the group Al-Jama'a al-Islamiya, apparently as an example of the kind of counternarrative humour for which they are arguing. After he was killed in a police raid on his home in Jakarta, the Indonesian government circulated details of a forensic autopsy in which they claimed to have found 'an anomaly in Noordin's anus … indicat[ing] that somebody had sodomised him'. Following this, mocking and, of course, deeply homophobic videos began to circulate online, portraying the Islamist photoshopped into feminine clothes.[36]

The potential risks of ridicule backfiring have not gone unnoticed in debate within the CVE community. Anne Speckhard and Ardian Shajkovci, researchers who have played a prominent role in developing counternarrative materials based on videoed interviews of former IS members, note that 'confrontational counternarratives, which engage directly with a narrative to expose, correct or ridicule it, run the risk of being automatically rejected'. For their part, they insist on careful measures to ensure they never ridicule Islam nor treat '…subjects who are willing to tell their true stories of life inside ISIS with ridicule or any disrespect'.[37]

Counterextremism agencies commissioning bespoke material from professional comedy writers could comprise a more promising approach. A major exponent of this approach is Priyank Mathur. Possibly the person in the field of counterextremist comedy with the best credentials, Mathur has worked variously as a counterterrorism official for the Department of Homeland Security, with the advertising and PR giant Ogilvy Red and as a writer for *The Onion*.[38] His start-up Mythos Labs, described as a 'strategic communications and production company', works in a number of ways to produce 'comedic content that counters violent extremism'. (A second mission is to similarly take on 'gender stereotypes'.) One way it does this is by creating partnerships with comedians who produce relevant content which they host themselves. Mathur notes that, apart from being funny, there is the added advantage that the comedians Mythos works with are already 'social media influencers' in their own right. Another is to hold 'digital literacy and video production workshops in areas that are vulnerable to radicalization', with the aim of helping local comedians to become better at creating and distributing their own content. According to one comedian he has worked with, Mathur is 'doing the hardest job that exists in our industry, which is finding the people who have the money and getting them to meet the people who have the content'. To date, he has secured funding from sources, including the DHS, for projects in Bangladesh, India, Indonesia, Malaysia, Kosovo and the Philippines, as well as an unknown country in the Middle East.[39]

A notable example of the fruit of such partnerships is East India Comedy's *I Want to Quit ISIS*. Self-described as 'India's premier comedy collective', East India Comedy is a multi-religious group of stand-up comics who perform live and produce regular videos, including *Outrage*, a 'John Oliver-style straight-to-camera monologue dealing satirically with current affairs. When Mathur approached the group about the possibility of creating a sketch addressing terrorism, the group's response seems to have been warm from the outset, perhaps not least because they had previously concocted an idea for a sketch based on the concept of the 'corporatisation of ISIS'.

The slick, well-produced and gag-packed video is based on the premise of IS (or ISIL, or ISIS—the changing acronyms are a running joke in the video) as a typical Indian company (complete with a traditional *chai wallah* (tea seller), played by Muslim comedian and EIC member Kunal Rao), conducting the inevitably painful corporate ritual of the exit interview. In an office bedecked with inspirational posters depicting past successes such as 9/11, a disillusioned extremist tries to explain to his superior why he wants out, with ultimately fatal consequences.

While the central conceit works on one level because of its apparent incongruity, like most effective satire, much of the strength of the concept can be said to derive from the fact that it caricatures an underlying truth. Studies of Al Qaeda and IS have shown them to be organisations obsessed with bureaucracy and record keeping, to an extent that sometimes verges on the bizarre, such as keeping meticulous lists of members' identities, which all too easily fall into the hands of their enemies when they are forced to retreat from territory in a hurry.[40] For many IS members, life in the caliphate really has looked more like an episode of *The Office* than the fast-paced video games and action movies which their propaganda sought to imitate.

The relative transparency of the relationship between Mythos Labs and collectives such as East India Comedy is not, however, typical of the way in which counterextremism has come to operate. Instead, the model that has apparently come to predominate relies on state backers staying very discreetly, if not secretly, in the background. This, it would seem, is characteristic of the approach of the United Kingdom, which has been given a leading role in the propagandistic aspects of the Global Coalition Against Daesh's operations. The Research, Information and Communications Unit, the UK's secretive cross-departmental unit charged with counterterrorist communications, apparently understands its role primarily as 'help[ing] to support counter narrative products for civil society groups and local partners already interested in helping to campaign against radicalization'.[41] This frames the activities of the unit in passive terms. 'Help', however, can imply a spectrum of facilitative relationships. Sometimes support for 'grass-roots' counterextremism initiatives means the provision of training or equipment. In others, it can extend as far as providing monthly stipends, in return for which counterextremism content producers must submit to regular evaluations by government handlers who vet the appropriateness of their content.[42] This does not mean that those in receipt of such assistance are not 'already interested', but it does invite a measure of scepticism as to how independent these influencers are once they have entered into such arrangements.

Indeed, investigative reporting has, in some instances, revealed specific links between ostensibly independent campaigns against Islamist radicalisation (especially in relation to IS) and state agents. For example, investigations by Ben Hayes and Asim Qureishi for *OpenDemocracy* and journalists writing for the *Guardian* have revealed numerous campaigns—not all of which have an obviously anti-jihadi emphasis—that have been used by RICU as vehicles for the targeted delivery of counternarrative messages. In one particularly controversial case, Help for Syria, a humanitarian campaign soliciting donations for victims of the civil war, was apparently used as a front by PR company Breakthrough Media to target thousands of students with anti-IS material.[43]

Such reporting has made it possible to identify a handful of examples of known front campaigns such as these which have made use of comedic talent. For example, online searches for IS content often turn up the website of the British state-backed initiative 'Open your eyes, ISIS lies'. This campaign presents short videos of influential Muslims expressing their opposition to IS, among them British-Somali comedian Prince Abdi and American-Iranian Baba Ali. (It is worth stressing here that there is no reason to think that the actual comedy routines of these artists have in any way been influenced by this project.)[44] There are also examples of cartoons created specifically to try and counter the potential appeal of jihadis. These include the 'urban' looking AbdullahX, and his approximate American equivalent 'Average Muhammad'. While the artistic style gives the faint impression of an attempted comic framing, these are not comedy—at least not intentionally.

Nevertheless, it would seem that counterextremism initiatives along these lines have also included the cultivation of comedy material. Interviewed specifically on the subject of the use of comedy by British and Global Coalition Against Daesh counterextremism initiatives, a former British civil servant who had occupied a senior position helping to formulate counterideological operations against IS described to us a contest between different members of the coalition racing to snap up credible existing platforms, 'whether that be a blog, or a Twitter page, or a video or just some kids who've got their own YouTube channels then try to find the untapped talent that hasn't been discovered yet by all the other governments'.[45]

It is unlikely that this online talent hunt was the only way in which networks such as the Global Coalition Against Daesh sought to promote counter violent extremism. The West's wealthy Arab allies, such as Saudi Arabia and the United Arab Emirates, have become increasingly committed supporters of the CVE agenda, and this has extended to increasingly overt anti-jihadi material airing on Arab media channels controlled by these states—a point we will pick up on in chapter 5.[46] On the other hand, in poorer countries which are recipients of Western aid money, Jordan and Iraq being notable examples, there are numerous Western-funded programmes aimed at countering or researching CVE. Allegedly (drawing on non-attributable conversations with individuals who claimed to be directly involved in such processes), this includes substantial resources devoted to shaping and influencing domestic media programming.[47]

Given the existence of this modus operandi, it is possible to surmise that a good deal of ostensibly independent comic material dealing with IS could well be in receipt of direct or indirect support from a state sponsor. Certainly, there are examples of somewhat mysterious videos and other materials lampooning jihadis, about which it is tempting to speculate. In this book, however, we generally seek to resist this temptation except in cases where the political affiliation and aim of the comedy is already well known. Particularly in the Arab world, accusations of being in the pay of foreign powers are extremely dangerous, and even with sound evidence, it would often be irresponsible to draw such connections.

But such speculation also somewhat misses the point. It is a commonplace of critical media studies that mainstream media, even in pluralistic democratic countries, routinely end up reproducing narratives favourable to the agenda of those in power. As such, it is possible to identify material as fitting the general model of counternarrative without any need to assume that agents of the state are directly pulling the strings. Take, for example, the sketch 'Real Housewives of ISIS', which aired in 2017, allegedly to much controversy, on the sketch comedy programme *Revolting*.[48] While the spoof-reality TV sketch attracted criticism for what some saw as its insensitive treatment of radicalisation, sex-slavery and suicide bombing, others observed that the sketch actually contained a great deal of genuine detail about the actual experiences of women who had travelled to join the group.

While there is no reason to think that 'Real Housewives of ISIS' sprang from anything other than the minds of its writers, Heydon Prowse and Jolyon Rubenstein, it is nevertheless 'masterfully scripted to debunk every recruiting technique employed by ISIS to lure vulnerable women and girls to join their cause',[49] according to a review written by Matthew J. Daniels, a counter-radicalisation expert at Washington graduate school the Institute of World Politics. Incidentally, this is the same conservative-leaning institute where anti-terrorism comedy advocate and former undercover insurrectionist Waller also once taught.[50]

This might be contrasted with another controversial sketch featuring Dakota Johnson which aired in 2016 on *Saturday Night Live*. In the sketch, Johnson plays a young girl whose father frets about dropping her off with a group of heavily armed jihadis in a Toyota pickup. The sketch plays on the same basic subject and the same basic anxiety as the BBC one—the recruitment of national citizens to a terrorist group—but it does so without anything like the same level of detail or apparent didacticism.

In any case, it would appear that a key method of counternarrative in the digital age is the curation, or playlisting, of examples of pre-existing material. We understand that one proposal considered (but not taken forwards) by British government counterextremism experts was the creation of a 'hub' that would have provided a 'repository of satirical material' theorised to be effective at undermining the 'corporate pomposity' regarded (by those proposing the initiative) as a key feature of IS propaganda.[51] While this particular project may not have seen the light of day in this form, there are certainly others that appear to resemble it. Moonshot CVE, a counterextremism communications company based in London, specialises in maintaining a list of existing online materials that show groups considered to be violent extremists in a bad light. In partnership with search engine companies, items on this list are shown to people who enter particular key words in web searches.[52] Although most of Moonshot's playlist consists of serious material, we understand that some satirical content is also included.[53]

All this serves to blur the line between counter-jihadi comedy deliberately created by counterextremist policy networks and content that simply happens to meet their requirements. As policy wonks often like to remark, 'it takes a network to fight a network'.[54] This suggests, for example, the potential relevance also of seemingly spontaneous online campaigns such as Anonymous's operations #OpParis #OpISIS #OpIceISIS and #OpTrollISIS,[55] all of which fitted well with the US objective to 'take back the internet', regardless of the spontaneity of their origins. These campaigns were primarily jamming and, to a lesser extent, intelligence gathering operations, whose satirical intent was strictly secondary, aimed at taking down pro-IS accounts on Twitter. Nonetheless, sub-campaigns such as 'troll day' involved the promulgation of memes which, for example, imposed images of ducks, troll faces, yetis or gay rights symbols on images of the group and its fighters. In another example, the Twitter account ISIS Karaoke captioned pictures of jihadi fighters with lyrics from well-known pop songs.[56]

Perhaps a particularly surreal example of this mobilisation of internet culture is the abovementioned ISISchan, a Japanese-style manga character in a black garment with a face and head-covering characteristic of conservative Islamic women's attire, cut salaciously short to reveal thighs and stockings. Functionally, the campaign was primarily an example of 'Google-bombing'—the aim being to obstruct people searching online for genuine IS propaganda by means of a character who was intended to subvert the group's hyper-masculine, hyper-violent image. For example, ISISchan images quite often showed the character cutting a melon, in order to demonstrate what knives ought to be used for.[57]

Similar examples of online jihadi-baiting could be cited almost inexhaustibly, but it is impossible to resist mentioning one final one: the satirical remix. This particular form of online humour is premised on the popularity of the *nashid*—a type of Islamic hymn—among supporters of jihadi groups. Because jihadi-Salafis usually take the highly conservative view that all musical instruments are forbidden in Islam, *nashids* are sung a-cappella, though they do make liberal use of multitracking, digital vocal editing and various sound effects.[58] Popular *nashids* can become the equivalent of hits in other musical contexts. Various anonymous online musicians have created musical parodies of the form. In one, for example, a *nashid* regarded by some as the 'national anthem' of the Islamic State—*My Nation, Dawn Has Come*—was remixed into a bleepy 8-bit version, reminiscent of vintage computer game soundtracks. Another account (now sadly suspended, ironically for violating YouTube's guidelines on extremist content) was called In Jihad We Rock. The account took the unaltered original vocals of well-known jihadi *nashids*, alongside the artwork that accompanied them on YouTube—typically rendered in a dark, epic, medieval fantasy style—and added meticulously crafted heavy metal instrumentation over the top. Almost as much homage as parody, the joke was reinforced by the fact that the doom-laden combination of vocals and distorted guitars sounded so natural together.[59]

While Bono's appeal for comedy to be deployed against IS was in some ways naïve, not least because it revealed a lack of awareness of just how extensively comedy *was* being deployed for that very purpose, in some ways his off-the-cuff remark serves very well to crystallise the attitudes that seem to lie behind the use of comedy in CVE and point to some of the areas of unresolved tension within them. On the one hand, the notion of deployment carries with it the idea of 'weaponised ridicule',—of humour as a secret weapon that can be instrumentalised as a policy tool much as a state might make use of a cruise missile, a commando squad or a computer virus. Something that, in the leaked words of one private intelligence analyst, 'when used properly is more powerful than an aircraft carrier battle group'.[60]

On the other hand, Bono's invocation of an avant garde art movement using subversive humour to resist the Nazis conjures up a deeper cultural narrative: one in which humour is connected at some deep structural level to the cause of freedom and inherently antithetical to that of totalitarian militarism. Finally, in (jokingly) name-checking three zeitgeisty comedians, he implicitly links the subversive values of European radicals in the 1930s to the values of mainstream contemporary American popular culture.

This same outlook seems to lie not too far beneath the surface of a good deal of actual policy on the subject. As professional propagandists, CVE practitioners are naturally obsessed with the language of scientific measurement and targeting. The lack of a sufficient 'evidence base' for humour, or for other forms of intervention, for that matter, seems to be a commonplace lament. Viewed from this perspective, comedy tends to be seen primarily as a sort of delivery system—an attractive wrapping for arguments and points of view that might otherwise find it difficult to gain a target audience's attention and interest. Paraphrasing George Bernard Shaw, the comedian we previously quoted who was involved in creating counter-jihadi material for a state client made the point to us 'if you want to put a difficult point across, make someone laugh. Otherwise they'll kill you'.[61]

Indeed, as Mathur similarly suggested:

> I think comedy is disarming—you can use it to tackle controversial subjects with less risk of inciting controversy or offending people. Take our 'I Want to Quit ISIS' sketch, for example. It has a scene where the main characters quote verses from the Quran. Despite the sensitivity of doing something like that in South Asia, we got no negative comments or reactions from anyone in the region.[62]

We might also discern a similar attitude in the sketch 'Real Housewives of ISIS', where, perhaps paradoxically, the deeper 'joke' can be seen as lying in the fact that the apparently absurd and incongruous material is actually broadly accurate. This may suggests that one audience this 'comedy' was hoping to reach was not expected to laugh at all, but rather, within the context of an otherwise mainstream television sketch format, have its attention drawn unexpectedly to information of which it may already have been peripherally aware from more serious sources.

A slightly different claim about the effectiveness of humour relates to the unpredictability that accounts for some CVE experts' ambivalence towards using it. We have noted Goodall et al.'s view of humour as a 'narrative IED', a form of communication with the ability to lie dormant before suddenly exploding with subversive impact. But while they make their arguments in less operationally minded terms, there seems to be something not altogether dissimilar in the lines of thinking put forward by both Greenberg and Kraidy. Humour's power, they seem to argue, lies, at least in part, in its disruptive nature, its ability to shatter carefully constructed illusions without having to offer up anything specific to put in their place.

At the same time, however, there also appears to be a more idealistic stratum beneath this seemingly instrumentalist discourse. According to this line of thinking, humour is not simply a convenient tool, but something that relates to the deeper meaning of the struggle between the values of terrorism and those of liberalism and democracy (of which CVE almost inevitably sees itself as a champion, even where it may actually be working closely with or even in notably illiberal autocracies). Humour is not just a neutral weapon in this formulation. Its very nature—its disrespect for hierarchy and dogma, the liberating vitality of laughter, its power to overcome fear—means that it naturally aligns with the cause of liberty and will always be the enemy of the cause of terror. 'If you are scared of terrorists', Mathur opined in a video created by the Pulitzer Centre, 'they relish that. If you express hatred towards them, they feed off of that. But if you laugh at them, I don't think they know how to deal with that'. These kinds of views carry an implicit theory not just of comedy but also of terrorism. In answer to the perennial question of 'what terrorists want', they seem to posit that what terrorists want is simply terror itself. 'Let them hate', as Suetonius quotes Roman tyrant Caligula as saying. 'Let them hate so long as they fear'.

As we shall see, laughter did become an important refuge for communities that were directly threatened by groups like IS, and the power of laughter to counter fear does seem to be one of the commonly expressed justifications offered by Arab creators of anti-IS comedy for the value of their work. Even so, one might wonder whether counter-terrorism (or counter violent extremism) practitioners are always best positioned to advocate for this. Waller's argument, in particular, seems somewhat paradoxical in that, on the one hand, he is calling for the US to pour resources into 'fighting the war of ideas like a real war' while, at the same time, making an argument that closely resembles the often-expressed notion that terrorism, even the word itself, serves to fuel moral panics and distort policy by pandering to irrational fear. This suggests that the sort of comedy that should be applauded in this regard is not offensive humour aimed at undermining the jihadi enemy, but rather humour that helps to strengthen social cohesion and resist excessive securitisation at home. As the essays in Ted Gournelos and Viveca Greene's *A Decade of Dark Humor* help show, comedy after 9/11 played an important role as counternarrative in the United States, where it worked to counteract attempts by the US government and mainstream media to present Islamist extremism as a hugely overblown 'existential' threat and helped open up a space in the public sphere for critical discussion of foreign engagements and the erosion of civil liberties at a time when 'serious' media discussion did little more than rally round the flag. Similarly, comedians of Arab and Muslim heritage from Western countries have striven to transmute their own and their audience's anxieties into laughter.

A distinguishable but related idea concerns the notion that jihadis, as with other fanatics, are intrinsically too rigid in their own self-image to cope with the complexities of humour. As the former UK Foreign Office official quoted above told us:

> ...terrorists spend a great deal of time caring about their reputations. Always they want to represent themselves and their organisations as incredibly serious. They're always trying to secure credibility for themselves. Now, nothing undermines credibility better than humour.[63]

Similarly, the proposed 'hub' for anti IS satire which was considered (but rejected) by a 'sceptical' British civil servant apparently had a 'theory of change' along the following lines:

> Because terrorist organisations tend to be both sober and self regarding and pompous tonally in their communications, their corporate pomposity would be undermined by humorous material ... by demonstrating the absurdity of grandiose claims in the context of Daesh around state building or the likelihood of its conquering Rome in the near future. This would somehow provide a kind of strong narrative foundation for undermining the messaging of the organisation.

Here, we can note, that it is not just the terrorists' means (that is, their desire to terrorise) that is the ultimate subject of mockery, but also their supposedly absurd aspirations (the establishment of a caliphate, for example).

Finally, occupying the middle ground between the notion of humour as a persuasive tool and the understanding of it as more fundamentally aligned with a particular set of values is the notion of comedy as a specific form of implicitly (white) American soft power. Despite the fact that the comment was itself at least half meant as a joke, it was Bono's quip about Amy Schumer, Chris Rock and Sacha Baron Cohen that attracted to him the most withering comments. (Perhaps in part because Baron Cohen had specifically mocked Bono's alleged saviour complex in his film *Brüno* (2009), in which the shallow hero aspires to acquire celebrity status by solving the Israel-Palestine conflict on a flying visit to the Middle East.) And yet, according to Mathur, a standard part of his own, hard-headed pitch to policymakers is that 'comedy [is]… becoming more popular, especially in regions of the world that were vulnerable to radicalisation'. For groups like East India Comedy and many young Arab comedians, 'comedy' in this sense suggests American reference points similar to those Bono invoked: John Oliver and Jon Stewart, *South Park* and *Seinfeld*.

Ultimately, it is clear that comedy has already come to be accepted as a potentially promising method for combatting extremist groups like Al Qaeda and IS. The thinking behind such an approach is not frivolous, even though it is not always systematic. Nevertheless, it rests, at least in part, on faith as well as logic: faith in the intrinsic virtues of humour and the intrinsic alignment of its values with those of the 'liberal democratic' West. But is this faith justified?

2

LAUGHTER AND SLAUGHTER

USES AND ABUSES OF HUMOUR IN THEORY AND PRACTICE

In 1976, psychologist Charles Gruner reviewed the experimental basis of the proposition that humour increases the persuasiveness of a message—humour being understood as 'laugh-or-smile-provoking stimuli of a good natured sort'. He found, apparently to his surprise, no evidence suggesting that this was the case. He found satire, which he differentiated from humour, to be even less effective. Relying heavily on a study he conducted himself (right down to penning his own satire), he found this comic form simply went over the heads of average readers. In his conclusion, he was forced to admit that the most one could say was that 'the communicator who chooses to use apt and appealing humour in his discourse is likely to improve his image with the audience'.[1]

Another serious review of the question conducted fifteen years later came to similar conclusions.[2] Despite noting that up to a fifth of American advertising at the time of writing was 'intended to be humorous' (a figure that apparently remains accurate), it once again turned out that evidence supporting whether humour actually increased persuasion or comprehension was mixed at best. In so far as humour did have benefits, these seemingly arose from the relatively obvious fact that humour tends to be enjoyable. People were more likely to pay attention to messages couched in humorous terms. There was also evidence that humour might be more effective at changing behaviour as opposed to beliefs—this was based on a study where humorous and non-humorous messages were used to get people to attend an event. But that was about all there was.

In 2009, Martin Eisend published a meta-analysis of the advertising literature, in which he discussed and compared several previous reviews in the field. In common with these earlier studies, he found that humour as a messaging strategy does seem to have some beneficial effects. It 'creates attention and awareness, enhances source liking, attitude towards the ad, positive cognitions, and reduces negative cognitions'. On the other hand, he found no evidence for the suggestion that humour improves comprehension, recall, recognition of product or source credibility, and could only say that the evidence was 'unclear' as to whether it improved the one thing that presumably really matters to advertisers: 'purchase intention'.[3]

This is quite striking. It is hardly surprising that humour is a good way to entertain, getting people's attention and making them feel more warmly disposed towards the messenger. People like to laugh. One might as well say that handing out free chocolate is a good way of getting people to eat chocolate. And yet work in the area seems to doggedly resist confirming the seemingly reasonable expectation that, having got people to consume advertisements, humour might also succeed in getting them to take on board the message that the advertiser is trying to communicate.

Perhaps humour simply isn't a good way of getting a point across after all—at least not if that point is trying to convince audiences that they ought to buy a particular product. What is more likely, however, is that the problem is methodological. Studies such as those dealt with by the reviews discussed above typically work by trying to present experimental subjects (who are typically undergraduate students at Western universities—something now recognised in psychology as a problem in its own right) with otherwise identical versions of 'humourised' and 'de-humourised' texts. If you feel this idea seems in and of itself like a joke, then you are not alone. As linguist Paul Simpson has observed, the surreal idea that one can scientifically measure out precise dollops of humour under controlled conditions is reminiscent of the Monty Python sketch 'The Funniest Joke in the World'.[4]

A potential alternative is offered by qualitative research that examines not so much whether humour achieves a particular effect, but the linguistic nuts and bolts of how it might do so. And yet this line of enquiry has problems of its own. Rhetoricians, discourse analysts and linguists all have a great deal to say about such matters. But their conclusions don't necessarily point in any clearly discernible or actionable direction.

Cicero, the great Roman orator, thinker and politician, was well aware of the potential effectiveness of joking as a means to deflect criticisms and end arguments—'you're unworthy of your ancestors!' 'And you are worthy of yours!'—but he believed that only those with 'natural genius' could effectively use it.[5] Lucie Olbrechts-Tyteca, whose monumental work The New Rhetoric helped to revive the field in the twentieth century, saw value in 'the comic' as a way of establishing rapport with an audience—essentially the same thing concluded by advertising research.

Also in the field of rhetoric, Meyer has sought to identify four specific functions of humour in rhetoric which he calls identification, clarification, enforcement and differentiation. Ultimately, though, his argument is for humour's 'flexibility as a rhetorical tool'.[6] These four functions fall along a continuum, whereby 'identification' aims to create unity between the audience and some other group, while 'differentiation' aims to achieve the opposite. While surely true, it hardly narrows down our understanding of what humour can and cannot achieve. Simpson observes that humour has many different social functions: to relieve embarrassment or to signal aggression, to display individual resilience or as a means to influence and persuade others, or simply to offer the playful humourist some rhetorical wiggle room.[7]

In Simpson's study The Discourse of Satire, this broad characterisation of the accomplishments of humour serves to introduce his own contribution, which revolves around a theory of satire premised on three stages of irony. The satirist first introduces a 'prime'—effectively something that reminds the audience of the thing that is being satirised—then places the prime in an incongruous situation, and subsequently proceeds to develop the incongruity.[8] Hodgart, in an earlier monograph on the same subject, notes that satire, unlike invective, requires the combination of 'a high degree both of commitment to and involvement with the painful problems of the world and simultaneously a high degree of abstraction from the world … an element of aggressive attack and a fantastic vision of the world transformed'.[9]

But even such seemingly unarguable ideas are not universally upheld. Innocenti and Miller, for example, have examined what they believe constitutes persuasively effective humour in the context of political rhetoric, focusing on American suffrage campaigner Anna Howard Shaw.[10] On one occasion, they note, Shaw mocked American opponents of women's suffrage by comparing them to children who feared goblins under the bed. On another, she pointed out the incongruity of a female anti-suffragist opponent who was going on a lengthy speaking tour in order to argue with force and eloquence that a woman's place was in the home beside her husband, and that women lacked the mental capacity to make decisions in political matters. The former, Innocenti and Miller argue, is merely 'unfair… childish buffoonery' with no effective persuasive content. The latter, on the other hand, is persuasively effective humour precisely because it isn't fantastic, but on the contrary makes a factually accurate and perfectly logical point.

But this, too, would seem to be contradicted by an experimental study which, interestingly, draws its hypotheses from ancient Roman tradition. According to Holbert, Hmielowski and Jain the study of persuasive humour effects has been inconclusive, in part, because of its failure to differentiate between 'Horatian' satire, which, like the work of the golden age Latin poet, pokes fun at its object in a gentle manner by contrasting the humble level of everyday life with the pretensions of the great and powerful; and 'Juvenalian' satire, which goes straight for the jugular, bombarding its target with a withering tirade of sarcasm. The study found that a custom-written Juvenalian satire works better than its Horatian equivalent or a non-humorous control text, mainly because its acid put-downs make it difficult to formulate a counter-argument. (Or did so for the students who took part in the study, at any rate.)[11]

In short, drawing clear conclusions about whether humour works as a messaging strategy is more difficult than one might imagine. So far, however, the research we have considered, whether experimental or interpretive in nature, commonly focuses on the communicative effects of humour in an artificially narrow sense. And yet when humour is actually for political effect, it is never deployed in a vacuum, but always in a particular context. Indeed, experienced political activists have long held a practical belief in the effectiveness of humour as a campaigning tactic. Community organiser Saul Alinsky is famous to the point of cliché for having said, 'ridicule is man's most potent weapon. It is almost impossible to counterattack ridicule. Also it infuriates the opposition, who then react to your advantage'.[12]

But this sound bite only makes sense when considered in the context within which Alinsky places it. For him, the above precept (rule five of his *Rules for Radicals*) is simply a logical development of a tactical insight (rule four, which he presents simultaneously with rule five), which sits at the heart of virtually all theories of civil resistance: 'Make the enemy live up to their own book of rules. You can kill them with this, for they can no more obey their own rules than the Christian church can live up to Christianity'.[13]

In practice, whenever ridicule is mentioned in the context of an action in *Rules for Radicals*, it turns out to be a by-product of this mechanism, not simply a freestanding rhetorical technique.

Alinsky's intellectual successors in the present day continue to see humour as potentially integral to the logic of nonviolent action. In the Serbian revolution that brought down the genocidal dictator Slobodan Milošević, the Otpor resistance movement became legendary for its use of humorous political tactics. Activists painted Milošević's face onto a plastic barrel and placed it outside a shopping centre along with a baseball bat and an invitation for passers-by to donate a coin for the privilege of giving the president a pummelling, with the result that police, unable to find the original culprits, were forced to arrest the barrel.[14] On another occasion, the group released turkeys adorned with a white feather, parodying the style of Serbia's first lady (the Serbian word for turkey is apparently 'one of the worst things you can call a woman').[15] Once again, police were forced into the undignified task of rounding up the offending turkeys. In a more theatrical action intended to protest shortages, activists pretended to queue up for cooking oil in a park. Eventually, someone arrived with a tiny bottle of oil and distributed a teaspoon to each person.[16] Following the success of the revolution, Srđa Popović, a leading figure in the movement, established an activism training centre called CANVAS, from which he has trained activists who have taken part in nonviolent mobilisations from the Maldives to the 2011 Egyptian revolution, and from Damascus (where tiny speakers playing anti-regime songs were apparently placed in rubbish bins and hundreds of ping pong balls were released to roll down narrow medieval alleys),[17] to Venezuela.[18]

Popović's approach is what activists today would describe (not always in a complimentary sense) as Alinskyan. He urges activists to take a practical, focused approach to insurgency, always seeking ways to unite the largest possible coalitions, seeking achievable, incremental successes, and favouring practical impact over ideological purity. He encourages them to think of their struggle against oppressive ruling powers in terms of the free-market metaphor of branding. By using humour, activists can make their brand look 'cool' and attractive—especially if authorities are goaded into over-reaction, making themselves look joyless and clumsy by comparison.[19]

The role of humour in activism has also been theorised in a rather more conventionally scholarly manner by Majken Sørensen, who has typologised what she calls 'humorous political stunts'[20] as corrective, naïve, absurd or provocative actions. Corrective stunts involve pretending to agree with dominant practices in order to push them to subversively ludicrous extremes. Naïve stunts occur when protestors feign innocence and unawareness of the controversial or political nature of their action. Absurd stunts involve doing something so baffling that those in power struggle to work out how to respond. Finally, provocative stunts involve directly insulting those in power, laying down the gauntlet in a more conventionally oppositional manner.

Janjira Sombatpoonsiri, a political scientist who has studied the humorous tactics of Otpor, also seeks to draw some theoretical lessons about how political protest humour works. Similar to Alinsky's argument about forcing the enemy to live up to their own rules, she proposes that political humour directly challenges its targets' ideology by 'annexing its form' and recasting it as absurd parody. Secondly, it creates an atmosphere of cheerfulness as opposed to antagonism at protest events. Third, within the movement itself, it creates a carnival atmosphere which offers a foretaste of promised freedom.[21]

There is no doubt that stories of humorous stunts pulled by activists make for great anecdotes. And this in itself may say something about their effectiveness. Nevertheless, it seems that there is still something missing in these theoretical accounts. In Popović's excitement about 'branding' we appear to have gone full circle to the humorous advertising campaigns whose actual effectiveness is seemingly so difficult to demonstrate. But there is perhaps a deeper problem. Many of the things that are cited as particular virtues of humorous campaigning appear to be difficult to distinguish from the basic strategies that all civil resistance follows. As social movement theorist Charles Tilly put it, protest movements almost inevitably seek to project what he called, using what has to be one of the worst acronyms of all time, WUNC, or worthiness, unity, numbers and commitment.[22] Activists will always try to broaden their appeal, make it hard for authorities to stigmatise them and create a foretaste of the change they claim to stand for by adopting symbols and performances with a broad social resonance— but this doesn't have to mean being funny. It could equally entail adopting the language of patriotism or moderate religiosity. What makes humour different?

Popović's answer to this question is that belief systems like patriotism and religion are potentially divisive. Only humour is truly inclusive.[23] Sørensen, on the other hand, argues that non-humorous protestors 'care a great deal about the reactions of states and companies and thereby indirectly recognise their power and the rationality they represent'.[24] Humorous protestors, on the other hand, refuse to grant this kind of recognition.

Both of these analyses seem interestingly telling. Why would humorous rhetoric be inherently less divisive than other types? After all, ridicule can antagonise as well as unite. In another place and time, Otpor's turkey stunt might have raised accusations of misogyny, for example, even among potential well-wishers. In fact, Sombatpoonsiri found that support for the use of humorous tactics wasn't universal even within the Serbian revolutionary movement. Sørensen's claim, on the other hand, appears to claim simply that humorous protestors (typically) make their points ironically rather than directly, which is almost a tautology. Indeed, she herself notes that actions she categorises as provocative come very close to conventional protest. To cite one of her own examples, in June 2010, Russian activists painted a penis on one half of the Leiteny Bridge in Saint Petersburg, so that when the bridge was

JOKING ABOUT JIHAD

raised the phallus erected itself right in front of the Federal Security Service (Russian intelligence, abbreviated as FSB) headquarters.[25] Aside from the fact that drawing pictures of willies is always hilarious, how is this really different from if the activists had instead written words to the effect of 'down with the FSB'?

Underlying these difficulties is a conflict that we touched on in the previous chapter. On the one hand, theorists of humorous protest wish to treat humour much as propagandists or advertisers do—as a neutral technique. This again brings us back to the same problem encountered by the studies we considered previously: the implicit notion that humour is an objective property of particular texts or performances that can be rationally manipulated in order to achieve particular results. Indeed, it is not just those interested in the instrumental deployment of humour who tend to hold this opinion. It is a presupposition of entire swathes of humour research. For example, Salvatore Attardo, a leading figure in the linguistics of verbal humour and the creator of the General Theory of Verbal Humour, insists that one of the key aims of his theoretical work is to make it possible to objectively distinguish humorous from non-humorous writing.[26] Using the theory developed by Attardo and originated by his collaborator Victor Raskin,[27] which relies on the idea of a sudden frame shift between two opposing 'scripts' that could be used to interpret a text, anthropologist Alexander Kozintsev successfully demonstrates that the New Testament account of the Last Supper, with its frame shift between mundane and mystical texts, is clearly a work of comedy. As he writes, 'the main lesson to be drawn from the age-long history of attempts at formulating an essentialist definition of funniness is that these attempts are futile'.[28] For Kozintsev, words like 'funny' are a hoax. They appear to refer to a judgement that a particular property exists in an object. In reality, people either laugh or they don't.[29]

But theorists of political humour are also pulled in another, different direction, one at which Popović's claims about the unifying power of comedy only hint. Similar to the end of the previous chapter, we again find ourselves drawn to the idea of humour not as a morally neutral technique, but rather as a particular ethic—one that is isomorphic with the goals of the campaigner for social justice.

In a less-often quoted part of *Rules for Radicals*, Alinsky reflects on humour not just as a propaganda tool of insurrection but as a necessary

40

personal quality of the successful organiser—something with spiritual, even metaphysical importance. A sense of humour, he insists, enables the organiser to 'maintain his perspective' and 'see himself for what he really is: a bit of dust that burns for a fleeting second.' It protects her from 'complete acceptance of any dogma, any religious, political, or economic prescription for salvation'. It acts as a way to 'maintain ... sanity' and even as 'a key to understanding life', enabling one to accept the inevitable contradictions of life. 'Essentially,' he concludes, 'life is a tragedy; and the converse of tragedy is comedy.' Only when one is equipped with a sense of humour can one make sense of this paradoxical quality of reality. [30]

Where does this attitude towards humour come from? The capacity to laugh, even about the most troubling matters, is surely a human universal, as are many of the other things Alinsky touches on. And yet there is reason to think that the particular role he gives to the 'sense of humour' is quite specific. The distinction is important, because it pertains to an issue we considered at the end of the previous chapter. When comedy is promoted as a means of opposing violent extremism, are we talking about the activation of a fundamental instinct, or rather the export of a particular value system?

In *The Senses of Humour*, historian Daniel Wickberg argues that the idea of humour and the sense of humour as positive accompaniments to political freedom arose hand in hand with the development of the word itself. [31] In Shakespeare's day, 'the humours' were bile, phlegm, blood and melancholy—secretions believed under ancient medical lore not just to cause, but to physically constitute human temperament. Laughter, on the other hand, was typically regarded with the default attitude that it was something ignoble and cruel, directed at the poor, the weak, the mad and the deformed—those at the very bottom of society. For Wickberg, the story of how this changed is, essentially, the story of the emergence of political liberalism, through the English Civil War, the Scottish Enlightenment, the American War of Independence, the Industrial Revolution and, ultimately, the emergence of the United States as the world's most advanced capitalist economy, in which the cultivation of a sense of humour became for the first time a highly desired and even marketed quality, deemed essential to getting by in a uniquely competitive and egalitarian society. As a result, Americans (and eventually the British) came to see their sense of humour as emblematic of their freedom and their self-appointed mission to bring it to others. Wickberg ends his story with American comedians like Bob Hope enthusing that, 'as our armed forces flow in to stop the world's decay ... where Hitlerism and Fascism and Tojoism have set in, they take with them... their sense of humour'.[32] This is not a million miles from the suggestion of deploying Chris Rock or Amy Schumer abroad.

Despite the apparently contingent nature of this history, there has been a tendency within Western scholarship to universalise and idealise the concept of humour. Indeed, the interdisciplinary field devoted to studying jokes, laughter, comedy and the like is usually referred to as humour studies, implying that 'humour' is a neutral master concept that can be used as a vantage point from which to consider these phenomena across all cultures. As scholars have begun to question this tradition, they have noted two important parallel implications. On the one hand, there has been a tendency to try to elevate the technical, cognitive aspects of 'humour' over the physical, pre-rational phenomenon of laughter, so much so that some scholars have sought to argue that humour is simply an aesthetic phenomenon that has no real connection to laughter at all.[33] Linguists like Raskin and Attardo, in looking for structural, universal explanations for humour in texts, have been correspondingly reluctant to admit that offensiveness or hostility could play anything other than a supporting role in the semantic clockwork they think comprises jokes.[34] Meanwhile, other scholars have idealised the social consequences of humour, cheering on the thesis of humour as the sword, shield and herald of liberty. For example, in his book *Comedy, Tragedy and Religion*, humour scholar John Morreall seeks to assess to what extent different religions represent what he identifies as the contrasting ethics represented by the comic and tragic visions. While not explicitly claiming that one is superior to the other, Morreall insists that the comic vision aligns with values of peaceful conflict resolution, socio-economic egalitarianism and gender equality.[35]

It is tempting to see the ideas of liberalism and the Enlightenment as playing a major role in shaping the outlook of contemporary humour scholars, both in terms of the instrumentalist and individualist mentality that lies behind a lot of linguistic, psychological and marketing research, and also the idealistic claims that we find in the writing of scholars such as Morreall. And indeed, the breach that work such as that of Wickberg has helped to open has since been widened by the growth of 'critical humour studies', a body of research which has, particularly over the last twenty years or so, set out to call into question the benign assumptions that have characterised so much scholarship.[36] Critical humour scholars take issue with the idea that humour can be understood in terms of objective properties of texts, arguing instead for its situation in culturally constructed, continually shifting and politically contested frames or modes, and, in particular, with the idea that humour is intrinsically liberating or benign. Michael Billig, a leading figure in this regard, makes extensive use of Wickberg's narrative both directly and in terms of the general contours of his history, showing how the development of the incongruity theory of humour from the eighteenth century to the present day has helped to obscure the darker sides of joking in favour of the notion of humour as the handmaiden of social progress, an antidote to the darkness of primitive fanaticism.[37]

Sociologists like Billig and, before him, Michael Mulkay[38] posit that the idea of humour as a crucial virtue of both individual and society ought to be understood not as a transcendent or mystical truth, but rather as connected to the historical development of Western capitalist societies. This contention coincides with the growing concern in experimental social psychology that assumptions once thought to be universal may have been distorted by overwhelming reliance on so-called WEIRD subjects—people (typically students) from Western, educated, industrial, rich and democratic cultures—leading to the burgeoning development of studies aiming to introduce more cultural diversity.[39]

This has had implications for understandings of the social role of humour. Kazarian et. al., for example, have examined whether the theory of 'humour styles', originated by the psychologist Rodney Martin, applies to students in the 'collectivist' culture of Lebanon.[40] The original theory holds that people make use of humour in four basic ways, two of which are positive and two negative. Aggressive humour antagonises others, affiliative humour seeks to create and sustain friendships, while self-enhancing humour fosters individual psychological resilience along lines similar to those Alinsky touches on, by helping a person gain some objective distance in relation to misfortune. On the other hand self-defeating humour undermines and weakens self-esteem.[41] And yet it appears that the Lebanese students in the study (Kazarian, appropriately or otherwise, seeks to draw conclusions about Arab humour in a wider sense) did not, in practice, differentiate between these different conceptions of the role of humour.

Yue, Jiang, Lu and Hiranandani, a group of psychologists based in Hong Kong, have also investigated the idea that certain positive ideas about humour may be exclusive to 'Western' cultures.[42] Their thesis is rather essentialist in itself. They seem to posit an eternal distinction between 'Western' and 'Eastern' attitudes to humour, which can be traced, respectively, to the supposedly positive view of humour held by Aristotle versus the supposedly more sceptical view held by Confucius. Ironically, scholars such as Morreall emphasise the characteristically hostile attitude to humour seen in most of 'Western' history, especially, but not exclusively, after the coming of Christianity, and look eastwards in the belief that 'Eastern' traditions like Zen Buddhism are more accommodating of the 'comic vision'.[43] Nevertheless, their study does appear to show a consistent distinction between how Chinese, Canadian and 'bicultural' students think about and value humour.

The authors happen to open their paper by recounting a telling example of intercultural difference with regard to the role of humour in public life. In 2008, US President George W. Bush was giving a final farewell press conference in Iraq when a journalist called Muntadhar al-Zaidi removed his shoes and hurled them at him, one after another, before being seized and marched away by security. Bush, who had successfully ducked both shoes, quipped to his shocked audience: 'To those of you apologising on behalf of the Iraqi people I want you to know it doesn't bother me. If you want the facts, it's a size ten shoe that he threw.'[44] As the authors of the paper observe, Bush's attempt to brush off the incident with humour stands in contrast to another protest event that occurred less than a year later in which a shoe was also thrown—perhaps in imitation of Zaidi—by a Tibetan independence campaigner at Chinese Premier Wen Jiabao while he was delivering a lecture in Oxford.[45] This politician was notably less amused, even though he urged for a calm and measured response to the indignity.

But the original incident in Iraq is perhaps worth considering further. What Bush apparently understood as a political stunt of the kind he was familiar with from the US, Zaidi carried out in profound earnest. Throwing his shoes at the president was, for him, an action expressive of the deepest contempt imaginable, a judgement against Bush's responsibility, as he saw it, for the ruin of his country and the death of millions of his countrymen. For him, it was inconceivable he could be allowed to live after such an act. He fully believed himself to be on a suicide mission.[46] Bush's laughter in response was simultaneously an indication that he did not fully understand the gravity of the insult intended, and at the same time that he simply refused to participate in the system of meanings that invested it with such gravity. Either way, for many Arabs (and for that matter many anti-war Westerners at the time), the president's breezy reaction was seen not as an admirably democratic tolerance for freedom of expression, but rather a callous and contemptible trivialisation of the injustices that had prompted Zaidi's outrage. Bush's response here can be seen as emblematic not just of culturally reductionist ideas of 'Western' versus 'Eastern' attitudes to humour, but rather of how the pro-humour attitudes of a thin, un-reflexive form of (in this case, neo) liberalism can find itself at odds with profoundly held beliefs and values that demand to be taken seriously.

However, there is a different origin story for subversive and liberating laughter, one that seemingly collides head on with the notion that it is a child of the Enlightenment. As Mikhail Bakhtin argues in *Rabelais and His World*, laughter underwent a fundamental change after the Renaissance. During the Renaissance, he argues, laughter had a real philosophical significance, one through which, he insists, 'the world is seen anew, no less (and perhaps more) profoundly than when seen from a serious standpoint'.[47] By the seventeenth century, however, laughter had lost this 'universal, philosophical form' and was seen as incompatible with anything 'important and essential'.[48]

Bakhtin's narrative, then, is the exact opposite of Wickberg's. The point at which Bakhtin believes laughter reaches its high-water mark with the work of Rabelais, Cervantes and Shakespeare, is where, for Wickberg, humour begins its transformative journey. His story of humour's ascent to cultural domination occurs almost in parallel with the process by which, Bakhtin sees laughter begin to wither on the vine. In a sense, the story Bakhtin is telling is no less parochial than that of Wickberg. His concern is the tradition of laughter in medieval Western Europe, and more specifically, this tradition as it contributes to understanding a single novel: Rabelais' *Gargantua and Pantagruel*.

Nevertheless, Bakhtin's medieval laughter, unlike Wickberg's humour, does not begin at any definable point, fading rather into the mists of the Dark Ages, into the thinly documented folk culture of classical paganism and, beyond that, into practices that belong in the speculative realm of comparative mythology. This means that Bakhtin's work can be—and has been—linked with other folk humorous practices in traditional societies the world over. Wickberg's on the other hand—in another curious symmetry—begins in a very specific place and time (late sixteenth century England) and ends with the humorous tradition of the US toeing the threshold of world domination.

Unsurprisingly, then, Bakhtin's characterisation of medieval laughter, especially the institution of the folk carnival, has become a widely drawn on alternative, more radical model for how laughter can underpin popular resistance, not least because his description of the nature of medieval laughter is so attractive. Marked by 'exceptional radicalism, freedom and ruthlessness', Bakhtin saw medieval laughter as a universal popular counterculture, one which took the oppressive ideologies of feudalism and religion and turned them upside down.[49]

A key part of what Bakhtin contends is that, with the development of more controlled and less ambivalent forms of humour and satire in subsequent centuries, the culture of medieval laughter would come to be misunderstood. For example, there are features of the tradition which may to us seem macabre or horrific, such as the motif of the dance of death; or simply revolting, such as the fixation on what he calls 'the lower bodily stratum'—in other words, toilet humour.[50] Bakhtin insists forcefully that this is because we fail to appreciate the way in which these features fitted into the 'regenerative' character of medieval laughter. The same goes, he thinks, for the extreme and ridiculous violence found in the work of Rabelais. This isn't meant to be taken literally, for Bakhtin—it's simply another symbol of 'regeneration'. In a deflection characteristic of the political radical, he insists that the real violence in medieval culture was inherent in the system.

> The serious aspects of class culture are official and authoritarian; they are combined with violence, prohibitions, [and] limitations and always

contain an element of fear and of intimidation. These elements prevailed in the Middle Ages. Laughter on the contrary overcomes fear, for it knows no inhibitions, no limitations. Its idiom is never used by violence and authority.[51]

There is no doubt that those in political authority in medieval times (if not all periods) relied on the use of violence to subordinate the population. However, many have noted that Bakhtin's attempt to wholly exonerate the institution and the idiom of the carnival from violence and any role in asserting authority is suspect. For example, he identifies the *charivari* as a medieval practice that was cousin to the carnival. Charivaris were noisy parades typically used to shame and intimidate members of a community who had violated the typically conservative norms regarding sex relations. Sometimes they culminated in murder.[52] In France, up until the eighteenth century, a popular carnival practice was to burn live cats, which were viewed symbolically as a proxy for witches (or women in general), with the burning understood as a kind of symbolic 'mass rape'. Cultural historian Robert Darnton touches on one example of this practice, writing: 'Although it seems strange to us … the cat massacre was the funniest thing that ever happened to the workers in the Rue Saint-Séverin'.[53] These were popular practices, no doubt viewed as liberating by those who participated in them; but they were also designed to assert authority and to 'inhibit and limit' others.

In the previous chapter, we noted Waller's thesis that ridicule is an effective weapon for the US to use against Al Qaeda, on the grounds that Osama bin Laden himself said that it was 'worse than death'. And yet, in the speech Waller is referring to, the Al Qaeda leader is not just talking about ridicule in an abstract sense, but specifically about (among other things) Abu Ghraib prison and Guantanamo Bay.[54] Presumably, this is not what Waller had in mind by ridicule. However, as one former Guantanamo Bay guard recalled:

> During call to prayer, many times soldiers would mock and laugh at the detainees. Many would also try to sing along to the call for prayer, trying to be funny. I also know that sometimes, during call for prayer, water would be given out to the detainees in their bucket, and some would spray the detainees with water during prayer, then stating it was an accident.[55]

Similarly, a former Abu Ghraib detainee has testified that US Army Specialist Charles Graner was 'laughing and whistling' as he forced him to eat from the toilet. As he put it, 'they were torturing us as if it was theatre to them'.[56] Echoing Darnton, as appalling as such behaviour seems to us, it was apparently funny to people like Graner at the time. Furthermore, in a sense, what they were doing was a version of what Waller recommends—using ridicule to destroy the dignity of their 'terrorist' captives.

Stating that laughter is not always benign is by no means a new observation. But it is perhaps worth driving home just how shocking and disturbing some of its associations are. After all, there is a strong defensive tendency, a sort of defensive cultural reflex, that can kick in when we are challenged with the idea that laughter and slaughter can really go hand in hand.

As philosopher Simon Critchley writes, 'a true joke, a comedian's joke, suddenly and explosively lets us see the familiar defamiliarised, the ordinary made extra-ordinary ... the real rendered surreal and we laugh in a physiological squeal of transient delight'.[57]

Critchley says this in order to distinguish 'true jokes' from other jokes that he recognises as 'reactionary'—in other words, jokes that express viewpoints Critchley disapproves of. And yet, as Simon Weaver, a scholar of racist humour notes, at least one of the jokes that Critchely specifically cites as an example of a 'true joke' (because it is a feminist joke aimed at men), was originally told as a racist joke aimed at black people.

When laughter occurs in what seems to be absolutely inexcusable circumstances, there is a tendency to invoke mental illness as an explanation, not unlike the tendency to apply this language to terrorists and other violators of social norms. In his classic study of the intimacies of violence, *On Killing*, former US Lieutenant Colonel David Grossman describes the folk psychological belief, prevalent among American soldiers, in a form of madness called 'Ganzer syndrome' which causes people to 'make jokes, act silly, and otherwise try to ward off the horror with humour and the ridiculous'. The case he cites derives from a 'personal narrative' about a US soldier in Vietnam who entered his tent with the severed arm of a Vietnamese person. With the arm, which he named Herbert, he proceeded to horse about, inviting his friends to shake Herbert's hand and attempting to pick his nose with it.[58] The problem is that Ganzer syndrome apparently does not exist. There is a rare psychiatric condition called Ganser syndrome, but it is not associated with inappropriate humorous behaviours.[59]

What is striking about this story (and what may underlie the need to invent a psychiatric condition to explain it) is that there is a recognisable joke. There are plenty of accounts of individuals laughing while, for example, carrying out gun massacres. But such laughter may be explained away as fundamentally different to the laughter that accompanies humour. And yet there are plenty of accounts of appalling and atrocious violence accompanied not just by laughter, but by things that look grotesquely akin to 'humour'. In their book *Soldaten*, historian Sönke Neitzel and psychologist Harald Welzer examine the remarkable archives of audio recordings, which the Allied Forces secretly made in World War II, of ordinary conversations between Nazi prisoners of war. The conversations are a particularly valuable resource because they show how perpetrators of violent atrocities view such events when they inhabit the social and ideological frame of reference in which they carried them out. Often, it seems, soldiers would openly brag about acts of mass slaughter and worse, present them for the amusement of their peers. In one of many deeply shocking examples, eight German military officers are described as 'laughing their heads off' as an alleged female spy was raped, tortured and murdered with horrific brutality.[60]

This sort of laughter was by no means the exclusive preserve of Nazis. Philip Gourovitch describes how, in the Rwandan genocide, a favourite practice of Hutu death squads was to chop the feet and hands off Tutsi captives. This was a reference to the greater average height of Tutsis, who were in this way cut 'down to size'. The practice was seen as entertaining, and 'crowds would gather to taunt, laugh and cheer as the victim writhed to death'.[61]

Kozintsev refers to an essay called 'The Laughable' by Russian novelist Maxim Gorky, in which he recalls similar examples of what the anthropologist describes as 'chillingly aberrant laughter'. In one such case, a group of soldiers stole a peasant woman's cow—her only source of food. One of them wrote her a parodic receipt for the stolen animal. 'And he signed it, the son of a bitch, "The Lord"... And this occurrence made us laugh so hard we couldn't walk'.[62]

Numerous other examples could be cited. Indeed, as Donald Horowitz, an expert on inter-ethnic violence has noted, episodes of atrocious killing routinely amount to 'a holiday for violence, punctuated by laughter',[63] in which torture is carried out 'with hilarious and joyful abandon'.[64]

Confronted with this unutterably dark face of laughter, there appear to be two avenues open to us. One is to return to roughly where we were at the outset of this chapter, with the acceptance that humour is simply a tool that can be deployed to a variety of ends. And yet we have already sought to demonstrate the unsatisfactory nature of this view. To strip humour of its ambivalence, to try to transform it into a precision munition that can achieve one specific end and no more is to deny humour its essential nature. The only alternative is to embrace it, and consider the possibility that any power humour has against the darkest aspects of human nature arises perhaps because, not in spite, of its seeming complicity in this very darkness.

How can this complicity be understood? Writing in the aftermath of another atrocious conflict, the English Civil War (or more accurately the Wars of the Three Kingdoms, as Ireland and Scotland were also involved), Thomas Hobbes theorised laughter in what is one of the most quoted passages written on the subject. He wrote: 'Sudden Glory, is the passion which maketh those Grimaces called LAUGHTER; and is caused either by some sudden act of their own, that pleaseth them; or by the apprehension of some deformed thing in another, by comparison whereof they suddenly applaud themselves'.[65]

Laughter, for Hobbes, is essentially cruel. It results from one person's subjective elevation above another. Importantly, it is also mediated by group identity. Hobbes does not find the debasement of friends and relatives funny—only that of strangers and enemies.[66] In contemporary scholarship, this general view of humour has been termed 'superiority theory'.

On the face of it, superiority theory seems to offer a powerful explanation for the examples of murderous laughter we just encountered. The 'jokers' laugh in diabolical exultation over the sheer abjectness of enemies and strangers. For superiority theory, this is not a perversion of humour (although of course it is a perversion of humanity). On the contrary, distasteful as it sounds, it represents the essence of what humour is.

Hobbes' bleak thesis is mild in comparison with that proposed by Albert Rapp, a polymathic classicist who, in 1951, published a development of the superiority thesis titled *Origins of Wit and Humour*.[67] For Rapp, laughter first arose in humans not out of an uncharitable smugness, but from outright physical aggression. In his quasi-evolutionary theory of laughter, its origin lies in primitive man's 'cry of triumph in some savage jungle duel'.[68]

From this rather cartoonish origin myth, Rapp proposed that wit and humour underwent a gradual evolution—what we might call a sort of 'civilizing process'.[69] The original victory cry represented by laughter was later applied to those who had not actually been defeated, but who bore marks indicative of defeat—physical injuries or bodily deformities. Next, people learned the art of the verbal insult, using their wit to point out flaws and weaknesses in others. As this process developed, people eventually learned to produce gentler, friendlier humour, based on the playful, non-serious insult. Finally, people learned to laugh at themselves, or, rather, at past versions of themselves to whom they now felt superior.

In typical reviews of humour theories, the superiority account is followed by 'incongruity theory'. We already touched on this in an indirect manner, since the emergence of incongruity theory is usually associated with the rise of the liberal view of benign humour, and on the face of it, incongruity theory is unlikely to see an essential relationship between laughter and violence or hostility. Francis Hutcheson, widely considered to be one of the main originators of the theory, used it explicitly to ridicule Hobbes' view that laughter is inherently mean spirited and contemptuous. He insists that it is possible to laugh at someone while still respecting them, finding humour, for example, in the contrast between some small or temporary lapse of dignity and their admirable nature overall or, conversely, in flashes of relative nobility where we might not otherwise expected it—as, for example, when animals do things that remind us of humans. Nevertheless, some incongruity theorists such as Arthur Koestler do not consider this approach as incompatible with the idea that laughter originated in primitive aggression.

Another classic account we might turn to for an explanation of the relationship between humour and violence is 'relief theory', of which

Sigmund Freud is considered to be a key proponent. In *The Joke and Its Relation to the Unconscious*, Freud argued that much, though not all, joking can be understood as a means of releasing that which social norms force us to repress. As such, jokes can have a tendency to express sexual aggression, for example, or other forms of hostility. Laughter, then, represents the release of psychic energy previously required to repress these unacceptable urges.[70] Frantz Fanon, applying psychoanalytical approaches to understanding anti-colonial insurgency, would later explicitly link liberating moments of laughter to the emergence of the cathartic violence required not only to physically eliminate oppressors, but also to unshackle the colonised from the mentality of subordination.

> [t]he native ... laughs to himself every time he spots an allusion to the animal world in the [colonizer's] words. For he knows that he is not an animal; and it is precisely at the moment he realizes his humanity that he begins to sharpen the weapons with which he will secure his victory.[71]

Perhaps the deepest and most evidence-based account of the relationship between humour and aggression, however, is provided by a newer theoretical perspective, sometimes called 'play theory'. This account of humour is rooted in discoveries within biology and ethology. In the social sciences, such 'sociobiological' theories are often treated with suspicion, especially where they relate to violence. The concern is that they offer over-simplified explanations to justify a fixed view of how society must be. In the case of laughter, though, there is reason to think that the opposite is true. Understanding that the origins of humour are likely biological and evolutionary reinforces the 'critical' view of it as something inherently contested and culturally constructed.

For Aristotle, humour was a defining characteristic of humanity, one so intrinsic that medieval Christian theologians later struggled when faced with the fact that Jesus was not recorded as laughing in the New Testament, hinting that he might not be fully human after all—a heresy.[72] Their solution to the problem was to argue that when he said 'woman, my time has not yet come', in response to Mary's demand that he do something about the shortage of wine at the wedding at Cana, he must have delivered the line as a dry wisecrack. As recently as 2005, Michael Billig made the same claim in his book *Laughter and*

Ridicule. 'Hyenas may make laughter-like noises', he scoffs, 'but that is an acoustic accident'.[73] In fact, it is now widely accepted that laughter preceded and extends beyond humans. Chimpanzees and bonobos laugh, which means that our common ancestor presumably did as well.[74] Rats also laugh,[75] and dogs may too,[76] as do many other species.[77] The fact that such different lineages of mammal have the equivalent of laughter or smiling suggests that, in all probability, our forebears were laughing as far back as the time of the dinosaurs.[78]

What counts as laughter and smiling in apes and other mammals are vocalisations and facial expressions specifically designed to signal that a particular activity is understood as playful. For example, young chimpanzees enjoy chasing one another for fun. Where this is the case, the chimpanzee that is being chased will begin 'play panting' to signal to the other that it understands that this apparently aggressive behaviour is not really aggressive, but just play.[79]

Animal play comes in various forms. Ethologist Owen Aldis called his important early study of the phenomenon *Play Fighting*, but this is something of a misnomer, as he also identifies other playful activities undertaken by animals, like pretend hunting or exploration.[80] But what all of these have in common is that they imitate behaviours that would, if done for real, involve a significant amount of risk. There isn't certainty as to why animals play, though there are numerous theories. One is that play helps with learning. As Bateson and Martin observe, research suggests that play rewires the neural connections of young animal brains.[81] Another theory posits that play is important when it comes to learning to manage anxiety.[82] But it is interesting to note what play isn't. For example, play does not appear to be connected to the enforcement of social hierarchy.[83] On the contrary, it tends to invert hierarchy, so that an animal low in the pecking order may jokingly attack one that is much higher. Play behaviours and the symbolic aggression of status display behaviours, though they superficially resemble one another, are seemingly quite different things.

The implications of this for how we try to understand the emergence of human laughter are significant. For our pre-human ancestors, as Kozintsev puts it, 'the "recoding" signalled by laughter had an extremely narrow meaning. "I'm pretending to bite you, but it's just play." In humans, the meaning was extended to the extreme: "I'm pretending to violate all cultural norms and taboos, but it's just play."'[84]

JOKING ABOUT JIHAD

To understand the human, cultural phenomenon of humour (as opposed to the mammalian, biological phenomenon of laughter) we have to acknowledge two things: first, how threat and violation can manifest themselves as symbolic, rather than physical phenomena; and second, how these can be reframed (or, as Kozintsev expresses it, 'recoded') so as to be interpreted as playful rather than disturbing.

One example of how the play perspective can offer quite specific implications for how we understand particular humorous phenomena is in relation to satire. According to superiority theory (at least according to proponents like Rapp and Gruner), aggressive or mocking forms of humour ought to be quite far down the evolutionary tree—just one or two removes from laughing at one's fallen opponent. But if human laughter can be traced back to the observable play of our closest relatives, not just the cartoonish cavemen that Rapp imagined, then presumably things must be the opposite way round. Laughing at people, then, would require something more sophisticated, an ability to embed symbolic behaviours in more complex communications: perhaps— 'you're really trying to bite me, but I'm laughing to signal to you or my friends that it's as if it's only play', or, 'our friend is actually violating all your cultural taboos and norms, and look—there's nothing you can do about it!' This is why Kozintsev, in a paper on humour in wartime, insists that satire is an inherently unstable 'hybrid' genre. If it's real humour, it can't really be aggressive. If it's really aggressive, then it's invective, not humour.[85]

Writing in 1969, some time before the research on animal play provided a convincing account of the origins of human laughter, Hodgart intuited that the origins of satire 'probably go back beyond human nature, to the psychology of our animal forebears'. He sought to link the practice of satire to the maintenance of social hierarchy among animals by well-established means of threat displays. 'The satirist's aim', he wrote, 'is to make the victim lose "face"', thereby asserting his superiority in the pecking order.[86]

While we are not sure that the present consensus matches that of the late 1960s with regards to the sensitivities of horses and dogs, the idea that satire may, in part, have a distinct origin from laughter and humour seems possible. In cultures with strong oral poetic traditions (including Arabic) it seems that satire is often an institutionalised form of ritual insult regarded with great seriousness and invested with almost magical qualities.[87] In the Celtic tradition, for example, it was believed that satirists could cause their targets bad luck or physical harm. As recently as the seventeenth century, one particularly virtuosic woman poet was said to have literally killed a rival with her words alone in an insult battle on the Hebridean island of Uist.[88] Regarding ancient Arabic culture, satire (*hija'*) is stated originally to have been a kind of magic curse whose pronunciation was attended with various peculiar ceremonies'.[89] This may partially explain the often forgiving Prophet Muhammad's decision to punish one of his satirical opponents, poet Ka'b ibn al-Ashraf, with death—a precedent that served as the late jihadi ideologue Anwar al-Awlaqi's theological justification for urging his followers to take lethal vengeance against satires of the prophet by Western cartoonists.[90]

Maybe this casts some light on the difficulty of actually using ridicule against groups such as Al Qaeda or IS. If what we are really talking about is something akin to ritual insult—traditionally associated with the anathema and ostracisation of the wider community—then laughter or amusement is, at best, incidental to this. Of course, disgruntled communities can be a very important, even vital resource in undercutting support for jihadis, though this is just restating a truism. But the very instability of satire could also be an asset. As acts of symbolic aggression, insults can be understood as small but daring feints—tiny forays into enemy territory that can inspire a sense of excitement where the will and resources for a fully fledged rebellion do not yet exist. Even the most direct insults can be funny when walking the line between real and pretend danger. Indeed, the underlying logic of such attacks does not rely on their being humorous in and of themselves, but rather on the glee of the in-group as it realises that it can attack a potentially feared outsider and get away with it. When collective pillorying of an enemy in this way comes from a position of relative weakness, it may offer a way to rally resistance and build morale. Where the reverse is the case, however, or if the tables are suddenly turned, the examples referenced above show how this mentality can turn into something uglier.

While such insult-raids may serve to gradually bolster confidence in more explicit and risky action, this is not the only way humour may be effective against fear. Play, in its essence, entails reframing an apparent threat as something benign. For humans, the perception of threat often arises because of a symbolic violation of the systems of meaning that help to anchor people securely in their lives, rather than an objective immediate danger. Instead of trying to directly quell such fears by refuting them in detail or, more laboriously, by taking issue with the meaning system from which they arise, humour can help deflect them by encouraging people to reinterpret them as play.

We previously touched on the concept of 'self-enhancing' humour, which, evidence shows, can lend those who possess a capacity for it increased resilience against trauma. But is it possible to create content that actually provides this sort of protection? There appears to be some evidence for this. A study by Proulx, Heine and Vohs set out to experimentally test Freud's theory of the uncanny in relation to a well-established psychological theory called the 'meaning maintenance model'.[91] The meaning maintenance model essentially holds that people cling to whatever meaningful frameworks are available to help explain the world around them. If they feel objectively threatened, by witnessing death, for example, they cling still more tightly to these belief systems. The reverse is also the case. If people experience a serious challenge to the coherence of their worldview, they tend to become existentially terrified, strongly reaffirming their commitment to any belief system available to them.[92] The researchers noted that this seems to relate to Freud's theory of the uncanny, arguing that people feel shaken by a sense of uncanniness not simply when they encounter things that are strange and surprising, but only when they encounter them unexpectedly, in otherwise familiar and predictable settings. Their paper compares the responses of subjects confronted with, among other things, a surreal anti-fable by Kafka and an absurd spoof of a British World War I adventure story that appeared in a Monty Python annual. One group was set up to expect a genuine wartime adventure story, while another was told that it was a spoof. Those who read the Kafka story and the Monty Python story without knowing they were meant to be a parody subsequently answered questions in ways that indicated greater attachment to national identity or conservative positions—through a more judgemental attitude towards prostitution, for example. The others did not.

Interestingly, this suggests a mechanism by which comedy could work against extremist narratives. We may note that in this experiment it was apparently taken for granted that the Kafka story was an example of serious absurdity, while the Monty Python one represented comical absurdity. Given that some interpretations of Kafka see his disturbing, surreal stories as deeply humorous, one wonders therefore how the subjects would have responded had they been primed to read the Kafka story as well as the Monty Python one as an example of surrealist comedy. While the comparison may seem crass, the propaganda of groups like IS often works hard to compound the effects of their horrific deeds by creating a sense of disorientation even on top of the horrific deeds it sometimes displays. For example, IS's notorious beheading videos have made use of visual effects drawn straight from horror films. As well as instilling terror within those the group views as its enemies, another function of these polarising videos may be to spark a sort of moral shock in Sunni Muslim viewers, which could cause them to cling more tightly to their own identity commitments and more rigid interpretations of religion, paradoxically making them more prone to radicalisation. Is it possible, then, that a travesty of the same things may have a prophylactic effect by priming viewers to accept the possibility of interpreting them as surreal and absurd? This seems akin to what Bakhtin said of medieval humour, which transformed even the horrors of death and Hell into the benign absurdity of the grotesque.[93]

If satire, depending on one's understanding of the term, entails a genuine, symbolic attack, then a staple and seemingly culturally universal form of humour involves offensive insults which, like play fighting or play chasing, are intended and understood playfully. Good-natured humour of this sort occupies a central place in the eighteenth century writings of those who sought to refute the aggressive understanding of laughter typically held by their predecessors. The term they often used to refer to this sort of egalitarian humour was *raillery*. Raillery is seemingly the opposite of pillory, which we just described, in that one uses play to place the target of attacks outside the group, while the other incorporates and reaffirms the target's group membership—broadly speaking, what Martin calls 'affiliative' as opposed to 'hostile' humour. While this may not play an obvious role in highly polarised situations where fruitful dialogue seems all but impossible, we would argue that there is another sense in which this sort of humorous process plays an important function in anti-jihadi humour. This is where playful insults are used as a way of humanising the enemy. In the previous chapter, we already noted that ridicule can strip jihadis of their mystique—a better alternative to more demonising approaches, which garner them the notoriety they aspire to. However, we think that attempts to advocate such interventions have not always made the key distinction between the hostile out-grouping intrinsic to pillory and humour, which aims to bring the subject down to earth without treading them underfoot. There is, however, an important implication of this, one which could serve as a test of whether it is actually raillery that is taking place (and if so, there is always the possibility, in principle, that one's opponent could accept the invitation to play, and respond in kind). This might seem rather hypothetical. In fact, we already discussed one example in the previous chapter. In recounting the US military's attempt to ridicule Abu Mus'ab al-Zarqawi by presenting him and his supporters as human and all too human, Waller seems to view Arab media outlets' ripostes on the militant's behalf as evidence that the tactic backfired. In fact, the possibility that it could do so was inherent in the logic of raillery. Brachman's mockery of his so-called jihobbyists naturally provided an opportunity for them to answer back. The satirical British film *Four Lions* is a particularly good example of raillery—it depends on a comic portrayal of British jihadis that is deeply humanising.[94] Many who have seen the film might imagine that the clownish, inept caricatures it creates would not be appreciated by would-be jihadis. And yet, just as the logic of raillery would lead us to expect, there are reportedly cases of jihadis who seem to enjoy the film, sharing clips of it among themselves.[95]

Insults, meant playfully or otherwise, are designed to insult rather than tell the truth, which is one reason why even serious insults can often be read as humorous. Sometimes, though, joking is also used as a way to actually tell the truth. While this is an ancient practice, this use of humour appears to be at the furthest remove from its apparent animal origins, one bound up in the implications of the human capacity for culture, language and complex interpretation of multiple meanings. Paradoxically, the ability to say serious things by means of joking is predicated on the fact that playful activities are often bounded by clear and unambiguous cultural signals of their playful status, thereby pro-viding collectively sanctified platforms, sometimes in a literal sense, in which speech enjoys special protection. An archetypal image of this is the medieval fool or court jester, the coxcomb, using the comic license granted by his position to speak truth to the monarch where others would not dare.

For coxcombry to work, such culturally sanctioned spaces for com-edy must be available. In his book *Subversive Laughter*, clown-scholar Mark Jenkins describes how in the Hindu culture of Bali in the 1980s, sacred masked clowns would use buffoonery to dramatise the threat modernisation and the growing tourist trade posed to traditional ways of life.[96] The clowns were explicit about the serious content behind their performances, and were sometimes invited to perform by local politicians interested in gaining insight into popular grievances. This relates to another distinctive feature of coxcombry: although, at times, it necessarily expresses negative views of particular people or groups, this criticism is still a serious claim, not merely an insult for the sake of amusement. Balinese clowns used their routines to poke fun at the transactional mentality of cash-flashing Western tourists, but their comic portrayal didn't dehumanise or attack them simply for the fun of doing so. Rather, it articulated a genuine concern about the impact they were seen as having.

In presenting these specific (though surely not exhaustive) ways in which humour may be effective in projects aimed at countering the appeal of jihadi groups, it may seem that we have returned again to our starting point, paring humour back to a series of tactics and tools which, it is hoped, will be able to achieve particular impacts. We don't claim to have solved the problems we have raised, as this would mean claiming to have the last word on the nature and meaning of humour itself, but we hope that we have added some conceptual depth to the discussion. Rather than viewing humour in essentialist terms as an objective property of texts that is distinct from other considerations, such as the message of those texts, we have tried to move towards the notion of humorous processes, rather than humorous techniques; pro-cesses that arise from an understanding of the underlying interactions through which we identify things as funny in the first place. At the same time, while we have tried to be appropriately critical about the idea of humour as inherently benign, we have also tried to avoid simply saying that humour has both good and bad applications. The business of actually being funny is, and always will be, inextricably entangled in the moral question of when humour is and isn't appropriate.

3

'LET HIM WEAR IT HIMSELF!'

HOW ISLAMISTS BECAME LAUGHABLE

In late 2011, a short black-and-white clip from a speech delivered by President Gamal Abdel Nasser in 1965 went viral on YouTube among Egyptian viewers.[1] The clip shows the Arab nationalist leader on top form, relaxed and charismatic, working a raptured audience with the practiced timing of a stand-up comedian.

With mock solemnity, the president of the United Arab Republic announces:

In 1953, we genuinely wanted to cooperate with the Muslim Brotherhood, so long as they went about things in the right way. I met the supreme guide of the Muslim Brotherhood, and asked what his demands were. What did he ask? He said that every woman who walks in the street should wear a headscarf …

The audience erupts in laughter at the absurdity of this proposal. One man heckles: 'Let him wear it himself!'

Nasser goes on:

So I said to him, 'Well, if that's what you say, then you want us to return to the days of Al-Hakim bi Amr Allah, who wouldn't allow people to walk by day, but only by night. I am of the opinion that each person in his own house can decide his own rules'. But he said, 'no, you are the ruler, you are responsible'. So I said, 'well, sir, what about your own daughter in the faculty of medicine? She's not wearing a veil. If you couldn't get one girl to wear a veil, how am I to get ten million of them to do it by myself?'

It isn't hard to see why the video struck a chord with many Egyptians in 2012. As one Egyptian comedian interviewed for this book observed, it conjures up nostalgia—among liberals, at any rate—for an apparently more secular past, one in which Islamists were treated not as serious political contenders but as people whose ideas and demands could be regarded as ridiculous.[2]

In 2012, Egyptians with secular inclinations had reason to hanker for this apparent golden age. Following the 2011 revolution, the country's first ever free and fair elections ushered in a parliament overwhelmingly dominated by Muslim Brotherhood and Salafi candidates.[3] Some months later, voters would bring another Muslim Brother, Mohammed Morsi, to power as president.

The year began with an ominous sign of what an Islamist-run Egypt may look like. In January, comedy actor Adel Imam—arguably the country's biggest celebrity—was sentenced to three months in jail, charged with 'insulting religion'.[4] A few months later, another court deliberated over the fate of a group of popular writers and directors facing similar charges: Wahid Hamed, Lenin El-Ramly, Sharif Arafa and Nader Galal. All had, in the past, produced work that outwardly criticised political Islam.

The writers and directors were found not guilty, while Imam was cleared on appeal.[5] It is also worth pointing out that the charges were not brought forth by the government privately, but by the activist Salafi lawyer 'Asran Mansur.[6] Nonetheless, the fact that the cases went to trial at all, and particularly the issuance of a guilty verdict in the most prominent of them, was disturbing not just because freedom of speech was seen to be stake, or even because the fact that an actor was being prosecuted for things said by characters he played (or had played alongside) was superficially absurd.[7] On top of all this, the offending films had been released nearly ten years earlier, in a political climate which had apparently welcomed them. For years, Islamists had been marginalised, humiliated and repressed. Now, the cases sent out a clear message: the boot was on the other foot. It was payback time.

But there is a problem with this neat analysis. In their almost ninety-year history (the organisation was officially founded in 1929), the Muslim Brotherhood and its numerous splinter groups, daughter organisations and fellow travellers has faced repression in almost every conceivable form. It has been outlawed, manipulated, violently oppressed and, occasionally, co-opted. Its leaders have been exiled and executed.[8] Its followers, their families and their neighbours have been beaten and bombarded.[9] And yet, for most of its history, this repression occurred, for the most part, offstage. Entertainment media, despite being used for propagandistic purposes throughout the Arab world, was generally slow to turn its attention to Islamists. Far from making them routine subjects of ridicule, for decades, entertainment media largely treated Islamists, militant or otherwise, as if they simply didn't exist. In this regard, Nasser's speech stands less as a product of its time and more as an intriguing false start. The film portrayals of Islamists in the 1990s, for which Mansur was seeking vengeance in 2012, were not the culmination of decades of humiliation. They were almost the first serious attempts by popular Arabic media to turn the weapon of ridicule against Islamism.

Reviewing the history of Egyptian film, we found forty examples that, in some sense, feature themes of problematic religiosity or terrorism. Of these, most do not address anything that could be described as Islamism, but focus on the supposed backwardness and obsolescence of aspects of traditional religiosity or on non-religious forms of terrorism. Of those that do address Islamism, fewer still are comedies; and even among these, most feature Islamists only peripherally. We did not find any film prior to 1994's *The Terrorist* (which is discussed further in due course) that can be said to directly address the subject of militant Islamism.

There are two questions to be asked in response to this. The first, and perhaps the most obvious, is 'why'? Why weren't Islamists an apparently suitable subject for mainstream comedy for such a long time, and why did that change? The second question, however, and the one that we address in depth in this chapter, is 'how?' When they were finally called upon to do so, how did Arab comedy writers go about negotiating social taboos and adapting the idioms of popular comedy to make Islamists an appropriate object of ridicule?

In a sense, though, there is nothing new about Arab comedians using their art as a cultural weapon against the encroachment of politicised religion. On the contrary, this history of Arabic literature and civilisation offers countless potential precedents.

We need to be cautious at this point. The clash between Islamists and 'secularists' in the Arab world is modern, not ancient.[10] This is because both Islamism and secularism are, to state an obvious truism from an academic point of view, both products of modernity.[11] Before European conceptions of the secular nation state were introduced into the Middle East, the issue of whether to institutionally and formally distinguish between religion and politics was not even on the table.

Nevertheless, the perceived roots of the cultural conflict between Islamism and secularism do stretch further back, even to the origins of Islam. From the point of view of Islamists (as we shall discuss in the next chapter), a particular, essentialised reading of Islamic history is all but a definitional necessity. *Muthaqqafun* (Arab intellectuals) on the other hand, while not bound in this way, have drawn on the rebellious heritage of their cultural history, looking to previous golden ages such as the Abbasid era, when the flourishing of art and learning was accompanied by a spirit of libertinism that stood in self-conscious opposition to the stern demands of religious purists, in cultural production characterised by praise of wine-drinking, hashish smoking, bisexuality, philosophical speculation and religious tolerance.

'Wine poet' Al-Hasan ibn Hakami, better known by his nickname Abu Nuwas (the one with the sidelocks), is emblematic of such precedents. Abu Nuwas' poetry, which incurred ire and punishment at the hands of the religious authorities in his time, routinely mocked the sacred rituals and principles of Islam. As one believing attendee quipped during a seminar held at St. Andrews University on Arabic satire, it contains 'blasphemy in almost every line'. Moreover, in lampooning the tiresomeness of the Ramadan fast, for example, or comparing the prostration of prayer to falling down in a drunken stupor, it has been argued that Abu Nuwas was not just being offensively funny. Rather, he was systematically advancing his own, mystical conception of Islamic piety.[12]

A more explicit example of classical Arabic humour that takes on Islam itself can be found in the work of Abu al-'Ala al-Ma'arri, a celibate and vegetarian, believed to be an atheist, who wrote poetry that outrageously sent up key Islamic tenets. He even produced a spoof of the Quran, *Al-Fusul wa Al-Ghayat (Paragraphs and Periods)*,[13] which seems to have been intended to refute the sacred text's key claim to inimitability, whereby Arab poets are challenged to produce even one *sura* (chapter) like it.[14]

While these poets belong to the medieval past, the ideals that they supposedly stood for continue to be of relevance today, as evidenced by contemporary cultural struggles. In 2013, Al Qaeda-affiliated fighters in the Syrian town of Ma'arra beheaded a statue of Ma'arri (though it isn't certain they knew who he was, and may simply have objected to the existence of a statue).[15] In 2015, the hand of Abu Nuwas, clutching a wine glass, was broken off his statue, located on the pleasant stretch of Baghdad corniche named after him. This action seems to have been incited by a local cleric who accused the statue of 'provoking Muslims by manifesting drinking alcohol, which is forbidden in Islam'.[16]

Perhaps the most important precedent for our present purpose is a less well-known writer: Muhammad Ibn Daniyal. Ibn Daniyal is remarkable for two reasons. First, he appears to represent the only obvious example of a medieval Arabic comedy dramatist—one who has specifically served as a model and inspiration for modern-day Arabic comedians writing for theatre and film.[17] Secondly, his writing didn't just serve to express a hedonistically liberal worldview. It seems that it specifically did so as an act of protest and resistance against a political project of religious intolerance.

There are other details of Ibn Daniyal's biography that resonate with contemporary events. He was originally from Mosul, which was allegedly renowned as a redoubt of the drinking, carousing culture that Abu Nuwas' poetry previously idealised. The city's fate, and that of Ibn Daniyal, were reshaped by the calamitous Mongol sacking of Baghdad in 1258.[18] When, after an uprising, Mosul was also ravaged, Ibn Daniyal took refuge in Mamluk Cairo, where he worked as an eye doctor and acquired a reputation as a comic poet.[19]

Egypt remained a bastion against the barbarian onslaught (as Arabs, Persians and Turks at the time characterised it). Its ruler, Mamluk Sultan Baybars al-Bunduqdari, had, in 1260, defeated the Mongols at the decisive battle of 'Ayn Jalut.[20] And yet, as is often the case, this crisis was accompanied by a reactionary wave of social conservatism. Seeking the political support of Cairo's Islamic scholars, Baybars launched a puritanical public morality campaign in 1267, which included the banning of wine drinking and prostitution. The campaign was apparently violently enforced: 'Taverns were smashed, brothels torn down, and offenders severely punished'.[21]

When, at a high-society dinner, the host was forced to announce that, due to the new restrictions, wine could no longer be served, Ibn Daniyal—a man renowned for his multifarious appetites—seems to have had enough. He responded by authoring a satirical poem sometimes called *Elegy for Satan*, a work which combines stunningly evocative portrayals of debauched carousing with deeply ironic humour, simultaneously spoofing the nostalgic spirit of classical Bedouin verse and offering mock praise to the sultan for his victory over the forces of darkness.[22]

Presumably on the back of this, Ibn Daniyal received an invitation from an unknown promoter of shadow puppet plays, seeking to commission some new writing from him. This was rather remarkable, since Ibn Daniyal was a high-brow writer—a semi-official court poet, even—while the shadow puppet play appears to have been regarded as a vulgar form of popular entertainment. This is akin to John Updike contributing to *Playboy Magazine*. Nonetheless, after considering the offer, he accepted,[23] going on to produce what can confidently be described as some of the most outrageously and hilariously obscene writing created in a trilogy of plays, brimming over with debauchery, prostitution, gay sex and even coprophilia, alongside plentiful lamentations by the sinful characters about the difficulties of Baybars' new regime. In one section, the hero enjoins his lover to anally penetrate him while he is fasting.[24] In another, a poem describes the goings on in a brothel in which a man '… jerks off alone … aroused by a headscarf'.[25]

Ibn Daniyal has been called 'the Arab Aristophanes',[26] but perhaps it would also be apt to call him the Arab Rabelais. Just as Rabelais—in Bakhtin's assessment—crystallised and preserved the spirit of medieval European folk humour in *Gargantua and Pantagruel*, so too does it seem that Ibn Daniyal's trilogy of plays drew heavily on a bawdy, vigorously alive folk culture in which he was very much a participant observer. This, it is important to stress, was a culture which, for all its profanity, was by no means anti-religious in its core principles, as indeed neither are Ibn Daniyal's plays (at least on the surface), in which the debauched characters ultimately declare their intention to mend their ways and make the pilgrimage to Mecca. Moreover, the institution of the shadow puppet play was part and parcel of the experience of the Ramadan fast, just as it was once traditional in Christian Europe to celebrate Christmas with the sexually explicit genre of song originally denoted by the word 'carol'.

Centuries later, when theatrical comedy returned to Egypt, it came, as before, in the wake of a civilisational crisis precipitated by an invasion. This time, however, the invader came from the West rather than the East, and it was Egypt itself that was occupied by Napoleon's forces. The political response to this shock was not initially religious conservatism, but rather vigorous attempts by the country's new rulers to modernise society along Western lines.[27]

The pioneers of Arabic comic theatre, nonetheless, found themselves in conflict with forces of religious orthodoxy. Marun Naqqash, a Lebanese Christian immigrant to Cairo, cautiously staged an adaptation of Molière's *The Miser* in his home, but the performance was interrupted when the mufti, who was present in the audience, started to yell out advice to the cuckolded husband he saw onstage.[28] Later, Ya'qub Sanua, an Egyptian Jew, got into more serious trouble by penning a play that made fun of the Islamic practice of polygamy when the ruling khedive (who had two wives) saw this as a personal slight.[29] But this conflict was initially interpreted—as it would continue to be for a long time to come, though increasingly disingenuously—as a straightforward one between forces of traditionalism and progress. In fact, Jamal al-Din al-Afghani and Muhammad Abduh, often regarded as the founding fathers of political Islam,[30] enthusiastically supported Sanua's efforts to establish a popular theatre (including a traditional puppet show alongside his Western-influenced live performances), seeing these as potentially powerful vehicles for politicising the masses.[31]

Indeed, when Egypt did begin to develop a vigorous domestic tradition first of theatre, and then of film, it was not initially Islamic political agitators who represented a major obstacle so much as the institutionalised religious establishment. In her study of film censorship in Egypt

Censorship: The Expressive Dilemma Between Writer and Producer,[32] Egyptian scholar Amal Fu'ad notes that laws enshrining the right of the pre-eminent theological institution Al-Azhar to oversee artistic production were established as early as 1911—a power successively renewed in a series of laws and decisions stretching over successive decades. In 1926, Al-Azhar blocked what would have been one of the first Egyptian films ever created: *Muhammad, the Prophet of God*. As the sheikhs of Al-Azhar increasingly mobilised behind a conservative political agenda, the situation reached a point where it seemed as if the official censors, who could, but were often afraid to stand up to the clerics looking over their shoulders, became as much the guardians of artistic expression as its primary obstacle.

This is not to say that the temporal rulers of Egypt adopted a laissez-faire approach either. Indeed, reflecting on the (already heavily censored) films that flourished after the 1930s, Egypt's revolutionary leader Mohammed Naguib complained primly about the 'silliness and indecency' of the country's performing arts. He opined: 'There is no film but that a belly dancer has arbitrarily featured in it. No wonder this happened, because it was just a reflection of the age we have lived in. However, nowadays, we cannot accept from arts industry and its sponsors anything like what happened in the past'.[33]

Caught between a clerical establishment deeply suspicious of the portrayal of anything pertaining to religion or religiosity, a political leadership demanding nationalist propaganda and a viewing public seeking entertainment, Egyptian entertainment media tended to settle on an escapist formula. The world portrayed on screen became a parallel universe depicting an absurd, carnivalistic fantasy of supposedly ordinary Egyptian life. For film scholar Iman Hamam, Egyptian comedies conform to what she calls the '*sha'abi* genre'—deriving from the Arabic word *sha'b* (people). The key feature of this distinctively Egyptian, popular genre is the way in which it provides 'a distorted view of an already distorted reality' by means of 'temporal dislocation', the 'haphazardness of events' and a 'formulaic and fragmentary storytelling, characterised by 'awkward beginnings, abrupt endings and unconvincing plots'. The films, she insists:

> …highlight common social concerns relating to compromised masculinity amidst corruption and unemployment. The hero's excessive and

unruly behaviour mocks social conventions, ruthless authority figures and the disturbed pretensions of class. And yet, for all their apparent subversiveness, these films ultimately end up reaffirming the status quo and maintaining the validity of those same institutions they mock.[34]

It is tempting to suggest that the carnival element at the heart of the *sha'abi* genre is a more or less direct inheritance from the spirit and style of pre-existing street culture, including that of actual popular carnivals, like the *mawlid* festivals celebrating various Sufi saints, or occasions such as the Prophet Muhammad's birthday or even, in previous times, the annual flooding of the Nile. If so, then there is a considerable irony.

Film, television and radio are, of course, technically 'modern' media. But more than that, they were used very deliberately and systematically by Egypt's nationalist rulers from the outset as tightly controlled propaganda with the goal of selling to Egyptians the idea of Egypt as a modern, forward looking state. Modernisation, certainly in its nationalist heyday, meant aggressively campaigning against the supposedly backward, embarrassing and un-Islamic institutions of *sha'abi* folk culture. In short, it seems that Egyptian television and film comedy both killed and preserved the elements of popular festivity similarly to how Hollywood's great silent comedies relied on the skills of entertainers who had cut their teeth in the same popular music hall tradition that cinema was rapidly making obsolete.

Another irony can be identified. In its incorporation of this premodern popular ethos, it seems that Egyptian comedy was playing a double game. On the one hand, in presenting a vision of Egypt from which religion and religiosity were largely absent—a merry world of cheeky chaps and curvaceous temptresses with hearts of gold—it may have been reflecting a vision of the progress of a modern, secular nation. And yet at the same time, hiding the sacred symbols and practices of religion behind a discreet veil was, in a curious sense, a characteristically Islamic (or Sunni Islamic) attitude to media representation. Under this approach, storytelling was not a mirror of society, but rather an organ of the social whole with important, if not necessarily praiseworthy, functions. It was a safety valve for jovial impulses that were sinful but also natural, and profanity was not a challenge to religious morality, but its necessary and constant obverse.

At this point, it is useful to make some very general points that will be relevant to the rest of the book, concerning how the media sector works in the Arab world. For a long time after their introduction, broadcast media tended to be heavily centralised and tightly controlled by the state. In fact, in the case of radio, the states concerned were often not Arab, but the Western powers that were controlling or contesting the region.[35] In a sense, authoritarian Arab media is an inheritance from authoritarian colonial rule. This began to change dramatically with the arrival of the first satellite television station[36] and then the internet.[37] With the emergence of pan-Arab media that paid little heed to national borders, came a large private sector with numerous competing channels. Nevertheless, it would be a mistake to imagine that these are free of political control. The satellites themselves (notably Nilesat and Arabsat) are owned by Arab governments (Egypt and Saudi Arabia, respectively) and the most important commercial channels are owned by tycoons who usually have a close political relationship with a state.[38] Often, it seems commercial considerations are secondary to the advantage accrued from these platforms in terms of media influence. Then, of course, there are the channels, often very popular, which are directly owned and controlled by political actors, whether these be states or movements such as Hezbollah in the case of the popular and largely mainstream Al-Manar TV.[39] For Arabs and other seasoned consumers of Arabic media, it is simply taken for granted that all channels ultimately exist in order to advance some propaganda agenda or other—a level of media literacy which, one could argue, remains comparatively lacking, but increasingly needed in the West.

Against this backdrop, despite changes in Egyptian society, the highly stylised forms of Egyptian popular entertainment came under increasing pressure. Anthropologist Lila Abu Lughod has shown how working-class Upper Egyptian women engaged with Egyptian dramas and the glamorous off-screen lives of their actors (particularly the women) without requiring or expecting that the lives and the values that governed them should in any way resemble their own. And yet, as pious ordinary Egyptians urbanised and began to establish a new, media-savvy middle class, this compact became more problematic. As Walter Armbrust, an anthropologist who specialises in Egyptian popular entertainment, points out, the numerous urban scenes in Egyptian films and television that featured few or any women wearing the hijab began to look less like a merry fantasy all could partake in, and more like a glaring and deliberate writing out of the experience of a vast swathe of people.[40]

There were other reasons that seemed to prompt the push for the representation of Islamists—at least of a particular sort—on screen. For decades, the regime saw dissident political Islamists, first the Muslim Brotherhood and later its more extreme and violent splinter groups, as representing a threat to national security. Islamists had famously attempted to assassinate Nasser and successfully killed his successor, President Anwar al-Sadat. The religious scruples of Al-Azhar clerics notwithstanding, there were sound political reasons for wanting to make cultural opposition to dissident Islamists visible.

Ahmed Salim, an Egyptian Islamist who has written about the cinematic representation of his ideological brethren, concurs, pointing out that Islamist characters in film and TV 'were very marginal and very weak until the beginning of the 1990s. Before that, neither Nasser, Sadat, nor even Mubarak in his first decade employed these two tools in their struggle with Islamists'.

Film scholar Hani Darwish offers an alternative perspective. In his view, the artistic motivation for making films about jihadis may not be as transparent as it seems. 'Terrorism', he points out, is an exciting, action packed subject that 'represents an excellent space for political thought' and is less likely to be confronted with 'the traditional censorship experienced by works which treat of political expression or dictatorship'. In short, it is important to be mindful of the possibility that films ostensibly about terrorists may be intended to, and may be understood as, indirectly criticising and targeting those in positions of power.[41]

However, at the beginning of the Mubarak era, when Egyptian artists were first attempting to introduce Islamist themes to their work, these were initially rebuffed by the censors. Salim draws attention to *The Elephant*, a novel by Fathi Ghanem that Yahia al-Alami turned into a TV series of the same name. 'In this case, the censors intervened to remove everything related to this character just a few hours before the series aired. Occurrences like this were repeated on more than one occasion.'[42]

This seems to imply that the religious establishment constituted the biggest obstacle, rather than a fundamental unwillingness on the part of Egyptian writers to broach the subject. Such things had happened before. Fu'ad quotes a former Egyptian film censor describing the struggle faced by 'the first film about extremism in the Egyptian cinema', *The Man from the Sixth District* (1984). Even after having 156 passages recommended for deletion, the film's backers struggled to get the film cleared, perhaps doing so by means of further concessions.[43]

Salim suggests some reasons for this. There is, he suggests, a 'dominant tendency in modern Arabic culture towards covering up and concealment, believing that disclosing and displaying wrongdoing risks tempting people towards the very wrongdoing it seeks to fight.'[44] This is a propagandist's dilemma that stretches well beyond Arabic culture.

Salim's second suggestion, one with which Darwish's account correlates, is, if not the most intellectually satisfying, certainly the most plausible. Despite everything that happened in the 1970s and 1980s, the assassination of Sadat notwithstanding, it was only in the 1990s that Islamism achieved enough momentum at every level of society that it became impossible for state media and the Egyptian media elite not to address it.[45]

As we just noted, some Islamists had posed an immediate threat to the heads of the Egyptian state since the 1950s. By the last two decades of the twentieth century, however, Islamism represented a more deeply entrenched and omnipresent threat to the established order. The most extreme manifestations of this were the campaigns of terrorist attacks launched by Al-Jama'a al-Islamiyya and Al-Jihad, both essentially offshoots of the Muslim Brotherhood. Often targeting the foreign visitors on whom Egypt's tourism industry depended, and sometimes killing Egyptians in the process, these attacks were a direct and palpable threat to sections of Egyptian society as well as political leaders. Attacks against individuals also escalated dramatically in the 1990s. In 1990, Rif'at Mahgub, the speaker of the Egyptian parliament, was assassinated by Al-Jihad. That same year, jihadis gunned down outspoken public intellectual Farag Foda. An attempted assassination of the Nobel Prize-winning novelist Naguib Mahfouz followed in 1994, and, one year later, President Hosni Mubarak completed the clean sweep of Egyptian presidents to face attempted assassination at the hands of militant Islamists.[46]

By this time, Islamist movements were also able to present a direct cultural challenge to Egypt's media creators, which was just as threatening in its own way. As a result, ostentatious public piety became increasingly mainstream—for example, a number of formerly prominent female actors decided to put on the veil and abandon their careers in what was now presented as an inherently sinful industry.[47]

As producers, actors, writers and directors began to fear for their careers and sometimes their lives, many began to see making a stand as essential. As a 1992 article in the *Christian Science Monitor* put it:

> Artists critical of Islamic extremism are not necessarily motivated by patriotism. It is also in their best interest to fight its spread. Muslim groups, critical of sex and immorality in the media, have an assassination hit list, which includes many artists. Adel Imam, the main character of 'Terrorism and Kebab' and the most popular actor in Egypt today, is on this list. Reportedly, he is under 24-hour police protection.[48]

In short, by the 1990s, the perceived interests of Egypt's creative industries and government cultural policy had aligned, presumably outweighing any scruples felt by the religious censors. Where (according to Salim) writers had been impeded by government censors in their attempts to present Islamist characters, now the government was eagerly pushing for anti-Islamist films, and Egyptian film-makers were obliging, out of a genuine desire to do so but also in the hope of placing themselves in the government's favour.

There are several notable examples of this new enthusiasm. The television drama *The Family* and the abovementioned film comedy *Terrorism and Kebab*, both written by veteran screenwriter Wahid Hamid, were two. The former addressed Islamist extremism, but not humorously. The latter was a notably successful comedy, but one that touched on Islamism obliquely, via the character of a Salafi government employee who used incessant prayers as a pretext to avoid work. Particularly important is the 1994 film *The Terrorist*, written by Lenin el-Ramly, directed by Nader Galal and starring Adel Imam, which is significant because it marks the first sustained portrayal of Islamist extremism in an Egyptian comedy—at least in the formal sense.

The considerable cultural significance of this film was recognised at the time and continues to be today. Despite being generally regarded as a work of indifferent artistic quality, it is among the most written about Egyptian films in the scholarly literature in English and, to a lesser extent, in Arabic. It features in numerous articles and books on Egyptian popular culture, notably by Armbrust,[49] Shafik,[50] Khatib,[51] Hammond,[52] Baker,[53] Allagui and Najjar[54] and Leaman,[55] and Ahmed Salim also devotes considerable attention to the film, offering the only extensive critique of it from an Islamist perspective of which we are aware.[56]

Despite the attention the film has received, however, it has not, so far as we are aware, been specifically analysed in the sense with which we are primarily interested in it—that is, as a work of *comedy*. This assumes that *The Terrorist* actually is a comedy—a point that could be contested. It is only sometimes referred to as such,[57] and, as we will consider in due course, a good deal of the content is clearly not intended to be funny. The film, as with other Egyptian comedies, contains elements that resemble generic serious action and melodrama more than humour. Even the more convincingly comic parts are typically played rather straight, especially compared with the over-the-top clowning one would normally expect.

At the same time, cinema audiences going to watch *The Terrorist* probably expected a comedy and likely interpreted at least some of the film through this frame. Imam was, particularly at this time, primarily known as a comic actor, and Ramly, the film's screenwriter, was known as a comedy writer. Moreover, the film's essential plot depends on what is clearly a comic premise. When interviewed for this book in Cairo, the late Hazem Azmi, a close personal friend and perhaps the most well-informed expert on Ramly's work, insisted 'the film is unquestionably a comedy—whether it is funny or not is, of course, another matter'.[58]

The Terrorist, then, marks a pioneering moment in the development of anti-Islamist satire. As a popular film with artistic ambitions, it upholds elements of the *sha'abi* comedy formula and violates others. Much of what Hamam sees as integral to the genre is present, including the 'body swap' topos, the 'unruly behaviour' of the male protagonist, pretensions of class and the problem of compromised masculinity arising from socio-economic challenges. However, the film's central reversal is, for the most part, used to re-assert the dominance of state sanctioned ideology rather than challenge authority figures. It is also clear that the film is trying hard to be meaningful and shed the label of 'meaninglessness' that is typically applied to Egyptian *sha'abi* comedies, often intended as escapist films.

The plot of the film, in brief, is this. Ali (played by Imam) is a violent Islamist extremist. We know that he is an Islamist extremist because he and his fellow extremists dress in uniform white robes with full beards and completely shaven moustaches. We know that he is violent because at the outset of the film we see him leading a group who smash up and torch a Coptic jewellery store and then a video shop.

Soon after, Ali is revealed to be a simple, uneducated man in the thrall of a sinister and hypocritical sheikh, who speaks in stilted classical Arabic and demands unquestioning adherence to his every word. Ali, as with the protagonists of countless other Egyptian comedies, turns out to be sex-starved and desperate to get married, a fact which the sheikh uses to manipulate and control him, parading a potential fiancée in front of him. However, his hopes of marriage are dashed when, after shooting up a busload of tourists, killing a nearby Egyptian child but none of the foreigners, Ali is forced to go into hiding, where he is tormented by sexual thoughts and aroused when he catches sight of a buxom woman hanging out laundry on her balcony—another commonplace burlesque motif in such films.

Subsequently, Ali is dispatched on another operation, this time to assassinate public intellectual Fu'ad Mas'ud (closely modelled on the real life Farag Foda).[59] In order to carry out this operation, Ali is obliged to shed his Islamist clothing in favour of jeans and a shirt, to shave his beard and to steal a car, which contains a briefcase belonging to the vehicle's owner. When the operation goes awry, Ali finds himself on the run from the police, but is run over by Sawsan, a wealthy and naïve young woman from a liberal, upper-class family. Panicked, the family bring the unconscious Ali into their home, with the help of their neighbour Hani, a Coptic Christian doctor.

Based on the documents they find in the briefcase, the family believe the convalescent Ali to be a poetry-writing philosophy professor from Cairo University. Ali is initially shocked and morally outraged by the family's liberal lifestyle but gradually finds his prejudices challenged. He also becomes acquainted with Hani who, in an ironic subplot, turns out to be henpecked by his obsessively religious wife.

Just as he is beginning to build a relationship with Sawsan, who has fallen in love with him after reading what she believes to be his poetry, Ali sexually harasses Sawsan's younger sister Faten due to her revealing clothing and gregarious manner, which he considers signs of sexual availability. Faten then becomes suspicious and investigates Ali's identity, discovering the truth by contacting the real professor whose identity he has stolen. Meanwhile, Ali attends Sawsan's birthday party, at which he drunkenly travesties a religious sermon before collapsing. Shortly after recovering consciousness, Faten returns and exposes him, forcing him to flee, holding the family at gunpoint.

Returning to his jihadi comrades, though he no longer believes in their cause, Ali discovers a fresh plot against Mas'ud. He phones him up to warn him of the plot, but the intellectual, refusing to be intimidated into changing his plans to appear in public, dies a martyr. An aborted escape attempt brings Ali to the house of his adopted family, where he is slain in a hail of bullets, calling out their names as he collapses before their door.

As we already pointed out, and as the plot summary will have reinforced, the film is not a comedy throughout. It is unlikely that this generic heterogeneity—the distribution of identifiably comical and serious moments throughout the film—is accidental. There is balance in the film between laughter and what, following Billig, we might call 'unlaughter', which, more than just the absence of laughter, is the clear expression that certain things are not to be laughed at.[60] This merits careful examination.

If we consider where humour is and is not made possible within the internal logic of the film, it seems that the key factor is the progress of Ali's character through four different incarnations. In the first, we are presented with Ali in his supposedly 'true' identity: an Islamist extremist and terrorist. These sections are fairly consistently melodramatic. Occasional flashes of comedy are permitted to peek through only when the rigid, fundamentalist personae slip a little, revealing the urges and frailties beneath. In a moment that could be interpreted as mockery, the sheikh character feasts on grilled meats, eating in a manner reminiscent of the culture of the Persian Gulf, one that is intended to appear savage and uncivilised to Egyptians. The moment is sinister and reveals an animalistic hunger beneath the veneer of religious propriety, but it can also been seen as comic. A more plausibly humorous scene comes later, when Ali finds himself sexually tempted. Though he is far from home and already operating incognito, Ali still has an Islamist appearance.[61] But the Islamist persona is already beginning to slip.

In his second incarnation, the protagonist is forced to disguise himself in order to carry out the assassination plot. An irony here is that, although Ali is supposedly in disguise, it is tempting to see this version of him as the 'true' one: resourceful, attractive, invested with agency—a model of capable Egyptian manhood in line with Imam's other leading roles in previous films.[62] These sections are devoid of even slightly comic moments. Instead, they follow the generic conventions of action movies.

The third iteration of Ali, which makes up the bulk of the film's plot, is the one in which the most comedy can be found. Here, Ali is forced to adopt not only a new appearance but an entirely false identity. This is a classic comic set up. So much so, that, according to Wickberg, it is quite literally the origin of the word 'humour' in its present sense in English.[63]

Finally, at the film's dénouement, Ali re-adopts an identity similar to his second incarnation. In this situation, he is no longer in the thrall of the Islamists, but must pretend to be in order to try to escape. Once again, he is presented as tough and capable, and this section of the film is a mixture of action with a touch of melodrama and even tragedy.

This tonal division of the film is revealing. Ali, understood as a sort of distorted representation of the *sha'abi* everyman, spends the bulk of the film occupying one of two essentially false guises. One of these gives him a horrific, hateful yet pitiable facet—another gives him a comic aspect. When, however, he assumes his true identity, he is neither horrific nor laughable. Stripping Ali of fundamentalist trappings and his action-hero skills is essential not just to setting up an incongruously comical situation, but also to making him a viable subject for comedy.

Thus, *The Terrorist* derives humour from Ali's situation in two ways. The first of these is familiar territory for Egyptian comedies: a working-class protagonist trying to fake it in an upper-class world. Unlike the pattern identified by Hamam, in which a cheeky, folksy anti-hero would exuberantly rise to this challenge, milking the situation for all it is worth and lampooning the stuck-up pretensions of those around him in so doing, in this case the joke is usually squarely on Ali, whose backwardness becomes an object of derision as he is baffled by seemingly ubiquitous products of the modern world like Nescafé.

There is, however, an arguably more sophisticated comic discourse also at play. Here, the humour revolves around a series of misunderstandings between Ali's inflexible, literal understanding of religion, and the more complex modalities of faith he gradually uncovers. In a lengthy discussion with Hani, Ali is pleased to find another person who takes religion seriously, unaware that their religions are not the same. On another occasion, Ali asks one of his hosts about a picture of Che Guevara hanging on the wall of his bedroom who, he is told, is:

'One of the most important *mujahidin*'.
'In Afghanistan?'
'In Cuba'.

In the linguistic theory of humour developed by Raskin and Attardo mentioned in the previous chapter, it might be said that the humour in these lines derives from a 'script opposition'. For Ali, the word '*mujahid*' carries a very particular set of associations, all of them deriving from a narrow, exclusionary attitude to Islam. For his interlocutor, on the other hand, the word carries a more general meaning of anyone fighting for a just cause. The two scripts are linked by a visual gag in this case—Guevara's unkempt beard, which fits with the narrow reading assumed by Ali.

Another theoretical resource from the discourse analysis tradition which can be usefully applied in this case is A.A. Berger's typology of the comic and the tragic.[64]

Fig. 1: Berger's elements of tragedy and comedy

The comic	The tragic
Chance	Inevitability
Freedom	Determinism
Optimism	Pessimism
Survival	Destruction
The social	The personal
Integration	Separation
Low status	High status
Trivial	Serious
Lowly characters	Elevated characters
Pleasure	Pain
Cathexis	Catharsis

The section of the film spanning from the car accident up until Ali's unmasking contains numerous comic elements. The accident itself involves the comic element of chance, bathetically undercutting and thus ending the first 'action' sequence of the film. Even though Ali is trapped by his injury and because he is on the run, he enjoys greater freedom than before, as he is no longer hemmed in by religious restrictions and the demands of his leader—something which, intentionally or not, seems like a metaphor for the often-promised trade-off between personal and political freedoms presented by Arab dictators. This section is characterised by Ali's sometimes inept attempts to survive and adapt in this situation and, ultimately to integrate into a new society—one which can be read as a stand-in for the Egyptian nation itself—a process involving numerous mishaps stemming from Ali's ignorance and low social status.

In sum, *The Terrorist* was a tentative step towards treating Islamist extremists as subjects for comedy. The film avoids being comical altogether wherever it directly encounters militancy or fundamentalist Islam, instead presenting their otherness as a melodramatically emphasised threat to the state. Similarly, in depicting the state's response, the film is never anything other than reverential. Comedy is confined to the domestic sphere and often the comparatively safe realm of class politics. But even here, a key ingredient is missing: neither Ali nor his upper-class hosts are capable of representing the rebellious, carnivalistic *sha'abi* spirit normally central to Egyptian comedy. This reinforcement of social order based on class hierarchy without any legitimised conduit for rebellion seems to lend the film a rather stifling feel.

One could counter that the awkwardness of the way *The Terrorist* juxtaposes traditionally comic and tragic-action elements means that it works as a sort of meta-comedy, inviting the viewer to choose whether to live in the broadly comic realm offered by existing societal structures, or in the tragic one that will inevitably result from rebellion of the sort initially chosen by Ali. The risk here may be that some could see the dignity the tragic arc grants Ali's character, even as a villain, as preferable to the sometimes humiliating comic role he is thrust into.

As Armbrust observes, *The Terrorist* was a watershed moment in the sense that, after its release, Islamists became relatively commonplace in popular Egyptian film and television—the taboo was, apparently, lifted.[65] However, most portrayals of Islamists on the screen before 2011 also tend to be even narrower and more stereotyped.

In comedies like *Hello America* (also written by Ramly, as the final instalment of his popular Adeela and Bakheet trilogy)[66] and Youssef Maaty's *The Embassy in the Building*, Islamists represent a more or less undifferentiated mob of fringe loonies, who serve as a punch line in their own right.[67] (Of these, the former is perhaps slightly more sophisticated in so far as it presents Islamism in the context of American hyper-individualism and consumerism.) Even in serious films with artistic ambitions, it is common to see portrayals without much more depth. Wahid Hamid's *Blood of a Gazelle*,[68] for example, despite featuring a radicalisation narrative, nonetheless presents Islamists as de-individuated and mindlessly violent. A possible partial exception is *The Yacoubian Building*,[69] which critic Ahmed Salim compares favourably with *The Terrorist* for its acknowledgement of brutality on the part of the security forces towards Islamists as a key factor in their radicalisation.[70] But even here, Islamism is presented as a reaction to poverty, exclusion and humiliation; very little is said about its actual attributes.

One interesting exception to this, which came at the end of the period with which we are concerned, is the comedy *Three Men Deceive Her*.[71] The plot of this film revolves around the misadventures of Nagiba, a young woman from a poor family who excels in academic studies, but is socially awkward and naïve. Entering university to study archaeology while holding down an elementary school teaching position, she is attracted, in turn, to three men: a Westernised playboy, a Marxist revolutionary and an Islamist television personality. Unlike most previous representations of Islamists in Egyptian films, the character of Sheikh Amir Hassan—probably a caricature of real-life Islamist Amr Khaled—is presented as suave and handsome, wearing a smart suit and with his own television programme. When Nagiba gets to know him better, however, this appearance turns out to be a façade. Amir's use of modern media is hypocritical—he scolds his adoring female followers for wasting time on Facebook, while simultaneously asking Nagiba to follow him. Even his eating habits display a similar double standard: he takes Nagiba out to a sophisticated restaurant, but proceeds to disgust her by eating simple Gulf style dishes of rice and meat, including bones and animal testicles (another trope present in *The Terrorist*). His teachings too are revealed as two-faced: on the one hand, he incites Nagiba to an act of rebellion, smashing pharaonic statues on the grounds that they are heathen idols (in shocking anticipation of IS's real life actions in this regard). But when asked to publicly comment on this, he condemns the act, using the smooth language of moderate Islam.

In its treatment of Islamism, *Three Men Deceive Her* represents a curious and, in some ways, jarring blend of the highly artificial world of Egyptian comedy and elements of realism, and not only in its central plotline. For example, various establishing shots throughout the film present groups of Egyptian students a significant number of whom, naturalistically, are wearing the hijab in a realistic modern style. The segment of the film dealing with Nagiba's dalliance with Sheikh Amir opens with her being consoled by two *muhajjibat* (women wearing the hijab) who are presented as pious, but not dangerous or unsympathetic. On the other hand, Nagiba (a working-class girl who, in real life, we would probably expect to wear the hijab herself, as well over 90 per cent of Egyptian women do) corresponds to the logic of film convention. For most of the film, she acts as if religion simply does not exist. When she does become religious, however, she immediately puts on an *abaya*, and transforms her school class likewise into a traditional-style religious *madrasa* (school). Nonetheless, the film is clearly innovative not only in the way in which it represents Islam and Islamism, but also in the way it extracts humour from the subject matter. While *Three Men Deceive Her* does invoke the old crude stereotypes of backwardness, savagery and ignorance, it relies more on incongruity than on simple mockery in order to obtain laughs. Islamists are funny now not so much because of their backwardness, as because of their duplicitous attempts to conceal their backwardness.

If Egyptian media took a long time to get round to representing Islamists on screen, it was still well ahead of most of the rest of the Arab world. Indeed, *The Terrorist* was seen as controversial enough for a number of other Arab states to ban it. This was not for a lack of appropriate vehicles for such an output. While Egypt was, and to a lesser extent it still is, the leading producer of Arabic entertainment media in general, most Arab states produced topical domestic comedy of their own. Operating within the limits of what Lisa Wedeen has influentially called 'licensed parody' or even 'licensed acts of subversion',[72] a number of such television shows gave voice to the frustrations of citizens, while stopping short of directly blaming governments or proposing systemic change. Notable examples included *Buqa'at Daw'* (*Spotlight*) in Syria, *Bas Mat Watan* (*The Nation Just Died/Smiled*) in Lebanon, *Watan ala Watar* (*The Nation on a String*) in Palestine, *Dababis* (*Needles*) in Jordan, *Caricature* in Iraq and *Tash Ma Tash* (*You Either Get it or You Don't*) in Saudi Arabia. As we shall see in the following chapter, some of these shows, or their successors, would go on to produce episodes tackling Islamist extremism—but only after the rise of IS had dramatically changed the cultural and political climate.

Where satirists did engage with Islamism, the examples conform to the same general pattern—it seems that Arab popular cultural production only addressed the topic when it became all but unavoidable not to do so. In Lebanon, *Bas Mat Watan* attempted a skit in 2006 involving a spoof interview with Hezbollah Secretary General Hassan Nasrallah,[73] though this example is perhaps a tenuous one in so far as, for many Arabs, the Shia Islamism of Hezbollah, together with its focus on Israel, makes it categorically different to the extremism of groups like Al Qaeda. More directly relevant, by this rubric, are the sketches making fun of Sunni militants that were incorporated into the Iraqi comedy show *Caricature*, reflecting the violence that followed the US-led coalition invasion of the country. In both cases, these comic interventions prompted violent responses: the creators of *Bas Mat Watan* were forced to apologise after an outbreak of pro-Hezbollah rioting in Beirut. In Iraq, Walid Hassan Ja'az, one of *Caricature*'s stars, was gunned down by unidentified militants.[74]

Probably the most important show to broach the subject of Islamist extremism was *Tash Ma Tash*. This is due to the fact that the series addressed the subject both earlier and more frequently than similar series elsewhere and also because it did so in the context of Saudi Arabia. This meant on the one hand that its creators were immediately face to face with the forces of Islamic fundamentalism at their most institutionally powerful, representing an important element within the Saudi state itself, and also that it was in a position to play a role within the wider context of the increasingly well-resourced and determined media campaign waged by the Saudi and Emirati states against Islamic 'extremism'.

On the face of it, Saudi Arabia was a radically different context to that of Egypt. While Egypt is a fiercely nationalist republic, Saudi Arabia is a monarchy run, at least theoretically, as an Islamic theocracy in which the Quran is the constitution and the Islamic *sharia* is the law of the land. Egypt had for decades been the most culturally exuberant Arab state, with a thriving film, music and television industry. Saudi Arabia's main cultural export, by contrast, was fundamentalist religion, while its traditional culture remained largely insular and unknown outside the country.

Even so, there were some notable parallels with the Egyptian situation. Saudi Arabia had its own history of anti-state religious insurgency, notably the shocking capture of the Grand Mosque in 1979 by millenarian radicals[75] and, like Egypt, it had initially dealt with this by trying to sweep it under the carpet to some extent. As in Egypt, cultured Saudi elites had to battle with the power and influence of fundamentalist religion from both above and below. According to Saudi critic Abd al-Rahman al-Nasir, *Tash Ma Tash* did not feature any women characters for its first three seasons as a direct result of clerical censorship, a situation which changed only after a direct intervention from the Ministry of Information. Again, like their Egyptian counterparts, these restrictions from above were matched by increasingly vigorous cultural challenges arising from below in the form of an Islamist movement—in Saudi Arabia's case the *Sahwa* or Islamic Awakening movement—which commanded a loyal following from among a broad swathe of the emerging middle class.[76]

Finally, in 2002, Saudi Arabia found itself dealing with a wave of jihadi violence bearing significant similarities to that experienced by Egypt in the 1990s.[77] Like Al-Jihad and Al-Jama'a al-Islamiyya in Egypt, Al Qaeda in the Arabian Peninsula was the offspring of a longer history of domestic radicalisation. Like the Egyptian groups, it carried out domestic violence with a clearly internationalist agenda.[78] In both cases, militants set out primarily to target non-Muslim foreigners within the country, but ended up killing locals in the process. Finally, and most significantly, both groups triggered concerted, if belated, efforts by the state to combat Islamist radicalisation by soft means as well as hard.[79]

JOKING ABOUT JIHAD

From 2003 onwards, Saudi-controlled media aired a number of documentaries and dramas on the subject of Islamist extremism, most of which treated the subject with great earnestness. These included *Al-Hur al-'Ayn*, a drama which was co-scripted by former Al Qaeda member Abdullah al-Otaybi and, apparently, actively facilitated by the Saudi government, which gave its writers access to state archives.[80]

In treating this subject with grave seriousness, the comedy show *Tash Ma Tash*, interestingly, was initially not exceptional—at least, not completely. From 2003 on, the show began to focus much more squarely on issues of religious extremism,[81] but it did so initially in two ways. On the one hand, there were episodes that dealt with absurd situations arising from Saudi Arabia's highly conservative laws and norms relating to issues such as the compulsory segregation of men and women or the prohibition on women driving. These episodes, among the most celebrated in the series, are bitingly satirical and extremely funny. On the other hand, however, the series also produced episodes which dealt with Islamist radicalisation and political violence head on. To begin with, episodes of this latter sort struck a very different tone, with comedy appearing to be all but absent, except occasionally, when very subtle black humour could be inferred.

These episodes (most of which were initially banned) include 'Nothing Makes Things Right Except the Truth', 'Oh Education!' and 'Blind Faith', among others. In each of them, Nasser al-Qassabi, a gifted comic actor and the leading star of the series, plays a moderate Muslim character pitted against the encroaching menace of Islamism. The Islamists are consistently portrayed as disciplined and cynical entryists, corrupting and co-opting Saudi institutions in order to brainwash young people into a militant and xenophobic mentality. In each case, these social processes are set against the backdrop of a changing and modernising society. Characters become vulnerable by, for example, travelling to live in an unfamiliar city, or by attending a mosque far from the family home. In 'Blind Faith', parents worry that it is no longer appropriate for their children to play out on the street, and so enrol them in a Quran recitation class which turns out to be presided over by a jihadi sheikh.

While, of course, they don't seek to be even handed, these episodes are significantly more subtle in their representation of the nature of

Islamism and Islamists than most Egyptian portrayals. While some of the same tropes are used, with Islamists presented as sinister, cynical, hypocritical, blindly obedient and violent, they are seldom presented as obviously coarse or backward. The model of radicalisation they seem to invoke is closer to models actually favoured by political scientists. In the Egyptian film narrative, becoming an Islamist is explicable only as a result of extreme ignorance or nihilism, where in *Tash Ma Tash*, it is more about belonging. Finally, in these episodes of *Tash Ma Tash*, there are often significant attempts to engage with actual theological arguments put forward by extremists.

It was not until 2006 that *Tash Ma Tash* presented an episode that dealt with Islamist extremism from an overtly comic angle, in the form of 'Terrorism Academy'. Despite striking a very different tone, the episode is in some ways a continuation of the earlier episodes dealing with similar subject matter. This time, Qassabi plays an idiotic young man from the city of Jeddah who is staying with his uncle in Riyadh. Looking for an activity to keep him occupied, his uncle enrols him in what he thinks is a youth club, which of course turns out to be dominated by extremists who promptly brainwash him and send him on a suicide mission to blow up the American embassy. Unable to find the embassy, Qassabi's character returns, to the exasperation of his handlers, who decide to set up a reality-TV style talent contest in the hope of finding better recruits.

It should be obvious from this description that 'Terrorism Academy' is not a total departure from previous attempts by *Tash Ma Tash* to address the issue of Islamist extremism. It plays, for example, on the same theme of social dislocation. Where, exactly, does the humour in the episode derive from, and what is its discursive significance? There are two basic jokes in 'Terrorism Academy'. The first one is the ancient device of idiocy and incompetence. Qassabi's character is a straightforward clown. He is brainwashed with comical ease, because he doesn't fully understand what is going on. When he is tasked with carrying out an act of terrorism, we don't need to take it seriously because he is incapable of carrying it out. But Qassabi's character is also a sort of wise fool. When he is radicalised, he takes to imitating his fellow extremists' habit of addressing each other as 'my brother in Islam'. When he gets lost on the way to the American embassy, he stops and asks a passer-by, whom he also addresses as 'my brother in Islam', for directions. This is, of course, correct, since he is a Muslim, but the fact that it violates the convention of the Islamists reveals them, at least implicitly, as *takfiris* who believe that only they are the true Muslims.

The larger joke of the episode, of course, is the incongruity of juxtaposing Islamic fundamentalism with the triviality and (for such fundamentalists, immorality) of talent contests like *Star Academy*. At a superficial level, the joke here is simply this: the incongruity between strict religious propriety and the sexualised glamour that is normal on television. More deeply, however, the contrast seems to make the claim that despite being superficially grounded in Islamic piety, Islamist extremism, too, is really just a kind of show business. Terrorism, like pop-stardom, is about the self-regarding pursuit of fifteen minutes of fame. Unlike *The Terrorist*, this comic device makes it possible to represent actual Islamist terrorists as objects of fun. And yet there is still an important underlying similarity. The comedy in both cases requires transplanting the terrorists from their own realm to the glamorous, make-believe carnival that is the world behind the screen.

We end this chapter, chronologically, at the threshold of the Arab revolutions and the seismic upheavals that followed. Up to this point, attempts by comedy writing in Arabic to tackle the subject of Islamist extremism and jihadism were still rare and tentative, especially outside of Egypt. Nonetheless, an important precedent had been set, a foundation to be built on. What, exactly, did this foundation look like? What lessons can be drawn from these attempts?

The first lesson is straightforward: whatever development there may have been in society and media, it isn't easy in the Arab world to laugh at Islamists and get away with it. Doing so has been and remains dangerous on a personal level. Islamists make vindictive and frightening enemies, and state protection—if and where it is offered—can seldom be relied on. We have noted the prosecution of Imam and the key Egyptian writers who took on Islamists in the 1990s. In Saudi Arabia, the actors and writers of *Tash Ma Tash* faced numerous death threats and state censorship.

Even once the matter of personal danger is set aside, there is the issue of public scorn or indifference. The public popularity of *The Terrorist* was never as great as the importance accorded to it by critics.

Today, the leaked version available on YouTube has a million views—respectable, compared with other popular Egyptian comedies—but of the four thousand people who have rated it, a quarter dislike it. 'Terrorism Academy', unlike other episodes of *Tash Ma Tash*, even previously banned ones dealing with extremism, is almost impossible to find online.

For those writers who have braved the subject, what are the key areas of commonality and difference? One important commonality is the way in which comedy has attempted to bring the fight with Islamism to the sphere of everyday life and the family. This is logical. Popular comedy is almost always concerned with everyman themes, and presenting itself as standing for the idealised everyman, triumphing against a mad and confusing system. But Islamism also seeks to base its power in this same realm, presenting family values and personal morality as under siege and their correction as the purifying step necessary to create a just society.

By pitting *sha'abi* characters against Islamists, or by placing Islamists in *sha'abi* contexts, popular Arabic comedy strives to reframe this, portraying Islamists as belonging to a perilous, strange world that sits outside the warm hearth of the comic realm, whether because they are literally foreign (as in the Egyptian association of Islamists with the customs of Saudi Arabia), or (as in Saudi Arabia) because they represent a source of social relationships with unknown strangers beyond the bounds of the local neighbourhood or the extended family circle. Despite claiming at one level to speak for progress against regression, what lies beneath is a clash of rival conservatisms.

4

LAUGHING TO THE BACK TEETH

HUMOUR AND ISLAMIC FUNDAMENTALISM

Often, when portraying Islamists, Arab comedians get into character by putting on an exaggerated scowl. This is hardly surprising as, for one thing, Islamist reactions to comedians' portrayals of them generally suggest that they don't have much by way of a sense of humour.

A typical conservative review would be that of Sheikh Khaled al-Jundi, a popular television personality on the religious channel Al-Azhar TV, who grumbled that Adel Imam 'has always shown the beard and *thawb* [a traditional robe favoured by strict Muslims] as symbols of terrorism and religious extremism'. He complained that the film *The Terrorist* was 'using Islamic terms in a comic way with the result that they have become popular catchphrases among ordinary people' and that its central character is '[a] split-personality that does not pray, likes alcohol after trying it, and desires to commit adultery'.[1]

More recently, Wajdi Ghonaim, another firebrand media cleric, went further, declaring Imam to be an infidel, a 'reprobate' and a 'whore'.[2] 'Some would say that I am excommunicating Adel Imam', he noted, stating the obvious implication of calling someone an infidel. 'Yes it is true. I only call a man an infidel because he is so', citing several verses from the Quran to support his accusation (Al-Tawba: 65; Al-Mutaffifin: 29; and 34 *inter alia*).

89

Moreover, it seemed that Ghonaim's objection wasn't just to Adel Imam having acted in films that could be viewed as hostile to religion and religiosity, but rather that he had acted at all. People like Imam were, he insisted *mushakhasatīn* (which literally translates to impersonators, but is also an archaic Arabic word for actor). According to Ghonaim, in earlier times, such people were not considered competent to serve as witnesses in court (presumably because of their skill at 'lying'). Worse still, Imam had appeared in plays and films in which he made the audience sympathise with *haram* (forbidden) things, like running away from the police or eloping from the family home.

The criticism directed at Nasser al-Qassabi, the star of *Tash Ma Tash* is no less harsh. In fact, Muslims are forbidden from watching the show altogether, according to an official fatwa from the Saudi Council of Senior Scholars. The fatwa denounces what it sees as the show's ridiculing of 'good and pious people' as well as its more general transgressions of 'stupidity and mockery' and its actors' wicked propensity for 'insulting virility by wearing fake beards'.[3] According to the current grand mufti of Saudi Arabia, Abd al-Aziz al-Shaykh, speaking on his own show *With His Eminence the Mufti*, aired on Al Majd TV network, '[the] series transgressed the [appropriate] limits and reached the highest levels of duplicity and misguidance'.[4] Later on, the celebrity preacher Muhammad al-Arefe, while presenting the religious Ramadan show *For Thee I Fasted* on Dubai TV, issued an impromptu boycott call when a viewer phoned in to complain about the series. His particular complaint related to an episode in which customs officials measure the length of arrivals' beards. This infuriated him because, as he opined, this does not actually happen in Saudi Arabia, but might lead people to think that it does.[5] Later on, another cleric, Sa'id bin Farwa, described the team behind *Tash Ma Tash*'s spin off series, *Selfie* as 'immoral and the dregs of the nation'. 'I swear to God' he warned 'that if you don't feel insulted by this series, there is a disease in your heart and it is to be feared that you yourself are one of the hypocrites'.[6]

These sorts of response help to cement a particular image of Islamic fundamentalism as something puritanical, literal-minded and profoundly hostile to laughter—or indeed any sort of fun and enjoyment, especially given that, being religious scholars (albeit with varying levels of official backing), these authorities typically bolster their objections with quotations from the Quran. A particularly popular one seems to be *Surat al-Tawba*, verse 65: 'And if you ask them, they will surely say: "we were only conversing and playing". Say: "Is it Allah and His Verses and His Messenger that you were mocking?"'[7]

There is a perception in some quarters that this hostility to fun and play reflects not just on certain schools of thought within Islam, but even on propensities intrinsic to Islam itself—a view that is not necessarily restricted to fringe Islamophobes. Humour scholar John Morreall, for example, while arguing that Islam has 'one major pro-comic feature' in 'its thoroughly social vision of life', which 'emphasises the family and the community, and rejects a celibate or monastic life', insists that this 'does not take it very far toward the comic vision' because of its 'overall solemnity and lack of playfulness'.[8]

In fairness, Morreall's critique is not meant to single out Islam. In fact, in some ways Islam compares favourably in his analysis compared to other Abrahamic faiths. His real claim is that scripturalist, monotheistic faiths are inherently suspicious of the ambiguity and the absence of final truth that he sees as an essential property of humour. By this standard, he thinks, 'Eastern' religions do much better, especially Zen Buddhism, whose meditative religious practices, focusing on *koans* ('what is the sound of one hand clapping?' etc.) seek to inculcate followers with an acceptance of paradox. (Other scholars of humour, in making roughly similar claims, have other favourites. Peter Berger, for example, is particularly enamoured of Taoism[9] while, in chapter 2, we made reference in passing to the sacred clowning of Balian Hinduism.)

Morreall's assessment notwithstanding, it is probably not helpful to try to characterise any religion along these lines in its entirety (Morreall, we ought to stress, would likely agree). Buddhism, for example, also has harsh and puritanical strains. On the other hand the Abrahamic faiths have all developed mystical traditions which would appear to delight in the complex nuances of the 'comic vision'. Judaism is, of course, legendary for the rich vein of comedy in the sayings of Hasidic rabbis, while Christian theologians would also develop the ascetic concept of being a 'Christian fool'[10] or 'fool for Christ', even seeing Jesus himself, through his self-humbling and riddling speech, as the original clown.[11] In Islam, Sufism—once so universal as to be effectively the default form of Islam worldwide—developed similar insights. Jalal al-Din Rumi, whose poems are crammed with hilarity, wrote: 'God said: the world is play, a children's game, and you are the children'.[12]

Similarly, the popular folk carnivals which we discussed in the previous two chapters in both European Christian and Islamic contexts were intimately connected to both of these religions. The shadow puppet theatre for which Ibn Daniyal wrote, despite its bawdy themes and spirit of rebelliousness against puritanical authority, was not just Islamic in the sense that the Ramadan fast provided its pretext. There was a deeper theology to it as well. According to Linda Myrsiades, puppets in the popular Islamic tradition—shadows on a screen projected from backlit forms manipulated by an all-powerful puppet master—were seen as providing a deep metaphor for God's all-pervading will, guiding His creations and the whole universe.[13]

As such, it is not a difficult task to refute the claim that Islam is anti-humour. But what is interesting is that even in the very forms of Islam which are seemingly most responsible for its austere reputation, it turns out that humour still has an important, if carefully circumscribed, role to play. Indeed, as we shall discover, even some of the same clerics we have just seen railing against the comedy of Imam and Qassabi are themselves noted among their own followers for their humorous abilities. To make sense of this apparent contradiction, we need, it would seem, either to revise our opinion of fundamentalist Islam or reconsider the relationship between comedy and what Morreall and others see as its essential spirit.

First, though, a quick word about terms. In this chapter, we are mostly concerned with Islamic scholars who might broadly be described as 'literalist', 'strict', 'puritanical', 'conservative' or 'fundamentalist'. All of these terms are perilous. The idea of literalism implies that religious texts have a single clear and obvious meaning which one might choose to gloss over by treating them 'figuratively'. This is of course not necessarily the case. Islamic scholars can and do disagree about the correct literal meaning of religious texts. The idea of strictness carries similar implications—that some are fully implementing the rules of Islam while others are not. But this, of course, also depends on what one interprets the rules to be. Conservatism, on the other hand, might imply that one is upholding a version of religion that was normal in the past, against attempts by reformers to change it. But conservatives in Islam, as elsewhere, are often themselves the reformers, seeking to change what is common practice and received wisdom to bring it in line with what they consider a more authentic ideal, perhaps practiced hundreds of years ago, if ever. Another relevant distinction is the one that anthropologist Joska Samuli Schielke draws between 'orthodox' Islam (with the quotation marks either used or heavily implied), as opposed to 'traditional' or 'popular' Islam of the sort that venerates Sufi shrines and holds *mawlid* festivals.[14]

Fundamentalism is itself a complex and problematic notion, something that is acknowledged by everyone who seriously engages with the term. Marty and Appleby noted at the outset of their discipline-defining series of edited books over the course of The Fundamentalism Project that the word is 'controversial' and not always 'congenial', but also that it 'serves to create a distinction over cognate but not fully appropriate words such as traditionalism, conservatism, orthodoxy or orthopraxis' and that 'no other coordinating term is as useful'.[15] One virtually universal feature recognised by the many scholars who contributed to Marty and Appleby's project was that fundamentalism seems to emerge as 'by definition a reaction to modernisation, although it is not necessarily a complete rejection of modernity as such'.[16] On the other hand, as Ernst Gellner suggests in the closing volume of the series, this does not mean that one cannot meaningfully observe 'continuity between fundamentalism and certain earlier phenomena'.[17]

In this chapter, we are concerned with contemporary and twentieth century Islamic scholars, whose pronouncements can be understood as in some sense a 'reaction to modernisation', if only due to the time and place in which they happened to be living. To see the living tradition of Islamic scholarship as purely reactive is problematic. Research has begun to cast doubt on the common narrative that sees 'Islamic modernism' as arising in response to Western colonisation, suggesting instead that the more textually rooted forms of religiosity that have become commonplace are rooted in a more organic development, arising from the beginnings of print literacy in late Ottoman times.[18] Historians like Michael Cook have also charted the ebb and flow of puritanical revivalist movements over hundreds of years of the history of what Gellner would consider an example of a 'Reformation prone' religion.[19]

Another word that roughly aligns with the sort of Islam we are talking about is Salafism, which derives from the Islamic term *Al-Salaf al-Salih*—the 'pious predecessors', meaning the first generations of Muslims.[20] Strictly speaking, Salafis are Muslims who reject traditional adherence to the canonical schools of law, in favour of returning to the original sources of Islamic jurisprudence: the Quran, and the orally transmitted record of the sayings (Hadith) and practices (Sunna) of the prophet and, secondarily, his companions. Although Salafism is often seen as a modern phenomenon, there are others who also identify it with medieval scholars like Taqi al-Din Ibn Taymiyya, a figure who is universally revered by Salafis today.[21] However, not all the scholars we discuss in this chapter can be comfortably classed as Salafis. For example, the wildly popular Egyptian preacher Muhammad Matwali al-Sha'rawi, despite being intellectually very close to the Wahhabi tradition of Saudi Arabia—which is often seen as almost synonymous with Salafism—was also the Egyptian minister of religious endowments and remained in other respects a bastion of a more traditional form of Islam. (Schielke records that, after his death, his son even instituted a carefully restrained and conventionally pious *mawlid* in his memory.) While Sha'rawi might be described as a 'conservative' or 'orthodox' figure,[22] these words, in turn, won't do for others we are concerned with, who would be better characterised as 'radicals'. These include Abdulhamid Kishk, seen by many Muslims in his day as 'a sort of Muslim Robin Hood',[23] to use Gilles Kepel's phrase, and Yusuf al-Qaradawi, a contemporary scholar closely associated with the Muslim Brotherhood, whose work exemplifies the group's combination of political activism and socially conservative piety combined with a relatively progressive and flexible approach to interpreting scriptures.[24]

Nevertheless, the scholars with whom we are concerned in this chapter have several important things in common. All remain, broadly speaking, deeply conservative in their social teachings despite variable degrees of flexibility in their theology. All would emphasise the apparent linguistic meanings of texts over esoteric understandings. All see the explicit teachings of scripture as having a direct bearing on social conduct. All are, at least at first glance, representatives of precisely the unlaughing face of Islam with which Morreall is apparently concerned. And yet they do laugh—at least among their own.

Regardless of what school of thought they belong to, Islamic scholars who make pronouncements about humour inevitably look back on the same shared set of Islamic sources and precedents, and to some extent a shared tradition of medieval Islamic scholarship dedicated to explaining and interpreting these sources. As such, it is useful to briefly consider the sort of material that is available today when it comes to drawing conclusions about what 'Islam' might have to say on laughter, joking and mockery. These are, as mentioned, the Quran (which Muslims believe to be the pure word of God Himself) and the sacred hadith traditions. We would like to stress that we are not Islamic scholars and that our intention in setting this out is to provide only a broad overview. We would also like to note that while we are not trying to favour a specific school of thought, we have drawn on stories and citations from key religious texts that we found to be popular and current in the religious media with which this chapter is concerned. It is possible, therefore, that the generally conservative tone of these media has had some influence on our own account.

The Quran is, of course, the first reference point for Muslims on all aspects of life, whether religious, political, social or even economic, but it would seem that it has seldom, if ever, been regarded by traditional Islamic scholarship as containing humorous material. Nevertheless, within the secular academic tradition of Islamic studies, there have been occasional attempts to identify humour within the text. Perhaps the best known example is in a paper by Mustansir Mir, which highlights three stories that, in his opinion, can be read as containing intentional comic absurdity.[25] The examples Mir finds are subtle, and it would appear that the humour he sees in them is lost on other scholars who have approached the same matter. George Tamer, while disagreeing with Mir's classification of these examples, offers a number of others in which he thinks humour can be observed. Tamer focuses on the less generous side of God's alleged sense of humour, discussing occasions where the Quran seems to engage in mockery or ridicule.[26]

When we turn to the traditions concerning the Prophet and his companions, things are more promising. Broadly speaking, these seem to support two, perhaps three distinct views of the early Islamic community's attitude to joking and laughter. The first of these presents Muhammad as an extremely sombre person who disapproved of levity in all its forms. The Prophet is recorded as saying, for example, 'if you knew what I know, you would laugh little and weep much', or is said to have lived in 'constant sorrow' due to his reflections on the punishments of the Hereafter. Another frequently quoted tradition is the Prophet's comment: 'do not laugh much, for excessive laughter deadens the heart'. The Quran even says, 'Do not exult; indeed, Allah does not like the exultant'.[27]

The second tradition presents Muhammad as seeing a place for joking and levity, but only in a suitably restrained and dignified manner. Muhammad, so it is claimed, would never laugh out loud, but would smile warmly when he heard a joke. In one commonly cited hadith, the Prophet's wife, Aisha, is reported to have said, 'I never saw the Prophet of Allah laugh fully… He would only smile'.[28]

The early caliphs seem to share this general attitude. A popular saying of Ali goes, 'the amount of joking should be like the amount of salt in one's food'.[29] 'Umar bin al-Khattab said, somewhat dourly but perhaps also correctly, 'whoever laughs too much or jokes too much loses respect'.[30]

Finally, however, there are also narrations that might be taken to support a third understanding of humour in the early Islamic community. According to these, the Prophet and his companions laughed uproariously, and involved themselves in outrageous and excessive jokes, well beyond the bounds of normal decorum. Numerous hadiths end with the prophet laughing 'until his *nawajidh* became visible'. Since this word, at least as it is now understood in Arabic, is usually taken to mean 'molar', this expression apparently implies loud laughter with a wide-open mouth.[31]

A particularly significant figure in this more burlesque set of traditions is Nu'ayman bin 'Amr al-Ansari. The hadith literature presents Nu'ayman as an extremely mischievous and apparently transgressive figure. At the same time, it is consistently made clear that he was especially beloved of the Prophet, who always took even his most outrageous pranks in good part.

For example, Nu'ayman would often buy Muhammad gifts from the market in Medina, and on one occasion, upon finding some delicious honey, he played a trick on the Prophet by sending it to him as a 'gift' without paying the vendor, thereby putting him in an intentionally embarrassing situation, to which the prophet responded by laughing and settling the bill.[32]

On another occasion, people tricked Nu'ayman and exploited his apparent naivety to persuade him to slaughter the camel of a Bedouin visiting Muhammad. When the Bedouin came out from the Prophet's residence, he did not see his camel and learned that Nu'ayman had slaughtered it and distributed the meat to people. Searching for the culprit, Muhammad found him hidden in a ditch, having covered himself with palm branches and leaves. The Prophet brought him out of the ditch, wiped his face and asked: 'Why did you do that?' Nu'ayman said: 'O Messenger of Allah! The ones who told you where I was are the same ones who told me to do it.' The Prophet laughed and paid the price of the camel.[33]

In a more extreme story, Nu'ayman used 'joking' as revenge to settle a minor grudge against Abu Bakr's cook, Suwaybit ibn Harmalah, by selling him into slavery, telling the slave caravan that he had 'a big mouth' and not to take his protestations that he was a free man seriously. Abu Bakr was forced to rush into the desert to bring Suwaybit back—creating a source of hilarity for the Prophet and his companions for a whole year afterwards.[34]

Most outrageous of all is a prank that took place after the Prophet's lifetime. A blind man asked Nu'ayman to show him out of the mosque so that he could pass water. The practical joker instead directed him to the corner of the mosque, where he urinated on the floor in front of the worshippers. Later, the victim of this prank began to ask where Nu'ayman might be found, hoping to take revenge on him. Hearing this, Nu'ayman changed his voice and directed the blind man instead to Caliph Uthman, whom he proceeded to beat with a stick. Uthman, like Muhammad before him, laughed off the incident.[35]

It is from this diverse and potentially contradictory set of traditions that Islamic scholars have attempted to weave a consistent understanding of the Islamic attitude towards humour. It would seem that from early times up until the present day, there has been a tendency for scholars to gravitate towards the middle ground—viewing humour with some suspicion, but accepting that it can be socially valuable in its milder forms. Discussing some of the very early opinions along these lines, the Israeli scholar Ze'ev Maghen even suggested that a number

of hadiths relating to less restrained laughter may have been manipulated—particularly those that seem to contradict the idea that the
prophet did not laugh out loud.[36]

In the present day, conservative clerics typically hold the position
that laughter is acceptable only within a clear set of traditionally recognised limitations. Perhaps the least surprising of these is that anything
that might be construed as mocking religion itself is unquestionably
forbidden. The austere but widely respected Saudi scholar Muhammad
ibn al-'Uthaymeen held the typically uncompromising view that 'deity,
prophethood, revelation and religion are sacred matters which are to
be respected. It is not permissible for anyone to mock them in order
to make others laugh'. He even went so far as to pronounce any
Muslim who does so an unbeliever.[37]

Another rule often laid down by conservative scholars forbids the
use of humour for harming people. A commonly quoted verse of the
Quran condemns humour used to belittle others.

> O you who have believed, let not a people ridicule [another] people;
> perhaps they may be better than them; nor let women ridicule [other]
> women; perhaps they may be better than them. And do not insult one
> another and do not call each other by [offensive] nicknames. Wretched
> is the name of disobedience after [one's] faith. And whoever does not
> repent—then it is those who are the wrongdoers.[38]

Another limitation is the idea—expressed in the belief that the
prophet did not laugh out loud—that even otherwise benign laughter
should not be excessively loud and boisterous. In order to square this
with the contrary tradition mentioned above concerning occasions
when the prophet apparently did laugh, scholars engage in some
semantic gymnastics, arguing that the word 'smile' is encompassed by
the concept of laughter.

Perhaps the most interesting rule commonly laid down is the idea
that joking should only be truthful. In a famous narration, the companions of the Prophet asked: "'O Messenger of Allah! Do you joke with
us?" Muhammad replied: "Yes, I do. But I only tell the truth"'.[39]
Conservative scholars have typically taken this not as a figurative reference to the use of humour as an oblique form of truth-telling, but as a
literal injunction against any form of joking involving fictional narrations, drawing on another saying of the prophet: 'Woe to the one who

tells lies to make people laugh.'[40] Clerics also argue that the Prophet adhered to this rule—albeit sometimes in a riddling manner. For example, on one occasion, he addressed Anas bin Malik as 'the one with two ears'. As the scholar comments, this is, of course, true. Humans generally do have two ears.[41] It is absurd, but only because of its obviousness. In another story, Muhammad jokingly said of the famously ugly Zāhir bin Haram, 'who will buy this slave?' This involved a play on words, rather than an outright lie, since the word he used ('ābd) means not only 'slave', but also 'worshipper of Allah'.[42]

The matter of how far to push this prohibition seems particularly contentious in the light of questions put to leading conservative clerics like Ibn Baz and Ibn al-'Uthaymeen on the subject. As an Arabic proverb goes, 'lying is the essence of joking',[43] and clearly some ordinary worshippers have felt constrained by the idea that humour must remain literally truthful. Nevertheless, Ibn Baz held an uncompromising view regarding the act of lying to make people laugh. Lying, he insisted, is evil and one must therefore equally avoid it whether one is being serious or joking.[44]

However, even the stern Ibn al-'Uthaymeen had a somewhat more nuanced view. When asked, 'when are jokes and anecdotes considered lies? And is it permissible to speak of a story that never happened for the sake of making people laugh?'[45] he replied that it is, provided that one mentions a story but does not attribute it to a specific person.[46] It is, he argued, acceptable to say something along the lines of, 'I cite the example of a man who said such and such or did such and such and the result was such and such'.[47] This does not mean, however, that he intended to grant broad licence for the use of fictional scenarios for joke telling. For example, he was against April Fool's day not only because it involved the sin of 'imitation of the unbelievers', but also because of its deceptive element.[48] He also condemned real-life examples of joking and teasing, such as telling people you had been 'jinxed' by their presence, or that they had 'brought bad luck' through a visit, regarding this as both lying and the sin of speculation in the Unseen' (rajman bil-ghayb).[49] Ibn al-'Uthaymeen worried that joking of this kind could develop into genuine and defamatory belief.[50]

In short, today's fundamentalist scholars seem broadly to concur with their ancient predecessors in seeking to endorse only the more limited and polite manifestations of Islamic laughter. As such, more extreme traditions, like those concerning Nu'ayman, have presented something of an interpretive problem. Ali Gomaa—Egypt's grand mufti until 2013 and therefore, in principle, the representative of a socially and politically quiescent, 'traditional' strand within Islam— seems to view Nu'ayman's wine-drinking as an opportunity to open up some interpretive space within Islamic sharia more generally, particularly when it comes to the prophetical commandment that:

> If he drinks [for the first time] flog him, then if he drinks for the second time flog him, then if he drinks for the third time flog him then if he drinks for the fourth time you should kill him.[51]

Noting the lenient treatment Nu'ayman received in response to his frequent drunkenness, Gomaa argues that Muhammad did not actually intend to kill people but, rather, to deter people from alcohol,[52] a position that could be used to buttress the comparatively liberal situation in Egypt, where, as in most Islamic countries, traditional *hudud* punishments (religiously mandated for particular crimes) like flogging are not applied.

An alternative approach is to see Nu'ayman as in some sense an exceptional character—someone who can be admired, but should not necessarily be emulated. A'id al-Qarni, for example, proposed that Nu'ayman's sense of humour should be celebrated as a natural gift, equivalent to a talent for management, public speaking or statesmanship.[53] Others have drawn less specific conclusions, arguing simply that Nu'ayman's pranks are evidence of a general good humour that ought to define correct Islamic conduct. For Muhammad al-Arefe, Nu'ayman is simply evidence that the original Muslims 'enjoyed their lives'.[54]

There are, however, scholars who seem happy to accept and even celebrate Nu'ayman's raucous legacy, using it as a means of broadening the possibilities for Islamic humour more generally in the context of its modern mass media manifestations.[55]

One scholar who explicitly describes Nu'ayman as the original Islamic 'comedian' is the modernist-Islamist Yusuf al-Qaradawi.[56] In his book *The Fiqh of Entertainment and Leisure*, Qaradawi sets out to challenge what he sees as the stereotypically 'grim' attitude of many scholars. He argues that laughter is integral to the meaning of what it is to be human—that 'man is a laughing animal'. Since Islam is a religion to which human nature is central, it follows that it must also be accepting of this natural tendency. Qaradawi writes that 'being the religion of instinctive disposition',[57] it doesn't deny the inclination towards 'fun laughter and enjoyment'. Instead, he argues, 'Islam welcomes everything that makes life better, and favours the optimistic cheerful Muslim over the pessimistic depressing one that sees life through a gloomy, black lens'.[58]

In arguing his point, the scholar revisits the matter of the apparent diversity of attitudes to laughter in the original sources, even going so far as to lay some of the blame for embedded misogelastic attitudes with the first caliphs. The early Islamic community, he insists, did not have any one single attitude towards humour, just as different individuals vary in their appreciation of humour, and other forms of recreation in the present day. However, the caliphs Abu Bakr and Umar bin al-Khattab held, he insists, an 'extremist' attitude about laughter, evidenced by a number of cases of hostility towards fun and enjoyment (often seen as interchangeable with laughter in scholarly discussions), which Muhammad himself was inclined to tolerate.[59]

Qaradawi's defence of humour extends to revisiting the traditional constraints discussed above. Even the matter of hostile mockery, seen as particularly unacceptable, is one that he insists deserves to be viewed with more flexibility. In particular, he actively endorses 'political jokes' that 'mock the rulers and their agents, especially in times of political tyranny'.

He also calls for a softer interpretation of the rule about 'telling the truth' when joking: 'It is not necessary that jokes are based on facts. They may be invented, just as storytellers and novelists make up stories'. After all, he insists, appealing for some common sense on the matter, 'people know that these events are made up'.[60]

Overall, Qaradawi is speaking to a deeper theological debate. In contrast to traditional reservations over virtually all forms of entertainment media, he and other relatively progressive Islamists are pushing a broader manifesto for what is known as *al-fann al-hadif* (meaningful art), which justifies its use of the suspect media of film, music or representative images by striving to convey a moral Islamic message.

While Qaradawi's views, compared with those of more literalist scholars such as Ibn Baz and Ibn al-'Uthaymeen, are notably progressive, it is also useful to consider areas of essential commonality. All seem to hold an underlying view that values moderate, pro-social humour in the context of a generally stable, well-ordered Islamic society. (Even if Qaradawi, unlike his quietist peers, may see this as requiring revolutionary political change to achieve.) They also all seem to reject those less restrained versions of 'holy' laughter connected to esoteric, introspective, ascetic or otherwise non-rationalistic approaches to religion. Indeed, Qaradawi couches his defence of humour precisely in the notion that Islam represents a moderate 'middle way', demanding only things that are compatible with human nature. This is very much in line with what Morreall calls Islam's 'thoroughly social vision of life'. Qaradawi insists that Islam 0'lives with people in reality and does make them live in the imagination and utopia. It does not delve into delusional idealism'. It 'stands with Man on the basis of truth and reality', its prophets 'live through what other humans live ... they laugh, get sad, cry, eat, drink, marry women, reproduce and walk in the markets'.[61]

Beyond theoretical debates about the acceptability of joking among Muslims, there are also scholars who have put Islamic joking into practice. Just like the jurisprudence of humour in Islam, clerical joking is by no means new.

An outstanding example is Abd al-Rahman Ibn al-Jawzi (1126–1200), a prolific scholar otherwise renowned for his puritanical orthodoxy, who nevertheless wrote a pair of what Ulrich Marzolph, a scholar of classical Islamic humour, describes as joke books—*Reports of Fools and Idiots* and its companion volume *Reports of Wits and Wags*. The latter of these, as well as demonstrating Jawzi's interest in humour, also contains a chapter that compiles the witty sayings of other religious scholars and 'wise men'.[62]

The question of whether these works are, strictly speaking joke books is of some analytical relevance. Jokes are a mainstay of humour research, with some key theories of humour based on analysing them. Salvatore Attardo sees their length as their defining feature, when compared to other humorous texts.[63] By this criterion, short, funny anecdotes and jokes are the same thing. And yet Attardo, as with Raskin, identifies a very particular structure in jokes, characterised by clearly distinguished set ups and punch lines in which contrasting 'scripts'—

possible readings of the text drawing on distinct and contradictory semantic fields—are resolved.

The idea of a distinction between jokes and funny anecdotes could be considered somewhat recent, and one that is, perhaps, particularly pronounced in English terminology. In French, jokes are commonly called *histoires drôles*—literally, funny stories. The great anti-government jokes of the Soviet Union were known in Russian as *anekdoty*. In fact, according to Ben Lewis, these tightly stylised humorous texts, very much in line with the Raskin and Attardo model, ultimately evolved from rambling comic stories told by peasants in Tsarist times that, it seems, really were closer to 'anecdotes'.[64] Even in English, the word 'joke' originally had a much broader meaning than its current sense, and joke scholars like Davies have traced how in particular cultural contexts, well-established forms of joke seem to have evolved from less obviously joke-like beginnings, such as the emergence of the 'Irish joke' from the 'Irish bull'—logically fallacious statements supposedly characteristic of Irish people, perhaps due to diglossia between the Irish and English languages.[65] On the other hand, ancient humour compilations such as the *Philogelos* contain examples of texts that are so similar to modern jokes as to dispel the idea that the joke in its narrow sense is a modern invention.[66]

One question that scholars of jokes seem to have seldom if ever considered is precisely one of the most pressing issues in conservative Islamic jurists' attitudes towards humour: namely the question of whether jokes need to be fictitious. It seems likely that the matter simply hasn't seemed important to most humour scholars. Even though of course some real life stories can be narrated so as to make them fit perfectly into the typical structure of jokes, it is usually taken for granted that jokes, especially the 'canned' jokes typically used for experimental research into humour, are not to be read as true accounts. Indeed, one commonplace observation in humour studies is the idea that humour systematically subverts the four maxims that the philosopher Paul Grice believed to underpin all meaningful discourse, including the 'maxim of quality', whereby a speaker is expected to be as truthful as possible.[67]

Nevertheless, Jawzi presents his material, at least formally, in accordance with the normal standards of Islamic scholarship. The stories he presents are all carefully sourced to a chain of oral narration, in essentially the same way as a hadith would be and, for the most part seem to be told as true. Where Jawzi perceives doubt, he indicates this through devices such as the formula *Allahu a'lam* (God knows best). In one place, he enters into a discussion of whether or not the famous wise-fool character Juha, the subject of countless anecdotes, was in reality foolish or clever, in a manner which apparently treats him as an historical figure.[68]

At the same time, Jawzi's material seems to be in keeping with a broader and older tradition of what Marzolph identifies as 'Mediterranean humour'.[69] His stories about idiocy and wit do, at least in a general sense, closely resemble classical material such as that found in the aforementioned *Philogelos*, which also concerns the deeds of fools and the comebacks of clever people. Moreover, traces of classical thinking can be identified in his own understanding of the material. For example, Jawzi seeks to define idiots (as appropriate objects for laughter) in contradistinction to madmen. Idiots are people who want the right things, but go about getting them the wrong way. Madmen, on the other hand, want the wrong things in the first place. The idea seems to be relatable to Aristotle's view in *Poetics*, where he defines comedy as being 'an imitation of baser men ... characterised not by every kind of vice but specifically by ... some kind of error or ugliness that is painless and has no harmful effects'.[70]

On the other hand, Jawzi sees wit as being about more than what we understand as humour, but as characterising a particular attitude to life. Witty people are distinguished by their eloquent use of language, but also by the care and attention they take with their appearance. Interestingly, despite his stern reputation (and his attacks on the more far-out strains of Sufism in his day) Jawzi seems more prepared than present day Islamic scholars to see wit as justifying a certain relaxation of social norms. He approvingly quotes Hassan al-Basri as saying 'if a thief is witty his hand will not be cut off',[71] and Ibn Sirayn's aphorism 'language is too broad to permit that a wit should lie'.[72] This, perhaps, can be interpreted as a hint about the extent to which Jawzi really believes his own compilation to conform to strict standards of truthfulness in joking.

At least in contemporary Arabic, Jawzi's comic anecdotes could be described as avoiding the word *nukta*—which refers to jokes in more or less the contemporary English sense—but rather as *tara'if* (singular: *turfa*), a term which, along with near synonyms like *nawadir*, can be closely translated using the rather quaint sounding phrase 'wit and humour', meaning a miscellaneous but supposedly truthful account of funny things said or done in particular situations by some individual or group.[73]

Tara'if in this sense continue to be recounted concerning leading scholars of modern times. It is perhaps surprising that, given his rather stern views about joking, one scholar who is often celebrated for his sense of humour is none other than Ibn al-'Uthaymeen. There are also stories dealing with his equally eminent contemporaries. Saudi Arabia's Grand Mufti Ibn Baz and Nasir al-Din al-Albani, the father of modern Salafism, sometimes even appear in the same stories together as a comic double or triple act. Among the Egyptian stories, most concern either Sha'rawi, the much loved former Egyptian endowments minister once described as 'the Billy Graham of the Islamic world',[74] or dissident firebrand Abdulhamid Kishk.

Unsurprisingly, the *tara'if* are diverse in nature, and those told about a given sheikh seem to have a lot to do with his social and political position. *Tara'if* about Ibn al-'Uthaymeen and other Saudi sheikhs are firmly located in the realms of religious teaching and everyday life. Those about Al-Sha'rawi bring him into sometimes satirical juxtaposition with figures like Sadat, with whom, given his senior position, he naturally associated. Stories about Kishk have a more rebellious edge, presenting the scholar as someone who made active and acerbic use of humour for socially corrective purposes. Occasionally, a *turfa* appears which looks suspiciously like a straightforward joke. In one seemingly popular story, Ibn al-'Uthaymeen is recognised by a man in hospital, who asks him what he is in for. The sheikh replies '*ahallil al-sukkar*', meaning 'I'm getting my blood sugar level checked'. Punning on the word *yuhallil*, which can also mean 'to make halal' the man replies 'but sugar is already halal. Come on, make something else halal for us!'[75] What makes this example atypical is that Ibn al-'Uthaymeen functions only as part of the set up to the punch line, and his place in the story could equally be filled by any well-known sheikh. By contrast, most *tara'if* seem to have the primary function of commenting on the virtuous character of the sheikh involved, revealing him to have qualities such as patience, diplomacy or humility.

More typical in this regard is another anecdote about Ibn al-
'Uthaymeen, in which he gets into a taxi in Jeddah. After chatting for
a while, the taxi driver asks his name. When the sheikh tells him who
he is, the taxi driver replies: 'And I'm Ibn Baz'.

'That can't be right', the sheikh replies, 'Ibn Baz is blind'.

'And Ibn 'Uthaymeen', the driver confidently insists 'is in Riyadh'.[76]

The humour in this story derives from the case of mistaken identity,
but it also presents Ibn al-'Uthaymeen as a man of the people—unas-
suming, and amused rather than offended by the taxi driver's accidental
impertinence. In some ways, it resembles a story from the opposite
end of the social spectrum concerning Sha'rawi, in which the great
man is invited to lay the foundation stone of a mosque in Italy. Learning
that he is going to Italy, the ministers of provisioning and irrigation
both ask him to bring them back some expensive Italian shoes. After
Sha'rawi's return, Sadat calls a cabinet meeting. The two ministers
arrive, wearing beautiful Italian shoes. A little later, Sha'rawi walks in
with very old and scuffed footwear of domestic manufacture. When
Sadat asks what happened to his shoes, the sheikh replies 'I left them at
home ... I'm only going to wear them on special occasions'.[77]

A very common theme of scholarly *tara'if* is the deft negotiation of
a clash between the sacred and profane. A typical story concerning Ibn
al-'Uthaymeen sees him leaving his house and walking to the mosque
with an incense burner in his hand. A young man approaches him and
asks if he can use the burner to light his cigarette—something a strict
Salafi like Ibn al-'Uthaymeen could be expected to see as *haram*. Instead
of upbraiding the young man, however, the sheikh politely acquiesces
to the request.[78] In another story, a man asks Ibn al-'Uthaymeen if he
can marry a poor woman as an act of charity. The sheikh, shrewdly
surmising the man's lascivious intentions, suggests that instead he provide the dowry so that a poor man can marry her, thus helping not one
but two people, and gaining double the heavenly reward.[79]

These stories concern figures who are often presented as stern and
judgemental, showing them in a markedly warmer light. This does not
mean that they conflict with the strict values promoted by these scholars. In fact, they help to illustrate how the standards of fundamentalist
Islam can be lived in practice, even when life presents conflicts and
obstacles. But not all stories come to such comfortable resolutions. In

one, for example, we see Nasir al-Din al-Albani confront a Sufi who claims he will prove that he is a man of God by miraculously passing a knife through his own body. Albani offers instead to not so miraculously pass a pin through the man's cheek—an offer the putative saint refuses. There is no negotiation of ambiguity here: the Sufi is simply a charlatan.[80] In another, Ibn al-'Uthaymeen snatches a student's pen and then asks whether he should be punished for theft.

'But you're only joking', the student protests.

'No I'm not', says the great sheikh, who pockets the pen and is met with an explosion of laughter from the students.[81]

As light hearted as the episode is, it asks, as presumably Ibn al-'Uthaymeen intended it to, serious questions about how literally to take rules not only about theft, but also about joking since, if he is joking, the scholar is doing precisely what he says a Muslim is not permitted to do even in jest: he is telling a lie.

This last anecdote is also an example of the use of humour as a form of instruction in a relatively traditional context. While jokes have always been used as a way to keep students engaged, as Islamic education has increasingly entered the media age (and increasingly the digital age), certain scholars have become famous for their comedic skills: perhaps lending relevance to a context where scholars can expect their work to be consumed as minutes-long YouTube clips, rather than hours-long *halaqat* (study circles).

Muhammad al-Arefe, seems to be particularly accomplished in this respect, frequently using jokes as a way to bring scholarly advice to bear on real-world problems. Speaking about marital relations, for example, he picks up on a hadith of Muhammad's wife, Aisha, which sees the Messenger or Allah getting drawn into a food fight.[82]

> I cooked *khazaira* for the Messenger of God. I said to Sawda [another wife of Muhammad] eat! But she did not. Then I said: 'If you do not eat it, I will spread it on your face'. She again refused. I grabbed some *khazaira* and smeared her face. Muhammad then said to Sawda: 'Take your revenge!' Sawda smeared Aisha's face. And the Prophet watched them, laughing.[83]

This serves as the jumping-off point for the preacher's own performance. Doing an impression of a stereotypical husband, he huffs, 'Why all these fights? I cannot even rest in my own house', contrasting this grumpy, self-important caricature with the Prophet's generous sense of fun.[84]

But sermon humour along these lines isn't always so well behaved. Indeed, it is often premised specifically on engaging with risqué contexts that might not be deemed appropriate subject matter for a man of religion. For example, Sulayman al-Jubaylan, a Saudi sheikh so renowned for his humour that his sermons have the quality almost of stand-up performances, tells a story about a conversation he had with a belly dancer in an Egyptian hotel. The essence of the anecdote is that the sheikh, unperturbed by the woman's scantily clad appearance, asks her if she prays, to which she replies that she didn't know she could, since everybody tells her that, as a dancer, she must be an unbeliever. The sheikh informs her, on the contrary, that while dancing is undoubtedly sinful, the prophetical message is that prayer cancels out bad deeds.[85] The humour in this skilfully told story is wholly situational, and arises entirely from the incongruity of the pious scholar speaking to the very embodiment of degenerate conduct. It is, in essence, the Islamic version of old jokes about strippers and vicars.

At times, the license apparently permitted to clerical humour extends to stories which, were they to appear in the mouths of others, might well be considered sacrilegious. Arefe tells a story about a Bengali who fainted during the Hajj and woke up in hospital. Seeing everything white around him, the man became convinced that he had died and woken up in paradise, and therefore mistook the nurse who comes to attend to him for one of the *hur al 'ayn* (or *houris*—the virgins of paradise).[86] The story, which Arefe embroiders with references to various crude racial stereotypes, is unmistakably a joke about ethnicity. The fact that the cleric selected a South Asian guest worker as the butt of the joke is in keeping with the theoretical predictions of ethnic joke scholar Christie Davies, who has argued that such jokes can be expected to be told about non-threatening groups that are at once social outsiders and insiders. In this case, the man is a Sunni Muslim, but not an Arab, and from a group that traditionally has a low socio-economic status in the Gulf context.[87]

The more surprising element of the joke—the apparently blasphemous invocation of the sacred virgins of paradise—can also be linked to a wider class of Arabic jokes (some of which we will encounter in a subsequent chapter) concerning the afterlife and, specifically, its sexualisation in the form of the *houris*. Omar Abdelkafy has also riffed on this subject. His joke envisages the believer entering paradise. Speaking to a congregation (in the second person), he sets out to describe the experience of the believer entering paradise as such: You see numerous women of exquisite beauty. 'Are these the *hūriyāt?*' you eagerly ask. 'No', you are told. 'These are only their serving girls.' Next, you see the *hūriyāt* themselves, incomparably more beautiful. Finally, when you enter your palace, you see your wife from your time on earth.[88]

The joke cleverly manages to be entirely orthodox (all of its elements come directly from commonly accepted Islamic traditions on the nature of the afterlife), and also, apparently, subversive of these. But of course the subversion is only apparent. The humour derives from the incongruity between the jealousies that would be normal on earth, and what will be the case in heaven.

As well as the use of humour by Islamic clerics, there is also the emerging genre sometimes called 'halal humour'. This involves the use of broadly 'Western' forms such as cartoons and topical news satire as a way to promote a particular Islamic worldview. The rationale for this can be found in modernist approaches, of which Qaradawi's discussion of humour is an excellent example. Occasionally, Islamic clerics participate directly in halal humour of this kind. In Jordan, Islamic studies professor Amjad Qourshah presented a series of videos for Jordanian comedy production company Kharabeesh. The series *Ehsebhasah*, which means, in conspicuously colloquial Arabic, 'apply correct Islamic ethical reasoning to the matter', saw Qourshah discuss everyday ethical dilemmas confronting pious (though not *unusually* pious) Jordanian young people. Qourshah's manner is familiar, worldly and sarcastic, and his lessons are accompanied by RSA-style cartoon animations. Although the material is not comedy in a clear-cut sense, it makes use of comic techniques and is obviously intended to have a light and playful feel.[89]

Egyptian satirist Youssef Hussein is another example. Hussein began uploading videos to his YouTube channel *JoeTube* ('Joe' as in Youssef, the Arabic version of Joseph) in January 2013, apparently seeking to imitate the style of various other topical satire shows in Arabic on the platform, including the early work of the soon-to-be-famous liberal

Egyptian satirist Bassem Youssef. Indeed, among at least some Egyptian liberals it is apparently taken for granted that Hussein's show was a deliberately organised attempt by the Muslim Brothers to offer an Islamist counterpunch to Youssef, whose comedy at the time was heavily focused on baiting Islamists.[90] Whether this is true or not, early *JoeTube* videos, contrary to Hussein's later media interviews on the subject, seem to have a clearly discernible Islamist flavour, to the extent that they pixelate footage of unveiled women. Moreover, the satirical format closely mirrors Youssef's approach, comedy that typically involved showing short clips of seemingly absurd political pronouncements from prominent Islamist politicians and religious clerics combined with sarcastic commentary. Hussein flipped this around, showing clips of prominent liberal pundits in which they appeared to hold religion or religious values in contempt.[91] It seems now that Hussein's rise to prominence as a seemingly Islamist-leaning comic helped pave the way for others in a similar mould, such as popular poet and now satirist Abdullah al-Sharif, seen with Hussein in one very popular video enjoying an Islamic *nashid* (hymn).[92]

The same general style of humour is also in evidence in 'Tales of Abu Jahl', a series of cartoons created by Egyptian artist and graphic designer Mohammed Sami. The cartoons focus on fashionably secular characters encountered in the course of everyday middle-class life in contemporary Egypt. In one cartoon, which serves as a sort of manifesto or explanation for the series, the cartoonist presents two figures: a clean-shaven man in a business suit and a scowling, comically diminutive, heavily bearded figure in medieval Arabic garb, holding a scimitar in one hand and a glass of wine in the other. (Ironically, perhaps, this figure quite closely resembles portrayals of jihadi fighters in various comedies, particularly those focusing on IS.) The text caption explains:

> There are people who imagine that Abu Jahl must have a frightful appearance, ignorant as an ass. Sadly, this is only the picture that the cinema has drawn of him. In reality, his appearance is very respectable—and these aren't just my words. This is exactly how one of the *sahaba* described the original Abu Jahl. Therefore, no one should be surprised should their colleague at work, or even their boss, turn out to be a big *Abu Jahl*, with a mobile and laptop, who speaks English and Japanese as well, wears an Armani suit, and yet he is an *Abu Jahl*. For the

most part, you'll find him constantly talking about the modern approach to religion, which he has, of course, discovered himself with his extraordinary intelligence, and how Imam Malik and Imam Abu Hanifa understood religious matters incorrectly most of the time. Of course, he didn't fall into any such mistakes. He starts by explaining to you that the reason for the backwardness of the Islamic *ummah* [community] is the women who wear hijabs and the men who pray in the mosque, adding that religion should be easy, meaning that you don't have to go off and pray every time you hear the call to prayer.[93]

The deeply sarcastic tone here, present throughout much of the rest of the Abu Jahl series, reflects not just a clash between the taken-for-granted values of religious and non-religious Egyptians, but also, it seems, a socio-economic conflict between young, pious and technically skilled subordinates resentful of the patronising treatment dispensed by older, more senior, upper-class managers who demand unearned respect for their degenerate and sinful ways.

The humour of the Abu Jahl cartoons brings us a long way from the old-time *tara'if* of scholars like Ibn al-'Uthaymeen and Sha'rawi, and not just because, in the strictest understandings of Islam, drawing pictures of the human form is unquestionably forbidden. The humour of these conservative scholars, while it may appear stifling or narrow-minded to outsiders, is reflective of a broader ideal of a society governed by the intimate bonds of family and friendship. It is thus instinctively hostile to abstraction and technologies of cultural reproduction, or to the impersonal institutions that require abstraction in order to effectively promote themselves. This is a kind of humour which, whether it concerns living religious scholars or semi-mythical figures (to non-believers) such as King Solomon, seeks to present itself as having the same quality as humorous anecdotes based on the real-life experience of personal friends. It is opposed to the savage laughter of what, in the previous chapter, we termed pillory, while its concern with truthfulness forbids travesty. Because it opposes theatrical performance, it is also suspicious of protected cultural spaces that make room for what we called coxcombry (although it does allow for the diplomatic, riddling use of language as a way to deal with situations in which one might otherwise have to tell an outright lie). It favours instead the egalitarian style of raillery, provided that it is being used in order to bring down to earth and humanise that which ought to be brought down to earth—namely, everything apart from God and religion.

Scholars with a more modernist outlook, as well as laypeople with Islamist sympathies, have come to favour and adopt the universal forms of modern globalised media, such as cartoons and topical television shows and, with them, the implicit idea of humour as a detachable technique. Humour of this kind most closely fits the model of coxcombry, in so far as it uses comic framings to convey essentially serious messages. However, it is perhaps fair to say that Islamist humour has yet to feel fully comfortable in these forms, with the possible exception of the cartoon. The desire to convey the religiously approved messages in ways that do not disrupt the dignity of things considered to be sacred means that often the end result seems to have been rather obviously 'humourised'.

Both forms of Islamic humour are organised around a fundamental opposition between sacred and profane. But here, too, there is an important difference between the two types. Humorous stories told about and by conservative scholars concern the contrast between an ideal life of perfect Islamic purity and a worldly recognition of the not-always-perfect reality. Islamic modernist humour, on the other hand, despite its promise of offering a clean alternative to profane joking, seems to have a hardness—even a bitterness—to it. Instead of contrasting a world of unobtainable perfection with forgivable lapses, it contrasts the taken-for-granted social values of more or less actually existing Islamic societies with the bafflingly, disturbingly different attitudes found in the wider world (especially in the 'West') and in the insidious activities of the minority of liberals within the Islamic world (or the Arab world, at any rate). It represents one of many front lines in the increasingly fraught battle for the cultural future of the region.

5

TERRORISM AT THE GATES

ARAB COMEDY AND THE ISLAMIC STATE

As we saw in the previous chapter, by 2010, the taboo on satirising Islamism had been broken across the Arab world: in Egyptian films and plays; in television comedy in Saudi Arabia, Lebanon and Iraq; and even, albeit somewhat obscurely, in Jordanian theatre. Nevertheless, most efforts had been tentative, and the topic was addressed by Arab comedians at their own peril.

The Arab Spring and the grim 'Arab Winter'[1] that followed it would provide the impetus for a dramatic increase in the prevalence of comedy dealing with the topic. As before, the obvious motivation for this was reactive, coming in response to huge, if sometimes short lived, gains by Islamists of all kinds—at the ballot box in the case of Islamist parties such as the Muslim Brotherhood, and with bombs, bullets and blades in the case of jihadi militias.

While Egyptian comedians got a head start, sharpening their wits on the Islamist politicians elected in 2012, the really transformational event at the regional level was the rise of the so-called Islamic State. It was previously referred to as the Islamic State of Iraq, a notoriously troublesome subsidiary of Al Qaeda, which occasionally received a scolding from the latter for bringing its name into disrepute with its excessive violence.[2] Almost moribund in its country of origin for a time, it managed to revive its fortunes through judicious investment in the carnage unfolding in neighbouring Syria. After attempting a take-over bid of its Syrian sub-franchise, Jabhat al-Nusra, it added another letter to its name, becoming the Islamic State of Iraq and Syria.[3] In June 2014, it returned home in spectacular fashion, shocking the world by capturing Mosul, Iraq's second largest city. Before the month was out, its leader—a bespectacled, bookish man known to the world as Abu Bakr al-Baghdadi—had anointed himself Caliph Ibrahim, asserting the right to political mastery of the entire Muslim world.[4] His organisation now referred to itself as the Organisation of the Islamic State or the State of the Caliphate. In this book, to strike a compromise between what the group calls itself and what it is, we refer to it as the Islamic State (IS).

The assertion of al-Baghdadi and IS of political mastery of the Muslim world was a dumbfoundingly grandiose gesture. If it wasn't to be taken seriously, then how else should it be interpreted? One alternative was laughter. Material satirising the group would now become increasingly ubiquitous. Even the name that most Arabs use for it—Daesh—rapidly became a joke. The Arabic acronym for ISIS (al-Dawlat al-Islamiyya fi al-'Iraq wal-Sham), the word is a near pun of words like da'asa (to crush) and dahasha (to penetrate sexually). It also lent itself easily to coinages such as Daeshi (plural Dawa'esh, a member of Daesh) or Da'ushi or Da'dush (its diminutive form), and so on. Da'asha even became a verb meaning 'to destroy completely', as in: 'I totally Daeshed the assignment!'

Humorous Arab responses to Islamism after the Arab Spring can be classified in a number of different ways, all of them revealing in their own fashion. Geographically, it is obvious that Arab comedians were influenced by the threats their own countries faced, as well as by local comic traditions and patterns of censorship, repression and facilitation. In terms of content, they differed in important ways when it comes to how best to address the group. A notable issue, one which we will take up later on, concerned the conspicuous attempts the group made to claim religious legitimacy. Should these claims be acknowledged and tackled head on? Or was it safer (and funnier) just to treat the group as another lot of thugs without any ideology to speak of beyond greed and violence? Violence, of course, was another issue. Just how black could humour about a group famed for its graphic depictions of massacres and amputations get before it went beyond the realm of humour altogether? Then there is the question of where the humour was coming from. A great many of the shows that turned their attention to IS in particular were, at least in spirit, Arab comedy of a more traditional sort, shaped by decades of state media control and (sometimes obliquely) nationalist agendas, packaged in formats and genres that reflected long-established areas of expertise. These, however, rubbed up alongside and sometimes blurred into comedy of another sort, inspired by recently imported American formats, online platforms and often times a more proactively secularist liberal agenda.

In this chapter, we will attempt to present an overview of the main types of Arabic comedy that have lampooned IS, while providing a number of detailed case studies of particular comedies, before finishing with an examination of some of the main commonalities and areas of difference in their approaches to making IS funny.

Many Arab states, as mentioned in the previous chapter, have at various times aired locally produced topical comedy programmes on national television. Sometimes, these take the form of anthology series, aired over Ramadan, with an ensemble cast performing a different story each night. Others take the form of sketch comedies. Lebanon has been particularly prominent with regard to this latter form. Lebanese media have long enjoyed greater freedom than in other Arab states, owing to both Lebanon's comparatively open and democratic political system and the balancing of power between different religious sects. It is also commonly regarded within the region as having a more open-minded and laissez-faire attitude to social issues and personal freedom.

Nevertheless, religion has typically been at least as much of a red line in Lebanon as anywhere else in the Arab world. The very fact that power is precariously shared by different sects means that there can be extraordinary sensitivity to anything that might be perceived as mocking the sacred tenets of one of them. Even issues that would seem to have no religious relevance at all can rapidly acquire a sectarian colouring. An example is the infamous garbage crisis, which has afflicted Lebanon (spilling over, quite literally, into the whole Mediterranean region) since 2015, in which arguments between different religious communities about the siting of new landfills paralysed the country's refuse collection infrastructure.[5] We already considered the consequences that followed the rare attempt of *Bas Mat Watan* to poke fun at militant group Hezbollah, which was interpreted by the group's irate followers as an attack on Shi'ism.

After the rise of IS, however, a plethora of Lebanese shows aired on different channels—*Bas Mat Watan*, (The Nation Just Died/Smiled) *Kteer Selbi* (Really Bad) and *'Irbit Tinhal* (Almost Sorted Out—raced to produce material mocking the group. *Bas Mat Watan*, fronted by the veteran comedy actor Charbel Khalil, is one of the longest-running comedy programmes in the Arab world. The show airs on LBC, a channel traditionally backed by the Christian Lebanese Forces militia, but now majority owned by Saudi tycoon Al-Walid bin Talal. In 2014, *Bas Mat Watan* dedicated a weekly sketch to ridiculing IS, and clips from the show went on to find a new life on the internet, with nearly one hundred of its IS sketches shared on YouTube—seemingly the most popular Arab content on this subject on the platform. *Bas Mat Watan*'s sketches, which are broadly similar to those of *Kteer Selbi* and *'Irbit Tinhal*, tend to rely on fairly simple humour, with generous helpings of smut, innuendo and the juxtaposition of pantomime jihadis with scantily clad glamorous actresses. One of the most popular clips of all (perhaps entirely due to artistic merit) is 'A Hundred Khalifas'.[6] The sketch plays on the name of now-retired Lebanese-American pornographic actress Mia Khalifa (who received threats from IS). *Khalifa* is the Arabic form of the word *caliph*—the 'commander of believers', anointed successor to the Prophet Muhammad and, of course, the title presumptuously adopted by IS commander Baghdadi on 29 June 2014. Mia is homophonous with the word for hundred in colloquial Arabic. Exploiting this salacious coincidence for all it is worth, the clip plays on the notion of the so-called 'sex jihad'—the allegation that young fundamentalist women were travelling to join groups such as IS to advance the cause by engaging in sex work, in effect.[7] Other sketches develop somewhat more serious and political themes, albeit in the same burlesque style. One sees Barack Obama and Baghdadi colluding, while the commander of the faithful enjoys a drink and a massage. Another sees Christians lining up to have palm ash crosses made on their foreheads by a jihadi. The crosses, it turns out, are to be used as cross hairs by snipers. Among the most popular IS sketches created by *'Irbit Tinhal* on Al

Jadeed TV channel—one of the few Lebanese channels not affiliated with a specific religious sect—is a clip titled 'Uncle Daesh'. A child (played by a chubby adult) defects from school to join IS because the organisation has banned schools.[8] Al Jadeed's anti-IS humour often has a political orientation. For example, one of its sketches satirising the Western backed political 14 March Alliance made light of the IS threat and even denied its existence, playing into conspiracy theories of IS as a group cynically created and controlled by outside powers.[9]

Watan ala Watar, (Nation on a String), which aired on the official TV channel Al-Filistiana before moving to the privately owned Jordanian Roya TV, is a Palestinian sketch comedy well known in the past for its bold satire of the Palestinian Authority.[10] Its best-known foray into anti-IS satire, which attracted attention from accross the Arab world when it was uploaded to YouTube, is a sketch dealing with an IS-style checkpoint. The sketch is clearly intended to refer to a specific, highly notorious real life incident that also went viral—when IS commander Shaker Waheeb stopped three Alawite truck drivers and shot them dead after they failed to answer questions on the details of Sunni prayers.[11] Indeed, the sketch showed actual footage from this original video, perhaps to reinforce the message that the satirists were not making things up. In the sketch version, the Alawite drivers are replaced by the characters of an Israeli and a Jordanian Christian. The Israeli is let pass because he is 'our cousin'. When it comes to the Christian, IS fighters argue over the privilege of killing him, and so reaping, so they think, extra heavenly rewards. Seeing this argument the Christian dies of a heart attack, confounding the fighters' hopes.[12]

Spotlight, presently on its thirteenth series, is Syria's pre-eminent comedy programme, and is notable for the fact that it has continued to be produced in the country despite the civil war.[13] While the series must ultimately have a clear pro-regime mandate, it is still capable of producing surprisingly balanced content, criticising the regime (albeit subtly) as well as its enemies. Prior to the war, religious topics were largely a no-go area for the series, the topic being especially sensitive due to the presence of several Syrian religious minorities, most importantly the Alawite sect of Shiism, which is the religion of the ruling Assad family and consequently of most military top brass. As the war became increasingly sectarian, however, *Spotlight* produced several episodes dealing in depth with the subject of jihadism, Islamist extremism and IS in particular. In keeping with *Spotlight*'s reputation for intelligent social satire and the subtlety permitted by its longer-form format, these have included episodes that delve deeper into the complexities and ironies thrown up by the occupation of portions of Syria by jihadi groups.

One of the show's most prominent IS-related episodes is titled 'The Road of Safety' (2015).[14] It tells the story of a Syrian couple who have to cross a succession of checkpoints manned by heavily stereotyped militia groups, pretending at each one to identify with the relevant ideology. The first group is a leftist one, whose leader quizzes them superciliously on their affinity to Che Guevara and their knowledge of the work of Marx and Lenin. The second is a jihadi group. Donning a white *thawb* (robe), a false beard, a prayer callus and a permanent scowl the husband, played by well-known actor Bassem Yakhour, gets so into character that he ends up excoriating the checkpoint guard for backsliding by refusing to condemn his own wife for speaking in the presence of men. The third is an image-obsessed group who have made the mistake of setting up their checkpoint but forgetting to previously adopt a political ideology. After some discussion as to who they are, they decide that they will just be all things to all people and set up a *nizami* checkpoint. The word would normally mean 'organised' or 'properly administered', but since the word *nizam* also means 'regime' (shorthand for the Syrian regime), it is tempting to speculate that a pun is intended.

As this single example illustrates, *Spotlight*'s jihadi comedy is often focused on exploring the minute absurdities that ordinary Syrians must deal with when confronted by the power of jihadi groups, and in particular the theme of role playing and double lives. The episode 'Secret Hideouts', for example, features a plotline in which a pair of hapless vice and virtue police are determined to catch out a cynical bookshop owner, but pounce on him only to find him praying.[15] Throughout the episode Syrians are shown enjoying the pleasures of secular life in secret, while adopting the religious stylings forced on them when they venture out in public. Another subtlety of the episode is that, rather than focus on the most extreme stereotype of the jihadi, it gently lampoons jihadis' own ideas about leniency, as the heavily bearded enforcers wrestle with trying to implement a gradualist approach. Meanwhile, a heavily bearded character who looks like a stereotypical jihadi grumbles that the stricter commander ruling his area has forced him to adopt this style. In 'Initiative', a comparatively early episode dealing with the sudden mushrooming of jihadi checkpoints in the Damascus area, two men dress up as Santa Claus as part of a children's charity campaign, only to find they have to cross a succession of such checkpoints.[16] At each one, they are allowed to pass only by further Islamising their appearance—first by exchanging their red costumes for Salafi robes, then by dying their white beards orange with henna, and finally by swapping bells for Kalashnikovs. Perhaps the most remarkable of these, however, is 'Photograph'.[17] This episode revolves around a man who has the exact appearance of a Salafi, but who believes that he looks like a secularist. After a series of (to him, inexplicable) encounters, in which everyone around him becomes suddenly and speciously pious, desisting from un-Islamic activities like listening to music, he goes to see a psychiatrist who informs him: 'We are all living this conflict … someone might be shaved on the outside and make himself out to be liberal, but his nature is religious, and vice versa'. Episodes that specifically focus on IS, rather than other jihadis and Islamists, pull fewer punches. In one, titled 'Religion Detector', IS invents a device that can detect people's inner religiosity. When it demonstrates that the group's leaders are in fact unbelievers, their technicians are forced to falsify the data.[18]

Following the rise of IS, a number of newly commissioned works were produced that were partially or even exclusively focused on the group. In the Gulf, Saudi Arabian Nasser al-Qassabi, now based in the less restrictive environment of the United Arab Emirates, starred in a new series called *Selfie*, which is in many ways a continuation of *Tash Ma Tash*. The series featured a double episode called 'The Devil's Egg'—a tragicomedy telling the story of a hapless father, played by Qassabi, travelling to Syria in the hope of bringing home his son, an IS recruit.[19] Stammering, apologetic and terrified, Qassabi's performance has the quality of a more innocent Woody Allen up until the episode's grim conclusion, when he is executed as a traitor by his own son. Another notable Saudi series is *Shabab al-Bomb*, which has, since launching in 2012, become hugely popular, probably on account of its relatively accurate portrayal of the lives of young people—something which has tended to be absent from much of Arabic popular media. A pair of episodes called 'Preachers of Satan' dealt with the issue of IS recruitment, but rather like *Tash Ma Tash*'s early forays into the topic, did so largely in the form of melodrama rather than comedy.[20]

In Egypt, the media went into overdrive. The election of Mohammed Morsi as president initially created a powerful incentive for the implacably anti-Islamist deep state to offer its support to anyone who might help dent the popularity of the ascendant Islamists. This led for a time to an uneasy truce between YouTube satirist Bassem Youssef and the de-facto powers in Egypt, who almost certainly played a key role in providing the space he needed to launch his revolutionary programme *Al-Bernameg* (The Show). *Al-Bernameg* was modelled most immediately on *The Daily Show*, presented at the time by Youssef's personal hero, Jon Stewart. However, the imitation was far from slavish. Rather, the creators made a conscious decision to bring together what they saw as the best aspects of a variety of American live prime-time shows.[21] After Morsi's ouster in 2013, Youssef and *Al-Bernameg* made the courageous decision to focus their attention on the new military-backed government of interim President Adly Mansour and, subsequently, former Commander in Chief of the Armed Forces President Abdel Fattah el-Sisi rather than continuing to function as what would have been in effect an anti-Muslim Brotherhood propaganda platform. The result was their rapid shut-down.

Nevertheless, in Sisi's Egypt, there was still plenty of scope for comic treatments of Islamism. In contrast to the reluctance to broach the topic directly, which we discussed in the previous chapter, now the Egyptian state and large sections of the country's domestic intelligentsia were united in an almost hysterical opposition to anything associated with the Muslim Brotherhood.[22] The rise of IS, particularly the organisation's Egyptian franchise in the Sinai Peninsula and its extensive presence in neighbouring Libya, provided such sentiments with useful cover—the group was the antithesis of attempts by moderate Islamists such as the Brotherhood to make themselves palatable in the context of mainstream politics. Indeed, as one well-known contemporary Egyptian comedian opined 'when we are mocking IS, of course we are often implicitly mocking the Muslim Brotherhood as well'.[23]

At least two Egyptian feature films have been made that exclusively focus on IS. *Da'doosh*[24] and *Al-Qarmuti in The Land of Fire*[25] are both stylistically traditional *sha'abi* (popular) slapstick comedies starring well-known Egyptian actors. Both of these films feature light-hearted comic protagonists who find themselves, deliberately or otherwise, inside the jihadi group. In the case of *Da'doosh*, the protagonist responds to an internet advert while on the rebound from being jilted on his wedding day. *Al-Qarmuti in the Land of Fire* on the other hand, concerns the character of *Al-Qarmuti*, a fast-talking, grandfatherly protagonist from an existing film franchise established with a previous anti-Iraq War film, *Sorry, We're Being Humiliated*.[26] In this case, an ill-fated boat trip sees him blown off course to an IS controlled region of Libya.

On television, one source of anti-IS comedy has been *Saturday Night Live Arabia*, which can be identified with the new wave of liberal, Westernised Arabic comedy pioneered by figures like Yousef, and which features comedy talent that cut its teeth on *Al-Bernameg*. *SNL Arabia* strives to offer a relatively balanced approach to satire, within a markedly more closed environment than existed during the brief period of the Morsi presidency. Jihadis are, however, one regular object of the show's mockery. The satire here tends to draw on relatively safe and familiar themes. In one video, an IS commander asks to see his suicide bombing unit drill. They crisply salute before self-detonating.[27] Another sketch, involving a fully veiled female interviewer who progressively uncovers, riffs on the idea of jihadi sex-obsession.[28]

A particularly controversial show, and one which is, arguably, at least as revealing as more acclaimed comedy, is hidden camera reality show *Mini Daesh*. Modelled on tasteless television prank comedy such as that of Ramez Galal (infamous for tricking Paris Hilton into believing she was about to die in a plane crash), each episode of *Mini Daesh* revolves around the same prank: tricking a celebrity into believing they have been captured by jihadis. With scenes showing terrified and traumatised actors begging for their lives, the show was condemned by horrified Arabic media commentators, with Egyptian Culture Minister Mustafa Bakri expressing concern that the show risked promoting the very ideology that it (presumably) intended to parody.[29] Nonetheless, the show was apparently popular with Arabic viewers.[30] By using the device of piratical, buccaneering jihadi stereotypes to pillory the glamorous and unapproachable world occupied by Egyptian film and television stars, the show in a sense seems to have dramatised the narrative of class warfare that, in part, helps account for what makes revolutionary Islamism popular.

Case Study: Dawlat al-Khurafa

The fall of Mosul was, of course, shocking. Not only had a massive city, manned by a theoretically formidable detachment of the Iraqi military, fallen incredibly rapidly, but in the weeks that followed, IS would push on through the Sunni-Arab majority provinces of Iraq and into Iraqi Kurdistan with a momentum and determination that led to speculation that the Kurdish regional capital of Erbil (whose defence was assisted by frantically mobilised airpower) and even Baghdad itself might imminently fall.[31]

When Muhammad Tha'er Jayyad (sometimes given as Tha'er al-Hasnawi), an Iraqi Shia mathematician and aspiring comedy script-writer, pitched a satirical series on the new threat, his project was swiftly green lighted by Al-Iraqiyya, the national channel.[32] Amply resourced by the standards of Iraqi television (reports vary as to whether the Iraqi government poured $600,000 or $750,000 into the project),[33] but very short on time, a team consisting of Jayyad as writer and artistic director, Ali Qassim as producer[34] and a number of well-known Iraqi comedy actors went into overdrive to get the show ready to start airing on a weekly Saturday evening slot by October.[35]

The show was called Dawlat al-Khurafa, mirroring the phrase Dawlat al-Khilafa (the State of the Caliphate). Khurafa means 'myth' or 'fantasy'—a play on words that cleverly acknowledged and subverted IS's most iconic ambition.

The launch of the series was met with well-wishing, but not, it is probably fair to say, unmixed enthusiasm beyond the show's immediate constituency. For Western media, otherwise eager to cover what looked like a positive story of plucky and, equally importantly, nonviolent resistance, misgivings immediately surfaced regarding the show's other targets, particularly with regard to a promotional music video accompanying the series' theme song, depicting an exuberant and surreal carnival in which an American cowboy marries Satan and Israel (or, perhaps, international Jewry), under the benign gaze of Qatar, in order to hatch a tiny, angry caliph out of an egg who is slavishly praised by a chorus of ex-Ba'ath Party military officers.[36]

In addition to this rapid-fire onslaught on America, Israel, Qatar and the remnants of the Saddam Hussein regime, *Dawlat al-Khurafa* also took a conspicuous swipe at Saudi Arabia, whose media, in Jayyad's view, also deserved a large share of the responsibility for spreading an extremist Sunni agenda. This lay behind the naming of the show's fictional Daeshi propaganda channel *Dam Bee Shee*—a reference to the Saudi-owned satellite channel MBC.[37] This may explain the apparently lukewarm, though generally not directly negative, coverage the show received in Arabic media, which is largely dominated by Qatar and Saudi Arabia.

Another strike against the show were certain apparent limitations likely imposed by a rushed writing and limited resources. As one American observer noted, comparing the show unfavourably to anti-IS material in the contemporaneous Lebanese sketch show *Kteer Selbi*, *Dawlat al-Khurafa* seemed to resemble the ramshackle sub-B-movie aesthetic of Ed Wood's *Plan 9 from Outer Space*.[38] Certainly, *Dawlat al-Khurafa* couldn't draw on the depth of experience available in Saudi Arabia, Lebanon, Egypt or even Syria. Nor did its creators possess the cultural capital of the new wave of American-style comics, including Iraq's own Ahmad al-Basheer, whose version of *The Daily Show* garnered glowing write-ups in the English-language media.[39] Finally, unlike some of its immediate competitors, *Dawlat al-Khurafa* was almost literally under fire as it was being produced to incredibly tight deadlines. Midway through shooting an episode, Jayyad reports, he was often still working on the script.[40] The haphazard nature of production also led to mishaps which are, presumably, more amusing in retrospect than they were at the time. The episode 'The Daesh Olympics', for example, contains a scene in which the jihadis conspire to take home a gold medal at the swimming event by electrocuting the competition.[41] (After which, their entrant, clad in black flowing robes, gleefully runs the length of the pool and mounts the podium solo, cheered on by an audience of fellow Daeshis.) To shoot this scene, the production had called up the manager of a swimming pool in Baghdad and arranged to book the pool for the necessary time. Unfortunately, the manager had neglected to inform the security guards, who ran away when they saw the apparent advance of the jihadis.[42]

Dawlat al-Khurafa does have a rushed look. Costumes and makeup often appear as if they come from a hasty raid on a child's dress-up box, while the sets would not look out of place in a school play. Graphics, which are supposed to parody IS's obsession with flashy visuals, are put to shame by the originals. Storylines are often stretched painfully thin and there is sometimes recourse to tired jokes, including ethnic stereotyping and the occasional use of blackface. In one episode, jokes are quite literally recycled, in a plot revolving around a Daesh version of a popular Iraqi joke-telling show called *Aku FadWahid*. The real-life comedians invited to perform crack already well-known jokes, somewhat bafflingly modified to include Daesh-related punch lines.[43]

And yet the apparent amateurism of *Dawlat al-Khurafa* is, at least to some extent, deceptive. For one thing, by Jayyad's account, some of it is deliberate. When asked about the often childish and seemingly naïve appearance of the show, he observed: 'In Iraq we say that children have most influence over television, because it's the child who is first to the remote control, so when I was writing, I had the idea that there should be something a child could enjoy in every scene'.[44]

As he went on to claim, this theory of change apparently paid off.

> In the titles we have a special thanks to the Ministry of Youth. A delegation from the Ministry of Youth from Mosul came to us and made a special appointment. I wondered—what is this about? He was talking about the influence of the series on the youth in Mosul. The children started to shout out of the windows 'Da'ushi' at the people who were dressed like that. So we were really happy that the Ministry of Youth people said that. Nearly everyone who had a television was watching us.[45]

Whether coincidental or not, it is perhaps worth noting that this claim seems strikingly reminiscent of the much-cited (and since doubted) Ku Klux Klan infiltration story popular on the counter-narrative circuit.[46] One chapter of *Freakonomics*, by Stephen D. Levitt deals with the supposed infiltration of the Ku Klux Klan in the 1940s by a man called Stetson Kennedy. This story seems to be favoured by counternarrative practitioners, and we heard it mentioned more than once—though not in formal interviews. The story claims that Kennedy was able to learn about the inner workings of the Klan, including their bizarre rituals and rank titles, and this then formed the basis of a Superman radio drama for children. The embarrassment felt by Klansmen when their own children were playing at being superman and defeating the 'grand wizards' and 'imperial dragons' of the Klan, resulted in a huge loss of prestige for the secretive organisation. Since then, Kennedy's account has been called into question, and Levitt has rowed back on it in a *New York Times Magazine* article titled 'Hoodwinked?'[47] Jayyad's claim seems oddly close to this story.

Aside from the insider testimonies from the show's originators, there is a case to be made that *Dawlat al-Khurafa* is greater than the sum of its sometimes ramshackle parts. To begin with, the show's very premise is interesting when compared with other attempts to lampoon IS. For most places making anti-IS material—Egypt, Saudi Arabia, Lebanon or Jordan—the threat posed by the organisation was primarily terroristic in nature. Media from these countries tends to focus on travesties of the radicalisation process or, sometimes, on portraying IS as straightforward buffoons. By contrast, *Dawlat al-Khurafa* stands out in its attempt to be a sustained situation comedy depicting life in a state occupied and run by a jihadi organisation.

In this sense, *Dawlat al-Khurafa*'s comedy is knowingly built on a humorous conceit that is, however absurd and caricatured other aspects of the show may be, genuinely reflective of an area of tension within actual jihadi thinking. As Jayyad puts it:

> …bad or good they were in control of areas, and if we were to take them seriously, they were calling for the establishment of a country. Of course it would have to be a country with trade, and a country with citizens and institutions. So I imagined that this country were to succeed and be established and accepted by the United Nations. The question then was, would this state work well for its people? So we supposed this fantasy. And we then thought what the conflicts would be between the underlying idea of this state and the lives of its civilians. My idea was that it wouldn't work for ordinary people—maybe it would work for people who were strict and believe in that sort of thing. So the idea was to make a comedy and a tragedy. The idea was to make a comedy focusing on the failure of the leader of the organisation, not in a caricatured sense but really as he is—the same costume, the same way of speaking, of sitting on a throne.[48]

Repeatedly, the series plays on the idea that IS is torn between wanting to tear down the structures of modernity and the nation state, and to appropriate them. Their inability to fully achieve either forces them to ally with those who can, including those who seek to cynically control them (military advisors from the Saddam era, for example), and those who are just trying to find a modus vivendi. This creates another layer of poignant humour as, little by little, the community of salt-of-the-earth Iraqi characters who appear to completely avoid incorporation into the Daesh project find themselves inextricably bound up in their hare-brained schemes. The incompetent supposed tyrants and the fed up but ostensibly powerless people they dominate become, over the course of the series, curiously entangled. It is only in a final episode, largely played straight, when the Daesh caliph oversteps the mark by trying to force the local *mukhtar's* (village head) daughter to marry him that the ordinary people feel truly obliged to move beyond grumbling and passive resistance, dramatically overthrowing the Daeshi regime.[49] In this sense, perhaps, the show is not just about IS, but a broader metaphor for the resilience and continuity of Iraqi society in the face of tyrannical but ultimately transient rulers.

We already mentioned Youssef and *Al-Bernameg*. His rise to stardom was clearly propelled by the Arab Spring. During the Egyptian revolution, he and his collaborator Tarek AlKazzaz created YouTube videos in which they mercilessly lampooned the contortions of the state-controlled Egyptian mainstream media that was seeking to defame and discredit the rapidly snowballing protests. However, Youssef's work was identifiable with a wider phenomenon of Arab comedy that emerged shortly before the Arab Spring and would, in one form or another, survive its demise.

One ingredient of this new wave of Arab comedy was the emergence of liberal, cosmopolitan talent with an unprecedented familiarity with American comedy formats. Since the 1990s, stations like the subtitled American-import based channel Dubai One[50] had introduced a generation of Arabs to American topical comedy, especially *The Daily Show*, on which they had seen the George Bush presidency and the War on Terror mercilessly lampooned. Another significant development was the introduction of stand-up comedy to the region. One key source of this was Arab and Muslim-American comedians who rose to prominence in reaction to the stigmatisation they faced following 9/11.[51] A number launched major world tours that included various dates in the Middle East, helping launch platforms for local and regional talent such as the Amman Stand-Up Comedy Festival. In other cases, the journey went in reverse. Saudi comedy star Fahad Albutairi, for example, acquired an interest in stand up while studying in the US, which he brought with him on his return (he has, since the writing of this book, allegedly been arrested by Saudi Arabia).[52] Meanwhile, a small Saudi stand up scene was being incubated among employees, expatriate and local, of the national oil company, Saudi Aramco.[53]

Another key element was the availability of new media platforms and, in particular, YouTube. Before the Arab Spring, young Saudi comedians, sometimes emerging directly from the country's small comedy scene, were beginning to reach an audience of millions with shows such as Albutairi's *La Yekthar* (Zip It!) or Omar Hussein's even more daring news satire show *3ala6ayer* (On the Fly).[54] These comedy entrepreneurs were under no illusions that their freedom of expression was unlimited, nor were they wholly independent of commercial and political backing. They did, however, enjoy a level of autonomy that could not exist within the structures of broadcast television. Within a few years, the big commercial Arab satellite channels were catching onto the success of their experiments, recruiting popular YouTubers as mainstream stars and replicating their style and formats.

In Iraq, Ahmad al-Basheer is a good example of this new brand of satirical humour. Debuting on the national television channel Iraqiyya, his show *Lifa Style* followed the format of a single presenter sarcastically responding to carefully selected clips of current events in a manner strikingly similar to the YouTube clips through which Youssef made a name for himself in 2011, influenced, in turn, by Jon Stewart.[55] In August 2014, shortly after the IS invasion, Basheer launched *The Albasheer Show*, initially uploaded to YouTube before it was picked up by the German Arabic-language channel DW Arabia. The first episode dealt primarily with issues such as sectarianism. By September, though, the series featured a revamped intro and an extended sketch inspired by the news that an 'IS cook' had 'been killed under mysterious circumstances'. Broadcast on DW Arabia, the show would continue to intermittently address the same subject matter, despite its host being forced to relocate to Jordan by violent threats.[56]

JOKING ABOUT JIHAD

Case Study: Dayaaltaseh

In 2011, Maan Watfe was studying engineering at the University of Aleppo. He didn't really want to be an engineer. He was more interested in media but, having excelled in high school, his family had pushed him to enrol in the prestigious course. Media work, they insisted 'won't put food in your mouth'.[57]

When the Syrian revolution began, however, the politically engaged young man rapidly found himself in the thick of it. Before the year was out, he was in jail, where he remained for seven months, frequently subjected to abuse and torture at the hands of the Syrian intelligence services.[58]

Maan left with a redoubled commitment to the Syrian Revolution but also, it seems, a determination to avoid violence and 'extremism in all its forms'. Fearing renewed arrest, he fled, like tens of thousands of his fellow citizens, to Gaziantep in Turkey, determined to work for the revolution by pursuing his penchant for creating media content.[59]

In Gaziantep he teamed up with an old school friend, Youssef Hillali, who had also fled Syria 'in a great hurry... in a matter of hours', after the public execution of a fellow activist.[60]

Together, the two young men founded the comedy collective 'Dayaaltaseh', a Syrian expression literally meaning 'lost the cup', used to refer to a clueless person, or someone who doesn't know what is going on. With Maan taking on most of the writing duties and Yusuf handling the more technical and visual aspects, the two of them (later on, other members would come and go) began to release a series of videos intended to raise awareness of the situation in Syria.[61]

Although passionately committed to the revolution, as time went by, the two friends became increasingly dismayed by what they saw as the increasing prevalence of extremism in the opposition to the Syrian regime. They watched the growing influence of Jabhat al-Nusra and its parent group Al Qaeda on many revolutionaries with dismay and, subsequently, the emergence of IS with disgust. Increasingly, their content began to address not only the violence of the regime, but also that of the jihadi groups taking over the rest of the country.[62]

This new direction made them fresh enemies. On one occasion, men with beards and guns turned up to a studio in which they had been working and attempted to break the door down until the Turkish land-lord came out to inform them that the people they were looking for were not present—opening the door himself to confirm the fact. The terrified man told his tenants, for the good of all concerned, to leave and never have anything to do with him ever again. Ultimately, Maan fled yet again to a country which, in the interests of his own security, we have not named.[63]

As with *Dawlat al-Khurafa*, Dayaaltaseh, though not physically in Syria, is another example of comedy taking on IS from the standpoint of those more or less directly in the line of fire. Aside from the physical risk they have run themselves, Watfe and Hillali stress the importance of this positioning in the content they create. In contrast to material made in Egypt or the Gulf, as they point out, their jokes about IS or Jabhat al-Nusra are informed directly by stories they have heard from friends and relatives who have encountered them in person or lived under their rule.

Dayaaltaseh are also distinguished by the fact that they are, like most Syrians, Sunni Muslims, something that Watfe believes differentiates them not only from the Iraqi series, written by Shia critics of IS who run the risk that their material will be interpreted through a sectarian lens, whatever their intentions, but also from overtly secularist comics. 'The Islamists accuse us of being secularists', Watfe once told Orient news, but the secularists accuse us of being extremists.[64]

The Syrian group are also set apart by virtue of their fierce loyalty to the fading cause of the Syrian 'moderate opposition'. A great deal of anti-IS comedy in Arabic is backed by large, relatively well-resourced networks. Other material, some of which we encounter in the follow-ing chapter, has been created seemingly spontaneously, by amateurs—but these examples tend to be one-offs. Dayaaltaseh have no identifiable external backer. The group's Facebook videos, which can receive up to half a million views (YouTube, being relatively unpopular in Syria, is not a primary focus), could be a possible source of monetisation for their content). Watfe alludes, somewhat cryptically, to money being available for 'occasional projects', but says that financing is usually a struggle and that the group is motivated by a spirit of political activism rather than any interest in commercial success.[65] As we saw in the opening chapter, it would not be out of keeping with the modus operandi of various Western countries to back the group's anti-jihadi content. But even if this wholly speculative possibility were true, such support would likely still be meagre. As such, the idea of the group as activist film-makers in an environment dominated by more top-down ventures is still seemingly valid.

In practical terms, this situation can be both a creative constraint and an opportunity with regard to content. Plainly put, the group cannot produce hour-long drama episodes or employ large teams of screenwriters. On the other hand, not being obliged to produce content on a strict schedule means that they are free to experiment with a wide range of formats, a diversity accounted for, as Watfe put it, by the fact that 'people have different tastes' and, sometimes, material considerations (*Daily Show*-style talk shows are cheap, he notes, because you basically only need a presenter, a guest, and a single computer-generated background). Much of the group's output takes the form of standalone sketches, but they have also attempted to create shows with more of a talk show format and recently (at the time of writing) a comedy series set in a psychiatric clinic.

It is the standalone sketches—eight relatively early examples of which are organised into a loose series called 'ISIS series'—make up the most important part of the group's output specifically concerning IS, although some of the talk show material also concerns jihadi groups.[66]

The sketches, early examples in particular, represent the struggle to find humour in the rise of IS at its most visceral. It is fair to say that they don't always wholly succeed and, sometimes, they don't even try. As Hillali observes, 'some subjects require tragedy more than comedy'. In the 'ISIS series', the main humorous technique used is simply to present IS violence as cartoonish and IS fighters as moronic buffoons who mindlessly repeat simplistic slogans before rushing off to incompetently carry out acts of brutality. Usually, this violence is shown as directed against the Free Syrian Army, who typically represent discipline, common sense and secular normality.

While the humour in these early sketches seems limited and simplistic, they nonetheless possess a disconcerting and rather surreal quality. IS fighters are crudely portrayed by actors who, equipped with obviously fake beards, flimsy robes, plastic swords and toy guns, come across as children merely playing at violence. This travesty of real life

IS violence is intended to accurately reflect the idea that IS are themselves a travesty, that their adoption of 'Islamic' clothing and mannerisms is merely play acting—a sort of historical re-enactment. In the first video, which depicts a group of IS fighters overrunning an FSA position after a rousing speech by Abu Bakr al-Baghdadi, this deliberately naïve and childish style is really all the joke there is.[67] In subsequent instalments, FSA fighters easily get the better of their accident-prone and none-too-bright antagonists. In one, an IS fighter, who mistakenly believes he is invisible because his face is covered, encounters an FSA man who is dressed, incongruously, as a cowboy. The FSA fighter outdraws him and shoots him with a revolver, before sweeping away his corpse with a broom, while saying 'this is Sparta!', a reference to the meme spawned by the film *300* (2006).[68] In another, an IS fighter's bomb fails to go off, as he stands endlessly repeating the IS slogan 'the Islamic State endures'. The FSA fighter, hearing a cry of 'finish him' from the *Mortal Kombat* video game franchise, proceeds to smack him, as if he were merely a naughty boy.[69]

These presentations are undercut by the fact that we know that in real life, at least at the time the videos were being made, that IS, buffoons or otherwise, were by no means on the back foot against the FSA, while the violent excesses rendered cartoonishly in the videos were no comic exaggeration but were absolutely real, and even understated. In this sense, there is something almost hysterical about the bedlam let loose in the Dayaaltaseh 'ISIS series' videos, as if they aim less to present IS as buffoons, but to vainly wish that they were simply buffoons. They could be seen as embodying humour in its role as the simple, desperate desire to escape trauma by retreating into the dream world of childhood.

As Dayaaltaseh's material has developed, however, it has arguably become more sophisticated, or perhaps just more capable of emotional distance from its subject matter. Two 'ISIS Mario' videos succinctly and comically frame a standard moderate opposition line on the organisation, the second in particular, as it shows an IS fighter, playing the role of Mario in the classic Nintendo platform game encountering the obstacle of a group of FSA fighters. In a subversion of computer game logic, the fighter does nothing to overcome this opponent, merely waiting instead for a Russian air strike to do it for him, before collecting a power up in the form of Syrian oil resources.[70] Another, titled 'ISIS 2080' shows elderly IS fighters, presumably after an IS victory, fondly reminiscing about the old days, when there were such things like electric lighting and running water. Another deeply ironic sketch called 'We Are All Julani' seems to refer to the leader of the Al Qaeda-affiliated Jabhat al-Nusra. In this one, a hapless civilian is bullied and robbed with impunity by a succession of balaclava-clad men who demand: 'do you know who I am? I am Julani!' Later, the victim discovers the same balaclava beneath a tree. Donning it, he in turn becomes 'Julani' and begins exacting tribute from those he meets on the road.[71]

At the time of writing, Dayaaltaseh are continuing to produce some material, despite the seeming obsolescence of their cause, including the occasional video targeting IS. The group's most recent videos on this subject focus squarely on the extremist group's violence and savagery rather than on wider political claims.

Satirical responses to IS have also come through other media and other means, not least from fighters who encountered them on the battlefield. Joshua Walker, a Welsh politics student who volunteered with the Kurdish People's Protection Units (YPG), recalls one occasion when IS fighters, dug into trenches at the front line, rigged up speakers from which they loudly broadcast *nashid* music—presumably to intimidate their opponents. The YPG volunteers, in response, rigged up their own speakers and played 'Fuck You, I'm Drunk' by Irish punk-folk band Bondo.[72] Raed Fares, the manager of the Syrian radio station Fresh.fm, responded to demands by local Jabhat al-Nusra fighters that he stop playing music that contained artistic surrealism by playing recordings of animal noises, ticking sounds, football chants, explosions and recordings of the chimes of Big Ben. When asked to stop broadcasting the voices of women presenters, he instead distorted them digitally so that they sounded like 'daleks, or robots', according to BBC reporter Mike Thomson.[73]

Another conduit for responses to IS, though one not quite so unconventional, is dramatic performance. 'Mawlid al-Sayyid Abu Bakr al-Baghdadi' by Lebanese band Al-Rahel Al-Kabir (The Great Departed) is a traditional-style religious festival song, which addresses former IS leader Baghdadi as if he were a Sufi master. The joke can be seen as doubly ingenious because it draws on precisely the kind of folk-Islamic tradition that Salafists like IS decry, and yet in actuality the leaders of jihadi organisations are often treated with an almost mystical reverence that is reminiscent of the veneration of Sufi saints.[74]

Theatre is yet another medium that has been deployed to challenge the specific IS threat. In the previous chapter, we looked at Egyptian theatre's relatively long history of challenging politicised religion. Another less immediately obvious place where theatrical performances have specifically challenged IS is the Hashemite Kingdom of Jordan.[75]

Case Study: Terrorism at the Door

Jordan occupies a curious position in Middle Eastern politics. In the-ory—and in the minds of many Arabs from more prestigious and ancient nations—the country is a byword for mediocre insignificance. It is not large or rich, nor does it have bountiful natural resources. It has no great ancient history to celebrate, no cities praised by medieval poets, no beautiful mosques or markets and few resounding cultural achievements. Its landscape is mostly of scrubland, a few scraps of forlorn forest and a lot of semi-desert. The stereotypical Jordanian is distinguished, according to regional lore, by the 'Jordanian frown'—an expression of glum resignation.

On the other hand, positioned at a crossroads between its larger and supposedly more interesting neighbours and with a tenacious habit of relative political stability, Jordan has a track record of occupying a larger role in political dramas than it would seem to have any right to.

In 2015, this was very much the case. Despite significant waves of protest by secularists, Islamists and Salafis alike, the kingdom had ridden out the Arab Spring revolutions with its usual mixture of brinkmanship, divide-and-rule, face-saving cosmetic reforms and the judicious application of repressive force. Now, however, powerful external forces were helping re-ignite internal tensions and threats. The kingdom was home to at least 600,000 refugees from the con-flict in Syria—the second largest concentration in the world, after Lebanon.[76] Many of these lived, often undocumented, in the cities, where they competed for scarce jobs. Others lived in northern camps, run by the United Nations, which were looking ever more like small cities themselves.[77]

As desperate people flowed into the country any way they could, Jordanian troops strove to lock down the borders. Dark rumours abounded. Over a beer or two in a relatively upmarket area of Amman, the deputy director of a respected local think-tank said he had it on good authority that the military had recently had to increase not only the weight, but even the calibre of its bullets: Syrian fighters, drugged up to the eyeballs on captagon—the new amphetamine of choice—didn't stop running when shot, but carried on lurching forwards, zombie-like.

Equally concerning to the government, however, was the flow of people in the opposite direction. For years, Jordan had been an important hub for an unusually vigorous, though carefully monitored, jihadi-Salafi movement. Jordan is home to world leading figures in jihadi-Salafism[78]—Abu Muhammad al-Maqdisi and Abu Qatada al-Filastini, arguably the prime theological authorities looked up to by Al Qaeda,[79] both hold Jordanian passports. Abu Mus'ab al-Zarqawi, a figure who acquired a talismanic status among supporters of IS and the wider movement that preceded and still surrounds it, was as Jordanian as it gets.[80] Beyond these rock stars of jihad was a robust network of local ideologues and organisers, such as the notorious Abu Sayyaf, who had spent years building infrastructure to support Jordan's many marginalised communities.[81] And beyond these, too, were numerous ostensibly more moderate Islamist figures who, passionately committed to the cause of the Syrian revolution, saw nothing wrong with volubly supporting jihadis such as Jabhat al-Nusra, even if they might draw the line at IS. A case in point was Amjad Qourshah—the trendy, British educated cleric we encountered in chapter 4, whose acerbic, colloquial videos for a trendy local production company packaged conservative moral guidance on contemporary youth problems in the language of stand-up comedy. In 2014, however, he had posted a pair of videos criticising the Jordanian government's participation in the international coalition against IS and urged people instead to support the Jabhat Al-Nusra against the 'infidel' Syrian regime. Two years later, due to the complex contingencies driving the politics of Jordanian security, Qourshah was arrested for this.[82]

Meanwhile, young people in Jordan were getting the message, as the country became the world's leading supplier of foreign-fighter recruits to jihadi organisations per capita.[83] Regarding large, marginalised cities such as Irbid, Zarqa and Rusayfa, worrying reports circulated of youth populations who seemed to perceive few options beyond drug addiction, foreign martyrdom or suicide.[84] In the city of Ma'an, south of the capital, a place dominated by tribes that would normally be seen as ultra-loyal to the royal family, walls were now scrawled with openly pro-IS graffiti.[85]

Hassan Sabaileh is a comedian very much of the old school. Tall and thin, with a lanky awkwardness that lends itself naturally to a certain sort of character comedy, and with a grandfatherly Arab nationalist moustache. After studying drama at Al-Yarmouk University in Irbid, he cut his teeth working as an entertainer in local hotels, in the absence of anything close to a conventional stand-up circuit. He had, however, as he puts it, always had bigger ambitions, distinguishing himself by making a point of writing his own material and striving to comment on issues of social importance.[86]

Eventually, Sabaileh got his break when Jordanian national television picked up his comedy series, *Dababis* (Needles). The show ran for eleven years (the last season was apparently in 2015),[87] putting out thirty episodes each Ramadan, each one commenting satirically on a different social issue through the misadventures of two central characters played by Sabaileh himself and Rania Ismail, who was also his wife. Za'l (the name refers to a perhaps particularly Jordanian emotional state somewhere between sadness, anger and general annoyance) and Khadra (which also means greenness and hence, liveliness and naturalness) are an everyman couple not a million miles away from Homer and Marge in *The Simpsons*, with the hapless, slow-witted Za'l struggling to assert his authority as a traditional patriarch, assisted by his more intelligent wife.

Sabaileh is not, as he describes himself, a particularly religious man. Nonetheless, in a process reminiscent of the experience of Egyptian and Saudi creatives we discussed in the previous chapter, he was shocked by the way in which, in Jordan's increasingly fundamentalist society, radical clergy began to treat him as a pariah.

> I don't pray, but I don't hurt anyone, I treat people decently, and I don't discriminate against Muslim or Christian. But I started to notice that there were people who would say that if you didn't have a beard and wear a *thawb*, then you were a *kafir* (non-believer).[88]

Things came to a head on one notable occasion when, Sabaileh said, 'I went to pray in the mosque, and the imam started speaking about *kafir* artists. I'd come to pray!'[89]

This, by the comedian's account, was what originally brought his attention to the issue of radicalisation. But it was not until 2014, with the fall of Mosul, that he finally decided that he needed to take specific action.[90] By this point, he and his wife had already built up experience of creating content with an overt focus on public interest, using their comic personas to promote causes such as public health campaigns for UNRWA[91] or Jordan's campaign against tuberculosis using dramatic plays and sketches.[92]

When Sabaileh turned his attention to the problem of youth radicalisation, however, he initially considered turning to a new medium: the internet. He created a couple of short CG animations in which he depicted Farhan, the son of Za'l and Khadra, being radicalised online, seeking to acquire status after his father humiliates him and tells him that he is nothing.[93]

Despite Sabaileh's profile, he found it initially difficult to make headway with this new subject matter. After offering his videos to the Jordanian government, he said he was rebuffed with the dismissive statement that 'we don't have a terrorism problem in Jordan'. Determined to push on, he instead took the videos to Ru'iya, a popular private channel with a Christian owner. Even so, the channel asked for payment in exchange for airing them.[94]

Despite being widely viewed online on the back of the publicity offered by Ru'iya, the reaction to the videos was apparently overwhelmingly negative, with abuse directed at its creator, including direct threats from at least one IS supporter. Concerned friends, including his wife Ismail, tried to warn him off the project, arguing that his material was dangerous because it did not also address Christian extremism. But in Jordan at least, to Sabaileh's mind, Christian extremism wasn't a problem.[95]

Sabaileh's next attempt came in the form of a play, *Irhab Ala al-Bab* (Terrorism at the Door). Featuring, as ever, the characters of Za'l and Khadra and their accident-prone family, the play built on the basic narrative of the animations, presenting Za'l as an out-of-touch and occasionally violent (though not intentionally cruel) father whose son becomes involved in extremism as part of a quest for self-esteem. The play, which was apparently met with more enthusiasm from the state, spent two years touring universities and local community venues in Jordan, as well as venues in a few other Arab countries, funded almost entirely, Sabaileh claims, out of his own pocket.[96] It was followed by another very similar production entitled *Dir Balak 'Ala Awladak* (Take Care of Your Children).[97]

The plot of *Irhab Ala al-Bab* revolves around Za'l, Khadra and their small, nuclear family, facing pressures typical of average families in Jordan and, for that matter, the world over. Short of money, Za'l takes a job as a guard at a local university where his son, Farhan, is also studying. Farhan's problem is not so much the lack of money (although he is short of that too), but prestige. His father constantly criticises him and makes him feel that he will never amount to anything. When Farhan meets an old friend who has recently returned from fighting with a jihadi group, he finds himself interested in the idea of joining up, in the hope of achieving something and making a name for himself. Unbeknownst to him, his father is simultaneously being courted by a terrorist recruiter, who appeals to rather baser instincts: money and the prospect of getting his hands on a pretty Ukrainian girl (once the conquest of Ukraine is completed). Issuing fatwa-style declarations, he proceeds to outlaw most of the electrical items in his house. Za'l eventually sees sense, but is too late to intervene in the radicalisation of his son, who ends the play revealing to everyone's shock that he is strapped into a suicide belt.

Irhab Ala al-Bab is what would be called a pantomime in the UK. It opens to thumping, *sha'abi*-style electro-folk music, including (during the performance Ramsay attended at the King Abdullah Cultural Centre in Zarqa in 2016) a reworked version of Korean rapper Psy's mega-hit *Gangnam Style*.[98] Actors work the audience, who are encouraged to boo, hiss and shout out advice to the clueless on-stage characters. But while this may sound simplistic, Sabaileh offers a thoughtful and articulate explanation for the form the production takes. A native of Tafileh—a Jordanian city considered such a backwater that it is the butt of the Jordanian equivalent of the ethnic jokes once told about Irish in Britain, or Polish people in America—Sabaileh presents himself as a self-conscious champion of popular values against a closed and

elitist establishment. In Jordan, he notes, there are two kinds of theatre—popular theatre, and what he calls 'experimental theatre'. Of
these, he alleges, the government only supports the latter sort.

> The experimental theatre says that the popular theatre is 'commercial',
> but they are the commercial ones, because they get 15000 JDs a show
> from the government. The government only wants shows in classical
> Arabic—things like translations of Hamlet. But people in places like
> Zarqa and Tafila aren't interested in Hamlet. But if you do a show for
> them in the Arabic of the street about unemployment, of course they
> are interested![99]

Sabaileh asserts that 'popular theatre' is as much rooted in Arabic
folk traditions like the art of the *hakawati* (traditional storyteller) as in
the Western history of drama—ironically, an argument reminiscent of
proponents of the sort of 'experimental' theatre to which he takes
exception. At the same time, there is much to be learned from the
Western historical experience. As he points out, actors and playwrights
were condemned by the church and sometimes banned outright by
guardians of public morality in Shakespeare's time.[100] Another tradition
Sabaileh explicitly aligns himself with is Augusto Boal's 'theatre of the
oppressed', a theatrical tradition in which drama is used in fluid inter-
action with a participating audience to analyse and propose solutions
to social problems.[101]

An element of participatory problem solving is explicitly built into
Irhab Ala al-Bab. When the play reaches its cliff-hanger conclusion, the
fourth wall is broken and the audience is asked for their opinion on
how the story can be resolved—a question which (at least in the performance attended during the research for this book) in practice,
turned into a more general session on the issue of radicalisation and
what should be done about it. Sabaileh reports that these sessions have
varied substantially from area to area, with remote audiences tending
to discuss issues of economic marginalisation, while audiences in certain Amman universities have been more politically aware and, at
times, more hostile to what they see as the underlying agenda of the
show. When Ramsay saw it, the audience—primarily made up of families rather than students—was somewhat unenthusiastic, and tended
towards cautious truisms about the need to right social injustice and
guide people towards true religion.

While none of the comedians we have discussed in this chapter escaped criticism—or worse—for their mockery of IS, the organisation's ascent allowed for the normalisation of mocking of militant Islamist groups, at least in the sense that this became something that average people could expect to see on mainstream television. But did it advance things in other ways? Earlier, we examined the fundamental obstacles that Arab comedians confront when satirising anything that purports to be a form of Islamic piety. We considered the various approaches that have been taken to try and solve this problem, including the ways in which humorous discourse can and can't get purchase on the issue.

We can conclude that in confronting IS, comedians faced very much the same obstacles that previous efforts in Egypt, Saudi Arabia and elsewhere ran up against. They had to find ways to steer clear of the accusation that by making fun of men with long beards who waved flags that said 'there is no God but God and Muhammad is the messenger of God', they were making fun of Islam itself. They had to find a humorous angle on very distressing subject matter: hostage beheadings, sex slavery and acts of genocide. Finally, they had to do all this, in most cases, in the context of authoritarian or sectarian political cultures that brought numerous other sensitivities into play. Despite this, there were other humourists flourishing under what one might consider even more unpromising conditions.

6

'WE'RE THE OTHERS!'

THE JIHADI SENSE OF HUMOUR

...Everything lively was banned. There were no musicians present to strum their instruments or to sing their songs. Those dancing feet were instructed to remain motionless. Laughter and jokes were discouraged. The evening never progressed beyond small talk.[1]

Speaking to biographer Jean Sasson, Osama bin Laden's ex-wife Najwa looked back on her wedding as exactly the sort of rigid, joyless affair that stereotype would lead one to expect. Years after this marriage, another took place, this time of Omar bin Laden—their eldest son. At the speech he gave on the occasion, as if in a riposte to his wife's future confessions, bin Laden[2] eulogised the new generation of global jihadi fighters emerging from his training camps as follows:

Its graduates never laugh. Their hearts are hardened. Our brother, the groom today, is a graduate of this camp. Here's the strange thing, though: the brother is laughing, praise the Lord! People who live in societies far removed from jihad, its strugglers, and the land of true bonds, often imagine the strugglers to be monsters ... If they only knew how the strugglers are a people of goodness and generosity. If they only knew how they ease the tribulations of all people, whether disbelieving or Muslim.[3]

Bin Laden's self-aware observation neatly encapsulates the complex place of laughter within the curious military utopianism of the jihadi movement. On the one hand, there is the outward facing image of puritanical toughness and militaristic ferocity. And yet, at the same time, there are ideals of kindness, generosity of spirit and even joyfulness, though still within carefully regulated bounds.

Laughter, for bin Laden, seems to have utopian implications not dissimilar to those supposed by some of the scholars we discussed in chapter 2. For him, it is something inseparable from the 'true bonds' that unite the community, from the virtues of 'goodness and generosity' that sanctify the *mujahidin* (fighters). It is, perhaps, a part of the almost mystical *halawa* (sweetness) of jihad referred to in much reverential jihadi writing. And yet, as we previously observed and as we shall see in the following section, jihadi laughter has by no means always been viewed in such generous terms—at least, by the 'disbelieving' standard that bin Laden himself holds it to.

Indeed, one reason for examining jihadi-Salafi humour is the complex and ambiguous place it occupies within the movement more generally. On the one hand, jihadi humour can be read as outward facing propaganda—a way to gain more recruits by putting a human face on the movement. On the other, it can be seen as offering insight into aspects of the internal culture of jihadi groups that seem to jar with the more conventional representations offered up by the media. Similarly, jihadi humour points in different directions. Sometimes, it relies on laughing at the crude denigration and even annihilation of the jihadis' enemies. At other times, however, it strikes a gentler tone, emphasising the human weaknesses and even seemingly innocent playfulness of jihadis themselves.

Jihadi humour is a broad phenomenon that can be found in one way or another across the global movement, encompassing different forms, styles, media and levels of involvement on the part of the humourists. In what follows, we will look at three main manifestations: first, the use of aggressive and satirical humour in the wider context of jihadi propaganda; second, comical performances by popular jihadi *nashid* singers; and, finally, comic literature in the form of the jihadi version of the *turfa* (witty account).

As we noted in chapter 2 (following Alexander Kozintsev), satire can be viewed as an inherently ambiguous genre that stretches from humour (essentially playful aggression) to outright aggression that just happens to be expressed in word rather than deed. Jihadi-Salafis are, of course, often verbally aggressive towards others. A key pillar—arguably the key pillar of jihadi ideology—is the principle of *al-wala wal-bara* (loyalty and disavowal).[4] Jihadis take it for granted that a crucial tenet of Islam requires true believers to rigidly distinguish between Muslim and non-Muslim, acting in loving and 'soft-hearted' ways towards the former, while actively hating and wherever possible dissociating from the latter. Jihadi expressions of defiance and contempt towards their enemies may sometimes resemble attempts at humour in their sheer vociferousness and their formulaic nature. But it is not always obvious that such rhetoric is intended to inspire laughter, rather than scorn or outrage.

It is not uncommon for the leaders and key spokespersons of jihadi groups to make comments that seem actively designed to goad their enemies, elaborating not only on their shortcomings and failures, but on the contradictory or absurd nature of their thinking. Typically, however, invective of this sort is delivered in a deeply serious and un-laughing manner. This creates something of a definitional puzzle, one which, in a sense, goes to the heart of the difficulty of defining humour more generally. Official public speeches by jihadi leaders are, as a strict matter of genre, 'serious' in nature. It would have been considered deeply inappropriate for a bin Laden, an Ayman al-Zawahiri, an Abu Bakr al-Baghdadi or an Abu Muhammad al-Adnani to actually laugh, even sardonically, while delivering any sort of official statement, however much it might seem to structurally resemble 'humour'. Hence the claim by Brachman that Zawahiri was 'deadpanning' in the interview in which he appeared to ridicule the analytical efforts of Westpoint's Combatting Terrorism Centre. At the same time, though, one might also suppose that a similarly serious and sombre attitude would be expected on the part of the ideologically committed listener. If a text is supposed to be delivered with total seriousness, and received in a spirit of total seriousness, is it still tenable to identify it as 'humour'? And if this means that the authors of the text's deliberately inserted passages that could be read in this way, does this mean that we can identify a certain element of mischief or even subversive wit even in what are supposed to be the most deeply serious expressions of groups which are, in theory at least, already famous for their total seriousness?

Or ought we to accept that, in the spirit of 'telling the truth when I laugh', there is room for at least a wry smile in even the most seemingly portentous of jihadi speeches?

Bin Laden, for example, made a laboured wordplay in his *Message to the American People*, based on the well-known fact that George W. Bush, after hearing the news of the 9/11 attacks, had continued to read out aloud from a book called *The Pet Goat* to a classroom of elementary school pupils: 'it seemed to him that occupying himself by talking to the little girl about the goat and its butting was more important than occupying himself with the planes and their butting of the skyscrapers'.[5]

This reads somewhat like a joke, and the impression of humorous intent could be reinforced by the probability that bin Laden learned about this incident (perhaps indirectly) from American comedian Michael Moore's documentary *Fahrenheit 9/11*.[6] But the humorous intent should not be taken for granted—the portrayal of a hapless Bush in the face of the blow struck by the 9/11 hijackers is as much a rhetorical flourish as a comical aside.

Zawahiri, as we have already seen, could also be said to have been partial to the occasional dry quip. In addition to the interview just mentioned, he was widely seen as having used ridicule against then President Barack Obama in a speech criticising Operation Pillar of Defence—the 2008–9 Israeli bombing of Gaza.[7] The crucial moment was when Zawahiri quotes Obama's claim that he was 'uneasy' about the level of force used by Israel in the conflict—a word that translates as *qalaq* in Arabic, which also expresses uncertainty and hesitancy. Zawahiri repeats and stresses the word, emphasising the diminutive compactness provided by its crisp pair of uvular consonants, making the phonetics of the word itself symbolic of the president's comically minimal gesture towards criticising Israel, let alone reining in its assault.[8]

IS speeches are, if anything, even more sententious than those produced by Al Qaeda's leaders. Even so, there may still be traces of wit. In his speech 'Nonviolence is Whose Religion?' late IS spokesperson Adnani described the gradualist approach of the Muslim Brothers in deliberately laborious and repetitive language dripping with bathos.

> They preached the claim that they would adopt these democratic methods as a pathway in order to implement the laws and principles of Islam. Then later on they departed from this position, saying that it was

not possible at the present time to implement the entire sharia. They said that 'we, from our position as legislators, will delay the implementation of some of the rulings of sharia according to what seems appropriate to us. Then after that, when it seems appropriate to us to implement them, we will then issue a new legal decree, and so on until at some year in the future we reach the implementation of the entire sharia. We do not expect that that year will be one of the four years permitted to us before the requirement for new legislative or presidential elections. But it will be some year in another four-year term, not this one. This delay in implementation will depend on what seems appropriate to us or what we plan or what we cancel, and the complaints can be addressed to God'.[9]

If these examples seem a little tenuous, it is because they are. Perhaps it is inevitable that one will find humour in a text if one looks hard enough for it. Moreover, given that their rhetorical purpose is to draw attention to the shortcomings of enemies, it is hardly surprising that sooner or later they end up describing them in a way that makes them seem laughable.

It becomes more possible to talk confidently about jihadis using satire and ridicule when we are dealing with texts and with speakers of less import. But here too, caution is needed. *Inspire Magazine*, an English-language publication affiliated to Al Qaeda in the Arabian Peninsula, has at certain times, deployed a tone described by Western counterterrorism experts as 'bratty' or 'snarky'.[10] It is plausible to suggest that English, as a secular, vernacular language in contrast to the elevated, sacred register used for most official Arabic propaganda, may be seen as more suitable for humorous or mischievous content. But the point shouldn't be stretched too far. *Inspire*, it has been noted, uses an irreverent, jokey voice only in its earlier issues, one which has been identified with the personal style of a particular individual: Samir Khan. After Khan was killed, this voice seemingly disappeared. Later issues of *Inspire* and other important jihadi magazines in English make little notable use of humour.[11]

If the identification of *Inspire*'s sarcastic voice with Khan is correct, it is probably significant that he was recruited (we might say head hunted) from the jihadi 'fan' community, from which he had previously launched his own DIY magazine, *Jihad Recollections*. Since that time, the general willingness of unaffiliated, online jihadi supporters to use humour and mockery in ways that were unlikely to be sanctioned in official publications has continued, unabated. An example of this is the emergence of distinctively jihadi memes and bad taste jokes that capture media attention, particularly when they are circulated in response to terrorist attacks. English-language jihadi memes, intriguingly, have adopted the same vocabulary of images and in-jokes as memes in general, including viral images such as 'first world problems woman' and 'bad luck Brian', using these to ridicule the efforts of enemies of jihadi groups like IS, in particular.[12] Such examples may seem surprising, but they are in line with a longer history (at least in the West) of 'culture jamming' by jihadis and political Islamists. On the hard drive of one young British Muslim arrested on terrorism charges was an image showing two aircraft flying into a skyscraper, their exhaust trails forming the Nike Swoosh logo. Beneath was the slogan 'just do it'. Interestingly, while Arabic-language jihadi memes also exist, they rarely seem so obviously comic in nature. This is beginning to change, however. A possible case of this is the Facebook group and Telegram community *Exclamation*.[13] While this group is seldom explicitly jihadi in its sympathies, it presents what appears to be a broadly jihadi discourse by mocking and laughing at the political alternatives. They direct ridicule at secular Arab governments, religions other than Islam, and Western countries, but also 'moderate' Muslims. For example, when Stephen Hawking died, the group circulated a meme lampooning rumours in certain Islamic circles to the effect that, before his death, the physicist had converted to Islam. The meme shows an individual dressed in typical Muslim Brotherhood-style garb, addressing Hawking in the hope that God will bless him. 'But I'm an atheist' Hawking replies 'I don't believe in God'. 'No', insists the Muslim. 'You are a Muslim, what do you know?'

One of the most successful cultural forms promoted by jihadi groups is the *nashid*—an Islamic hymn which, in principle, adheres to the strict principle banning the use of musical instruments. (In practice, jihadi *nashids* characteristically make lavish use of multi-tracking and studio effects.) Indeed, despite their pious lyrics on themes such as yearning for martyrdom, annihilating enemies and apologising to one's mother, for some years there has been a measure of concern among more staid members of the jihadi movement as to whether the popularity of *nashids* has become a liability, distracting fighters from more profitable activities like reading the Quran.

Despite their normally ominous or sentimental lyrics, *nashids* can have a lighter side. For example, in 2014, the IS *munshid* (nashid singer) Ahmad al-Shatteri uploaded a video in which he performed a satirical piece entitled 'Hey Band Head, Where Are You?' aimed at the late Saudi King Abdullah. Alongside him in the video were two other well-known *munshids*, Maher Misha'al and Abdul Karem al-Tunisi as well as Shaker Waheeb, an IS commander notorious for an incident captured in a widely circulated video showing him killing Syrian Alawite drivers after they failed to correctly answer questions about Sunni Muslim prayers.[14] All three men were laughing through the performance. Saudi loyalists responded in kind with their own parody. In response, Shatteri performed yet again, this time at an event at the former Syrian government headquarters in Raqqa, accompanied by numerous unknown laughing fighters.[15]

Sometimes *nashid* singing can involve a more playful style of humour. An example can be found in a performance by an unknown Saudi *munshid* who sings a compilation of *nashids* originally released by IS, adding a new, comical spin to originally serious lyrics.

The Russian *bear* is now history
He cannot beat us any more
Khattab broke the Russian bear's teeth[16]

As he sings these words, he emphasises the word 'bear', which in colloquial Arabic can also refer to a fat or slow-witted person, directing the word as a humorous insult at members of his audience. Later, he goes on to improvise new words of his own in a series of absurd punning call-outs to different locations, sending up a convention in jihadi *nashids* whereby the singer praises the attributes of different countries, regions and cities—such as strong faith, bravery or generosity. Here, instead, the singer mentions the less heroic attributes of famous dishes and vegetables, sometimes attributing food to the wrong countries just to fit the rhythm.

This year, in the tomato season (Ghouta) even the pigeon wore boots (*bouta*)
Greetings to people of Aleppo (*Halab*)… the masters of kebab

JOKING ABOUT JIHAD

Greetings to people of Homs ... the masters of hummus
Greetings to people of Tunisia (*Tunis*)... masters of rice and parsley
(*baqdunis*)

When he gets to Libya, he is unable to find a rhyme, prompting more laughter from the audience. The humour is not, of course, directly subversive of the overall aims and beliefs of the Jahbat al-Nusra jihadis watching him (it is unclear whether the performance came before or after the IS/al-Nusra split), but it is mischievous in the way it seems to parody the characteristic seriousness with which jihadis are supposed to regard themselves and their mission.

A perhaps more ambivalent example of a humorous *nashid* performance can be seen in a video featuring Amino, a former rapper from Tunisia who became a jihadi and joined IS. In this case, he is singing about a typical *nashid* theme—yearning for the beauty of the *Hur al-'Ayn* (virgins of paradise), and yet the manner in which he is doing so is clearly intended to be sexually suggestive, reminiscent of profane singing about romantic love.[17] This can be read in two ways: both as blasphemous mockery of a religious belief from the standpoint of sexual lust but also as the complete reverse—a mockery of the ordinary affections of the mortal plane from the standpoint of the transcendent rewards expected in the hereafter. Either way, however, both the singer and his companions are obviously amused.

Nashids, though not the humorous sort, are a staple of official IS propaganda. In fact, an important innovation of the group was to establish its own in-house outlet, Al-Ajnad, to produce what had formerly been a more organic expression of jihadi culture. However, the *nashid* performances we have just discussed seem to represent forms of expression which, though tolerated and perhaps favoured by jihadi hierarchies, were not formally folded into their centralised propaganda production. On occasion, however, IS and its precursors staged officially prescribed humorous performances. One example is the '*da'wa* (religious call) tent' established in Aleppo in 2013.[18] Here, alongside more serious preaching, popular *nashid* artists would entertain young people in performances that lay somewhere between compèring at a comedy gig and children's party entertainment. To give a sense of the kind of mild humour involved, in one particularly well-known video of the occasion, Saudi *nashid* singer Maher Mesha'al challenges a child to pronounce a tongue twister, prompting merry laughter from those around.[19]

Just as humorous *nashids* are a sub-genre of the *nashid*, it would seem that examples of humorous jihadi prose (which, following the conservative Islamic tradition discussed in chapter 3, jihadis refer to consistently as *tara'if*) can similarly be identified with the broader tradition of jihadi storytelling. While existing work on this phenomenon is limited, it would seem that jihadi prose literature also encompasses contemporary jihadi versions of broader Islamic traditions. These might tentatively be said to include *karamat* (miracles), the most famous example being the book *Signs of the Merciful in the Afghan Jihad* by Abdullah Azzam, which is a compilation of miracle stories involving jihadi fighters in that conflict. Less written about, but just as important, are *raqa'iq*—moving stories intended to move the listener to tears and 'soften the heart'. Another category might be the dream narrative, or the martyr biography. While a deeper examination of this is far beyond the scope of this book, this literature might in general be understood as a continuation of a concern with the much broader and older Islamic idea of *adab* (meaning both 'literature' and 'manners') as a crucial element in the cultivation of the virtuous Islamic personality.

Like these other examples, jihadi *tara'if* occupy a somewhat ambiguous space in relation to groups' more official productions. The stories circulate online, usually in seemingly informal contexts, cropping up in threads on forum discussions, on social media, or on posts to anonymous sites like Pastebin. But this does not fully answer questions about their relationship to more formalised propaganda campaigns. Researcher Hamud al-Ziyadi, for example, opined that the once-popular Twitter hashtag 'jihadi *tara'if*' functioned deliberately as recruitment propaganda for IS. However, this hashtag was also used to share stories by fighters from their rival Jabhat al-Nusra.[20]

In at least some cases, it is possible to identify *tara'if* with known jihadi fighters. These include, for example, Hamad al-Qatari, who collected stories of the martyrs in Bosnia and Afghanistan and whose collection was introduced by famous Saudi cleric Salman al-Ouda.[21] His collection also contains many non-humorous stories.[22] Another important source of humorous stories is Najm al-Din Azad (real name Adel Utaybi). This Saudi fighter was an active member of Jabhat al-

Nusra who briefly acquired notoriety when, in August 2013, he uploaded gruesome photographs of the massacred bodies of Alawite villagers in the countryside of the Syrian coastal city of Latakia.[23] Narrated in a lengthy series of tweets, and collected on his blog site, Najm al-Din Azad's 'Stories of the *Mujahidin*', sought to encourage the new generation of fighters by recounting his experiences of fighting in the Afghan jihad in the 1980s. Azad's stories, although intended to be stirring and inspiring, often have a mischievous feel, focusing on absurd and far-fetched events and comical occurrences. As such, they were shared on various sites as examples of *tara'if*.[24] A third example would be Al-Sultan Sinjer,[25] who reported a few stories mainly from Syria. On other occasions, online responses give us some insight into context, reception and, to a limited extent, authenticity. For example, forum discussions may involve groups of jihadi supporters (or people who claim to be current or former fighters) sharing stories and laughing together, even commenting to confirm the veracity of particular funny stories.

Do the stories as circulated online reflect what is actually typical of jihadis on the ground? While we did not personally interview former jihadis on this subject, our formal and informal discussions with people who were in close personal contact with jihadi fighters suggest that the sorts of humorous anecdote we have collected do chime with a sense of humour seemingly widespread among jihadi fighters, many of whom apparently have a sense of black humour and a penchant for amusing anecdotes. During the Libyan Revolution, Kirstie, a British aid worker, struck up a close friendship with two young Libyan fighters Hamdi and Sadiq, whom she met again in Syria shortly thereafter. Looking back, she describes them as two light-hearted young men, charming and polite, deeply religious but not fanatical, who were constantly laughing and joking. Often their humour served as a means of defusing awkwardness in relation to religious taboos (including those arising from maintaining a friendship with a single woman). They also took a good deal of amusement in how their jihadi style tended to alarm certain sorts of foreigner.

> Hamdi was very much into the idea of an Islamic State, [even] before the whole ISIS thing came out. He had this screensaver on his phone which was this Salafi flag stamped with the seal of Muhammad [proba-

bly the IS flag itself]. I remember I said to him 'Hamdi, what's that?' and he laughed and said 'When I was in Istanbul it was really funny. I was in the hotel and I had my phone on the side. There were these Germans and they looked at it and they rushed off!'[26]

Both men went on to fight and ultimately die for IS, their sense of humour growing darker and their attitudes becoming harder and more radical. But throughout this, Hamdi continued to share videos of the stray dogs and cats that he loved to rescue and look after.

What is it that defines jihadi humour? To our surprise, we generally had very little difficulty distinguishing humorous stories ostensibly by jihadis from other jokes (as will be considered in the following chapter) told about jihadis, despite the fact there can be a self-deprecating element to jihadi humour and the thematic overlap that can be found between jokes that laugh with and jokes that laugh at them. On the other hand, there is a slight grey area between properly 'jihadi' humour and that attributed to other radical Islamists. For example, one online compilation of audio recordings described as 'jihadi *tara'if*' that helpfully captures the roars of laughter from the audience on hearing these stories is actually substantially devoted to the wit and humour of radical Egyptian sheikh Abdulhamid Kishk.[27] Similarly, the joking practices of some notably 'jihadi' clerics seem to be very much in line with the general style of Islamic clerical humour encountered in chapter 3.

While of course there is not the same risk of mistaking one for the other, jihadi humour also bears a passing resemblance to cross-cultural examples of the 'squaddie humour' of troops. Jihadi humour is not as scatological and sexually explicit as, for example, contemporary British military humour,[28] but risqué allusions are important. More closely relatable is the black humour of people constantly in close proximity to death and the possibility of dying. Compare, for example, the following two anecdotes:

During the battle, one of the Chechen mujahidin was so zealous against the enemies of Allah that not one of the Nusayra (Alawites) remained on the battlefield. He killed all of them at that battle except for a single sniper. As the Chechen turned his attention to him, the sniper wounded him in the shoulder. The brother ran to the sniper's location and rebuked him harshly before killing him. He then returned very angry, muttering curses about the Nusayri. The brothers asked him why he had rebuked the Nusayri sniper before killing him, and why he was angry now. He replied in broken Arabic 'Sniper donkey. I tell him shoot here he shoot there'—meaning, he told him to shoot me in the head but he shot me in the shoulder.[29]

And:

A German sniper [was] firing at the Canadians in their trenches, shooting through the sandbags in the hope of hitting the men. One bullet nearly struck the colonel who was tramping through the lines. The enraged officer ordered one of his best scouts to go out and get the sniper. The man snuck out and eventually tracked down the enemy, catching him in a vulnerable position: whereupon the sniper, who spoke very good English, held up his hands and cried 'Mercy, Mercy,' but the soldiers said, 'No mercy for you, you missed the colonel'.[30]

These two stories differ in a crucial aspect: the soldiers in the second story (Canadians fighting in World War I) are (we assume, jokingly) angry at the sniper for failing to kill their commanding officer. The Chechen is angry at the sniper for failing to kill him, and in doing so granting him the gift of martyrdom. But the parallels are still obvious.

Finally, jihadi humour unsurprisingly brings with it elements of the humorous culture of the various societies from which jihadi fighters inevitably come. While jihadis, following strict religious convention, refrain from using the word joke (*nukta* in Arabic) to label their humorous texts, jihadi *tara'if*, such as the following, do appear to be recycled jokes.

In one of the training camps, the commander wanted to raise the morale of the men. Pointing to one of the recruits, Abu Haritha he asked:

'What's this, Abu Haritha?'

'This is my weapon', replied Abu Haritha

'This is your wife!' the commander corrected him

Turning to an Egyptian recruit he asked the same question.

'What's this?'

'This is Abu Haritha's wife!'[31]

This joke was current in Syria some time before the civil war and the rise of jihadi groups.

Jihadi *tara'if* exhibit considerable diversity, with stories relating to most important conflicts in which they have been involved. There are copious examples recounting events supposed to have taken place in the Afghan and Bosnian wars and some in Algeria and Iraq. *Tara'if* relating to the Syrian Civil War are particularly widespread, but this may well only reflect the ease with which these can be collected due to their recentness and the availability of social media to those sharing them.

In form, texts labelled as jihadi *tara'if* also vary greatly. Some are lengthy and well-developed stories—comic prose narratives, though usually written in a colloquial and conversational style. Other, shorter texts have a stylised quality that quite closely resembles the set up/ punch line structure of what would otherwise be called 'jokes'. Some texts record funny quips or observations made by jihadis on particular occasions. Others are very short records of mistakes or mishaps, whether made by the jihadis or their enemies. As prose narratives, the *tara'if* also overlap with other genres of jihadi story. Stories told for comical effect may involve reports of actual miraculous events or pseudo-miraculous events, meaning that they overlap with the tradition of the miracle tale. Quite a number of humorous stories concern accounts of martyrdom (or failed martyrdom).

Much of the underlying humour of jihadi *tara'if* comes in the form of what we have previously termed 'pillory'. Often the central joke is simply the death and humiliation of the jihadis' enemies, rendered as comical by their self-defeating stupidity. At other times, the emphasis is more on the wit and élan of the jihadis as they run rings around their dim-witted opponents.

The following tale from Afghanistan is related by Najm al-Din Azad.

You know that we used to annoy the Soviets in any way we could … I remember one time, when I had returned back here to Saudi Arabia and one of the brothers invited me to his farm. He had a swimming pool, and I said to myself: why don't we make a swimming pool for the *mujahidin* here? I got excited about the idea, so I went to the commander, Abdullah, and said to him:

'I have a request'.

'Tell me what it is'.

So I said, 'I want a swimming pool for the *mujahidin* so we can swim in it and keep it clean, and if we get tired, swimming will be a recreation'.

He laughed. 'Is there something the matter with you, Najm al-Din? Are you feeling ill?'

'No'.

'In that case where did the swimming pool idea come from?'

'I have a plan', I said.

'Come on, what is the idea?'

I explained to him in front of the *mujahidin*:

'First, we choose a place for the swimming pool. Then we provoke the Soviets. They will come with their planes, and you know the rest of the story'.

'We will ask the *mujahidin*', he said.

Everyone stood up and gave their agreement.

'Come on, let's put our trust in God and choose a suitable place and then go and harass the Soviets'.

Our raid was quick but painful, until we had ensured that the engineer (by which I mean, of course, the idiot pilot!) would carry out the project would finish his work. The planes came as always and gave the ground one hell of a pounding.

The day came around and we found that they had dug more than one swimming pool. Commander Abdullah said, 'The matter is finished! Now we have a swimming pool for the young men, and one for the older men—our elders. We've beaten them, thank God! Brother, the Soviets have done us a service, because they are fools. But I swear that this exceeds the international standards!'

Afterwards, we built a wall of mud bricks and put the swimming pools in and it became a prize.

But I wasn't content with this.

'I want', I said to the commander, 'I'm not sure what you call it, but I mean that board that you get onto and fly from into the swimming pool'.

The commander got my meaning.

'No, no! Where would we get one of those from?'

'It's easy—a helicopter rotor blade will do just fine, and there's lots of those lying around all over the place from the destroyed helicopters'.

'You're quite right!'

So he ordered us *mujahidin* to search for them, and we came back and brought them, and the old hands told us what to do. So we made a platform from mud and we set the rotor blade into the middle of it and put mud over it, and came back when it had dried.

Well, as you know, helicopter blades are very long, so it made a good diving board and when we tried it out, it worked well.

'Woe on the Soviets' said the commander. 'Don't they want to fight these young men? If they knew how they were making fun of them they would not stay one night in Kabul'.

And I said to him, 'Aren't these the Yellow Scorpion blades with which they fight us that we are now trampling beneath our feet—indeed, we have made them a source of mirth. Have you seen stupidity like that of the Soviets and Russians?' [32]

The central comic reversal of this story concerns the destruction and defeat of the apparently superior Soviet forces, whose broken war machines are literally 'trampled' underfoot. But the Soviets are here represented as an essentially impersonal enemy, whose only relevant attributes are their superior firepower, and their implicitly inferior intelligence and morale. Indeed, their mockery at the hands of the merry *mujahidin* serves simply to frame another humorous dimension in the story: Azad's own playful relationship with his commander, whose somewhat unimaginative scepticism positions him mischievously as a straight main foil to Azad's outrageous scheme.

This seems to reflect a broader pattern in stories concerning jihadi battles with foreign enemies from non-Muslim populations—especially, in the material we collected, Soviets and Serbs. The infidel status of these enemies is, of course, ideologically crucial, and the tales about them show no hint of reluctance or compunction about killing them. And yet there is little to indicate any really deep or bitter animosity. In Azad's stories, Soviet soldiers are presented as cowardly, foolish, inept and contemptible; but not as loathsome. He sometimes notes the Afghans' horror at the idea of polluting themselves by association with 'unclean' atheists. While he seems to regard this as commendable evidence of the pure and unsullied Islam of a simple and courageous people, he also tells stories which seem to contrast this with his own more relaxed attitude. This is evidenced in material relating to food. In one tale, the narrator, together with an Afghan friend, go on a daring scouting mission in which they succeed in liberating some roasting chickens from a Soviet field oven under the noses of the enemy—Azad describes at some length the relish with which they ate this meal. Later on, in another tale in his collection, he recounts the wife of a martyr refusing the gift of just such an oven, on the grounds that it would be shameful to 'cook food for the sons of a martyr in any oven from which pig was eaten'. In another, the author describes the acquisition of *ghanima* (a formal word for plunder, typically referring to the acquisition of heavy weaponry and powerful munitions) in the form of frozen hamburgers from a Soviet store. While the burgers appear to be a halal product also sold in Saudi Arabia, Azad seems to be rather amused by his fellow Afghan fighters' objections that they may contain pork. 'We're Wahhabis—it's fine as far as we're concerned', he breezily reassures them. The hungry *mujahidin* rush off to secure some burgers of their own.[33]

Stories about Americans are markedly sparser in our collection, but those that are available suggest a slightly more intimate relationship with the enemy. In one story, a US soldier in Afghanistan boasts in conversation to a *mujahid* that the Taliban have been defeated, immediately before diving for cover from a Taliban rocket. The following anecdote (another version of which concerns Syrian Alawite enemies) has a rather hard-boiled American flavour.

> The brother of a sniper said, 'a Crusader came out to smoke, so I killed him. After a quarter of an hour, another idiot came out to the same place, so I killed him as well. Smoking is dangerous to health and causes death'.[34]

A groaner like this, which one can easily imagine making it into a Bond film or a 1980s Arnold Schwarzenegger action blockbuster, might well be imagined as a deliberate attempt at a role reversal, casting the 'terrorist' in the role of the wisecracking hero, while the Americans become, in turn, either cannon fodder, or hapless buffoons, as in the next story.

> The interrogators in Guantanamo Bay asked a brother: 'Do you know Ibn Taymiyya [a medieval theologian]?'
>
> 'Yes', he replied.
>
> 'If you provide us with information leading to his arrest we will release you'.[35]

Once we move past stories concerning asymmetric conflict between *mujahidin* and non-Muslim militaries to the sectarian civil wars in Syria and Iraq, jokes about defeating the enemy become both more intimate and significantly darker.

> Some of the brothers and I were holed up in a particular place and we saw some of the Alawites. We'd memorised their faces, but the commander hadn't allowed us to open fire until he gave the order.
>
> We weren't allowed to do this because, as the commander said, they had many fat 'sheep' and we had to take things slowly so as not to lose out.
>
> We continued in this manner for two days, and after that we saw six Alawites who had put on Qandahari outfits (typical garb for jihadis)— the ones whose faces we had already memorised!
>
> They were close to a certain armoured car, getting out of it, and repeatedly shouting the slogan 'We are Islam! We are the Islamic State in every place!' We knew what their business was.
>
> But because of their extreme stupidity, they disgraced themselves of their own accord, through those mixed up slogans they were shouting. Two hours later, one of the brothers went to one of them and he was wearing the costume of a [regime] soldier.
>
> The brother, who was Syrian, asked them 'What's up, lads? Who are you imitating?' They said that this was a tactic nobody knew about.
>
> So the brother said, 'I will join with you in the tactic'. They agreed— how stupid they were! And the brother began repeating the slogans with them. And there was a slogan we had previously agreed upon which, when the brother repeated it, we were to attack. I shall keep that chant to myself. In the end, we attacked the place. The brother hadn't stopped playing his part to the fullest when the [soldiers' commanding] officer discovered what was going on. So there was nothing for the brother but to split the officer in two, and with him many of his comrades who entered their final sleep in this world—they weren't carrying weapons. Thank God, who fated us with victory in battle with these dramatic events.[36]

Fundamental to this anecdote is the (unsuccessful) attempt by the Alawites to imitate the jihadis and the escalating absurdity that leads to the sublime irony of jihadis imitating Alawites imitating jihadis—jihadis pretending to be themselves.[37] Indeed, the story plays out very much like a farce right up until its conclusion where, instead of a far-fetched resolution between the conflicting parties, the uncovering of the deception is resolved with extreme violence which, perhaps to the intended audience, adds further to the hilarity. As inappropriate as it seems, the ultimate liquidation of the enemy is actually essential to the functioning of this story as a humorous jihadi narrative, since it serves as a comfortingly unequivocal refutation of the disquieting fact that the two sides are able to imitate one another precisely because they are in virtually every respect the same.

In fact, the story above is an unusually lengthy and elaborate example of an entire sub-genre of jihadi *turfa* that seemingly originates from the Syrian civil war. Mirroring or recounting real-life examples of sectarian massacres, these stories revolve around desperate attempts by captured Alawites (or alternatively captured mainstream Shias) to pass as Sunnis and escape execution.

> On one occasion, the *mujahidin* got hold of one of the *shabiha* (Syrian state-sponsored militias) rats. He asked him 'are you Alawite?'
>
> He replied, 'I am Sunni. And the dawn prayer is two *ruka'at*, and the midday four, the afternoon four, the evening three and the night-time four'.
>
> One of the boys said to him 'We've changed the question now. How many times do you prostrate for funeral prayers?'[38]

Typically, difference in these stories is expressed, as here, through the device of mangled catechism. 'When the brothers captured an elderly Alawite in Lattakia', runs another one in this vein 'they asked him "what is your view on the companions of the prophet?" He began to curse them and insult Ali, thinking that we hate Ali'.[39] Another recounts how 'The mujahidin captured a Shia from the SWAT teams. He wanted to save himself, so he started to beg for help "O Umar, O Umar" and started cursing Ali'.[40] Or, in a slight variation 'the Shia whose own tongue accused him when he said, "by Bashar, I am Sunni"'. The point being made, of course, is not just that the enemy is ignorant of orthodox Sunni belief, but also that, in trying to replicate it, they end up (by the jihadis' logic) condemning not only themselves but also their own creed—Sunnis revere both Ali and Umar, but are not follow-ers of Umar in the same way Shias are followers of Ali. Of course, the willingness of the captives to forswear their own religion is also supposed to imply that their commitment to their religion, unlike the martyrdom-seeking jihadis, is only superficial and self-interested.

Another dimension to the stories is the more conventionally comic motif of stupidity and canniness. So much so, that it is sometimes possible to detect in these stories a trace of the same themes normally found in ethnic jokes.

> The *mujahidin* brothers entered a certain hideout of the Alawites, and there happened to be an Alawite soldier there pretending to be dead. One of the brothers passed him and said 'if he is an Alawite we will kill him, but if he is Sunni we will let him go'.
>
> The Alawite got up and said: 'I am a Sunni'. After that, the brothers sorted him out.[41]

The type of stylised idiocy in this story bears comparison, for example, to a Greek wartime joke, recorded by Davies, in which an Englishman, a Scotsman and a Pontian (the typical butt of Greek stupidity) hide from a Nazi in a box, a crate and a sack. The suspicious Nazi kicks the box, and the Englishman, imitating a cat, says 'miaow'. He kicks the crate, and the Scotsman says 'woof'. He kicks the sack and the Pontian shouts 'potatoes'!

In other cases, apparent ethnic stereotyping applies instead to the jihadis. For example, Egyptians have a reputation in the Arab world for light-heartedness and wit, which explains the significance of the Egyptian in the following (originally from an Egyptian play).

> The brothers caught an Alawite and one of the Egyptian brothers asked him: 'are you with us or with the others?' The Alawite said 'I am with you'. The Egyptian replied to him. 'We are the others'.[42]
>
> A Shia said, 'kill me at 2:00 so that I can have lunch with Hussein'. An Egyptian said 'we will kill you at 4:00 so you can wash the dishes for him'.[43]

Another ethnic stereotype, which Davies has identified as a common subject for humour, concerns 'warlike' groups. In some jihadi stories, Chechens seem to be identified with this role, carrying out acts which, even by jihadi standards, are particularly cold blooded.

> One of the Chechen *mujahidin* killed a *shabiha*. Afterwards, the *shabiha*'s phone rang. So he answered it and heard the voice of a woman saying:

'how are you my darling?' The Chechen replied (in accented Arabic), 'my darling is finissed, ha ha ha'.[44]

The presence of this stereotype in jihadi humour (which can also be seen in the story reproduced above about the Chechen confronting the sniper) is interesting in that it is also especially common in anti-jihadi humour of the sort mentioned in the previous chapter. For example, in *Dawlat al-Khurafa* and in several episodes of *Spotlight*, Chechen characters are presented as comically fanatical, a stereotype that presumably derives in part from the formidable reputation of Chechen fighters in the first and second Chechen wars, but perhaps also from the earlier role of Caucasians in filling the armies of the Mamluk and Ottoman states.

In the examples so far, we have caught glimpses of a more gentle and inclusive style of jihadi humour. Here, jihadis laugh not at their enemies, but rather at each other, tempering the mockery with underlying respect. These stories are interesting in how they touch on key aspects of the jihadi way of life including combat, martyrdom, marital relationships and the observance of religious ritual.

Jihadi-Salafi organisations face the task of integrating into a coherent unit with fighters from a wide variety of different backgrounds, including those of different ethnic origins, different levels of education and different levels of initial experience and fighting ability. Inevitably, this means that there are mistakes and misunderstandings which could potentially have fatal consequences.

We prayed the dawn prayer for the day, then some of the brothers went down to the basement to get some sleep. Some of them were up guarding. I was injured and went to bed late. The power was off and it was very dark, so I lay on my bed. I felt with my feet a solid object, so I just kicked it toward another brother. Immediately, I trembled and got up to check what the object was. Then I remembered that I had put a Russian defensive grenade near my bed. Where was it? It was between the brother's legs.

I instantly jumped on the grenade and held it to my chest, because I thought that the detonator was dislodged. (I had learned this technique from a story about a similar incident that happened during the jihad in Afghanistan when a brother held the grenade to his chest and it did not explode). I did the same but it did not explode because detonator was not dislodged. I held it with my hands and asked it: Do not you fear

Allah? Then I put it away from us. The brother was still asleep. When he got up in the morning I said to him, 'I want to tell you something my beloved brother'.

'O Sheikh!', he said, 'have you observed anything wrong I have done!'

'Of course not,' I said. 'You are one of the best brothers'.

He said, 'May Allah bless you, our sheikh'.

Then I told him what happened!

He knew I was reckless and always did some action at headquarters. When he heard the story he ran away screaming, laughing and saying

'Beware brothers! Breaking News! Abu Abdullah [the author] wanted to assassinate me'.

And every time he saw me he would say: I want to search you, sheikh.[45]

The laughter in this story seems to be a classic example of the relief function of humour—reflecting the anxiety of a close encounter with death. This is, perhaps unsurprisingly, a common theme. Whereas this story is told naturalistically, by a self-deprecating narrator, others instead serve to reinforce to comic extremes the stereotype of the jihadi as unafraid of death and consequently cool under fire.

One of our Syrian brothers related: 'we were under airstrikes and we had a brother from the Arabian Peninsula drinking tea'.

I told him, 'are you crazy? You are drinking your tea and we are under all this bombardment?'

The brother said, 'Do you think that if I put my cup down the bombardment will stop?'[46]

One of the brothers relates that when bombardment started we looked around to see a brother sleeping. We approached him and woke him up. He asked what the matter was. We told him that fighter jets were bombing us.

He replied angrily.

'Do I look like a surface-to-air missile?'

And he went back to sleep.[47]

Implicit in stories of the preternatural courage of jihadi fighters is the idea that they confront peril in the active hope of achieving martyrdom. This earnest belief may seem like an unlikely subject for humour.

In reality, a number of jihadi *tara'if* specifically focus on martyrdom. In fact, in some tellings, the story above is one of them, specifying at the end that the sleeping fighter died in the bombardment.

Other stories concern more deliberate martyrdom operations.

One of our brothers who was an *inghimasi* carried out an operation. He was not killed, but fainted. Afterwards, he got up to see smoke, ambulances, blood and human flesh everywhere. He finally made it to the camp by taxi.[48]

A *mujahid* was set to carry out a [martyrdom] operation. His friends brought food for him, and, with the food, Pepsi.

'No,' he said, 'I don't want Pepsi'.

'Why?'

'It causes osteoporosis'.[49]

These stories feel remarkable for the way in which they could easily be lifted and placed within anti-jihadi comedy. And yet they seem to be well attested as stories told and enjoyed by jihadis themselves. Of course, the stories do not directly mock the institution of religious martyrdom as such. In the first, the *inghimasi* (a special category of fighter whose function is to fight conventionally until his position is overwhelmed and only then detonate a suicide belt) fails in his task, but not through his own choice. In the second, the subtext may be a clash between two different repertoires of Islamist activism: on the one hand, the boycott of Western corporations such as Pepsi (which are associated with conspiracy theories and health scares), and on the other hand the rather more comprehensive commitment of jihad and martyrdom. If so, the joke is really a dig at the political correctness of 'moderate' Islamism.

The notion that the fog of war can serve to excuse occasional religious lapses runs through a number of stories, albeit subtly. At their most trivial, these anecdotes concern minor slippages in the use of religious formulas either under pressure or, in the case of non-Arabic fighters, due to possible ignorance. One story, for example, concerns a fighter who is waiting in ambush for an armoured personnel vehicle containing pro-Syrian government *shabiha* fighters. 'Brothers', he calls out, 'what's that thing called that we say before we shoot?' His initially uncomprehending comrades don't realise he is referring to the customary formula, 'And you did not shoot when you shot, but rather it was Allah who shot' (Al-Anfal: 17).[50]

Another story describes an occasion when, due to space constraints, dawn prayers were staggered, with groups of fighters being woken up successively to perform the ritual. As the first group heads out to pray, they inadvertently disturb a fighter sleeping on the floor, who groggily rises and joins them before returning to sleep. As successive groups head out, each one wakes him in the same manner as the one before and, too sleepy to remember that he has already prayed, the fighter ends up repeating his prayers several times. The anecdote records an innocent mistake, but technically Muslims are not permitted, except under very particular circumstances, to pray more than the mandated five daily prayers.

A similar case of a clash between the obligation of prayer and the contingencies of battle is recorded in the following story:

> During one of the Red Army's campaigns we had with us a young Afghan *mujahid*, who had arrived just two days previously to the front. He was studying in Peshawar in the Sharia Foundations there that had been set up there by the martyred sheikh Abdullah Azzam (may God have great mercy on him). This young man had—good for him, but it is all as God wills—memorised the Noble Quran, and he was excellent in theology as well. And it was he who was to serve as our imam in our prayers at the base.

> Well, the Red Army began to advance upon us and warplanes began to gather in large numbers, so many that one might imagine they were about to collide in the sky, and the bombardment began, as usual, fit to drive one mad, in preparation for the advance of their infantry. They were using huge rocket launchers of various types and sizes to rake the ground.

> My *mujahid* brothers and I were in our foxholes. Each one was big enough for just one *mujahid*, so we were spread out from one another. The time for *maghrib* prayer came, and this fine *mujahid* started calling out to the *mujahidin* 'the time for *maghrib* prayer has come!' Naturally he was speaking from his foxhole, and we were only listening to him, for no one was able to get his head out [to look at him] because it wasn't safe.

> So we said to him, 'Do the prayer in your foxhole!' And he said, 'No! Fear God! Are you afraid to assemble together to pray *magrhib*? Do you have no respect for almighty God?'

'Fine, we said. What do you want now?'

'Let us climb out, all of us, and pray together, but only after I have made the call to prayer [adhan]'.

So we said, 'make the call to prayer', which he did, singing a complete adhan while he remained in the middle of his foxhole. Then we got out—we were just nine mujahidin—and assembled for prayer just as we usually would.

No sooner had he said 'Allahu akbar' than rockets began to rake the ground once again. They were some way in front of us, but as we saw them falling they came rapidly closer to our position, falling in a line exactly parallel to ours.

The imam recited the prayers quickly, hastening to the next 'Allahu akbar'. [He prostrated himself], rose up to the kneeling position, and then back down again for the next prostration. Then he said his 'Allahu akbar' for the next repetition of the prayer sequence. All the while the rocket barrage was getting even closer, accelerating in our direction.

'Allahu akbar', said the imam, rising up to the kneeling position. And he spent a long time kneeling—so much so that the bombardment reached us, and the rockets began to detonate next to us. They were smashing and burning the trees around us, and countless rocks were flying everywhere, not to mention the dust and smoke which covered the whole place entirely. We braced ourselves for the full force of the rockets' barrage. And yet the imam remained kneeling, and we remained behind him.

But the kneeling had gone on for a very long time. I raised my head to have a look at him, and by God almighty! I had thought that he must have been martyred or wounded in the bombardment, but do you know what I saw, my beloved ones for the sake of God? I did not see the imam, because, may God reward him, as we had all prostrated, seeing that the bombardment had grown close and indeed was now upon us, he had fled and returned to his foxhole, and left us all prostrating. We did not sense him doing this because of the colossal power and noise of the rockets. So he had played his trick without the mujahidin realising.

'Mujahidin! Our imam has fled!'

We got up. There is no power and strength save in God! The mujahidin laughed and we sought forgiveness from our Lord for laughing. Then we returned to the maghrib prayer'. Indeed we added on an 'isha prayer as well.

When we had finished we returned to our foxholes and enquired after the imam.

164

'Are you alive, or are you a martyr?'

He replied 'It was good for you that you completed your prayer—but I was hoping to intercede for your protection during your prayer'.

We were laughing at him a great deal. And he was defending himself.

'May God combat ignorance. Do you know about the prayer that is called "the prayer of fear?" and that there is the prayer specific to jihad for battle time?'

We spent the entire night under bombardment joking with him and laughing at him, and he replied saying 'how little respect there is for the *ulama* (religious scholar) in your hearts!'[51]

The butt of the joke here is, of course, the religious scholar, whose ostentatious piety stands doubly in contrast to the attitude of the *mujahidin*, who, despite taking a more pragmatic approach, are the ones who actually follow through on the act of worship in the end.

Not all stories, however, show the jihadis in such a good light.

One of the Afghani *mujahidin* came back to his battalion that had fought the Russians. Not seeing any of the *mujahidin*, he guessed that they had defeated the Russians and left, because the neighbourhood was in ruins. He saw pieces of grilled flesh. Thinking that his fellow *mujahidin* had left them for him he began to eat with gusto. After he had finished, he looked at the area more closely and saw plenty of bones and skulls. He later asked the *mujahidin* about the grilled meat. They told him it was shredded flesh of Russian soldiers. Learning this, he said: 'It is halal: Islamic slaughter'.[52]

Given that this story is, to say the least, what Freud would describe as 'tendentious', it is perhaps significant here that it is told about an Afghan who, in keeping with the jihadi stereotype, is shown as naïve and ignorant. It has been observed that jihadi rituals related to beheading captives closely resemble Islamic rituals for the slaughtering of animals for food—and even the term used, *dhabiha*, literally means slaughter. Jihadi propaganda often uses cannibalistic metaphors: describing the *mujahidin* as 'hungry lions whose drink is blood and whose play is slaughter',[53] while the Islamic jurisprudence of jihad describes the blood of those who can be legitimately fought as halal— the same word used for ritually pure foodstuffs. Notoriously, one jihadi commander in the Syrian civil war was captured on video apparently eating the internal organs of a slain enemy.[54] In this story, the unintentional cannibalism of the Afghan, and his quip on learning of what he has done, seems to deflect with humour what is an otherwise difficult subject.

Off the battlefield, the realm of marital relations presents another site for potential conflicts between religious ideal and reality. Here, too, elements of ethnic humour are on display, as in this apparently very popular anecdote:

> One of the brothers married an Azeri widow. On the first night, she woke him up at 2.00 for the *witr* prayer, but he was lazy. So she poured water on him, and said: get up, you *munafiq* [hypocrite].[55]

Since the *witr* prayer does not have the same status as the five mandatory prayers, the laziness here is at least somewhat excusable, and the accusation of hypocrisy is of course overblown. It may be significant that, since most Azeris are Shia, the woman in the story perhaps has the zeal of a convert to Sunnism.

A *mujahid* from the Arabian Peninsula phoned his wife from Syria and said:

> 'I'd like to get married again'.

> 'You cheat!' she naturally replied to him.

> 'Relax and hear me out', he said 'I want to get married again so that I can have more children and bring them up to love jihad and store up merit for myself in heaven'.

> 'If you want to get merit', she said, 'why not do a martyrdom operation?'[56]

This story, by contrast, is more mischievous, since it subversively implies an ulterior motive to the two most sacrosanct life paths that a virtuous *mujahid* might take: raising sons to be fighters on the one hand, and martyrdom on the other. Since jihadi-Salafism famously accords great importance and literalism to Islamic doctrines of the virgins of paradise the ulterior motive can be understood as sexual in both cases.

In closing, we ought to consider one more outlet for jihadi humour. While we have already considered humorous visual performances captured on video such as the '*da'wa* tent' and various *nashid* gatherings, there are also some cases of jihadi fighters creating and circulating what are in effect short sketches. These have an informal quality and are better understood as a visual analogue to the *tara'if* than as semi-authorised jihadi theatre.

As seen above, it would appear that Egyptians are the most appealing 'performers', at least if we are to judge by the seemingly most popular of these videos, with 831,489 views at the time we downloaded it (the video has since been deleted). This video features a practical joke or sketch, in which a jihadi pretends to be dead or unconscious due to an unexploded rocket that has fallen next to him. Another fighter (also Egyptian) pretends to check the rocket's country of manufacture. After determining that it is not Russian but Chinese, he tells his fallen comrade Amr to 'get up' as it is 'not original'. 'Son of a dog', the now resurrected Amr addresses Syrian president Bashar al-Assad. 'Are you striking us with Chinese products?' Waggling his supposedly damaged finger, he jokingly threatens: 'I will send a message with the very same finger which you have wounded: what you have done is wrong. I will hold you accountable for my damaged finger and the [substandard] rocket'.

In another notable example, it is the Chechens' turn. Perhaps playing up their tough-guy reputations, this video involves a pair of fighters playing a trick on an enemy sniper by using a doll dressed in the black outfit and mask of the jihadi fighter, laughing out loud each time the doll is shot.[57]

The above examples may satisfy the worst expectations conjured up upon encountering the phrase jihadi humour. It is certainly true that a great deal of jihadi joking concerns the unrepentant and gleeful celebration of the kind of acts for which groups like IS have become notorious. And yet, it is also important to set such disturbing expressions of humour in context. As we saw in the second chapter, situations of sectarian civil war are often characterised by similar, and at times more appalling, examples of murderous laughter. Indeed, among the disturbing aspects of jihadi humour is not its exceptional brutality, but rather, in a sense, its ordinariness. Jihadi jokes about killing Shia and Alawites, for example, are quite often reheated versions of other jokes, some of which have cropped up in relation to other real life episodes of inter-ethnic slaughter.[58] This is reminiscent, for example, of the former

JOKING ABOUT JIHAD

Yugoslavia, where the genocidal killing of the 1990s is recounted today through gruesome jokes, seemingly told by people from the victimised groups as frequently as by those belonging to the groups from which the perpetrators typically derived. In the Bosnian Muslim city of Velika Kladuŝa, for example, the following joke is recounted (or at least it was, in the summer of 2000).

> To escape Serbian death squads, a group of Bosnian villagers hid in their township's well. A fighter strode up to it, leaned over into the shaft, whose darkness concealed the huddled fugitives, and shouted:
>
> 'Maybe they are in the well?'
>
> To mimic the effect of the echo there should have been, the villagers called back 'The well! The well! The well!'
>
> 'Maybe they are in the forest?' the fighter said, apparently satisfied.
>
> 'The forest! The forest! The forest!' came the echoed response once again.
>
> 'I guess I'll drop a grenade into the well anyway, just to be sure.'
>
> 'The forest! The forest! The forest!'[59]

Similarly, folklorist Alan Dundes collected numerous examples of Holocaust jokes told by Germans in the decades following the end of World War II. The jokes were, he noted, ambivalent as to whether they suggested that the Germans were at some level coming to terms with their responsibility for the atrocity, or were simply expressing anti-Semitic Nazi attitudes that were no longer appropriate in more serious contexts.[60]

Jihadi humour mostly occupies a rather unclear position in relation to the official propaganda of jihadi groups, but it would be naïve to deny that it has some role to play in recruitment. Indeed, its very informality may well be part of its appeal. Recounted in web forums, the *tara'if* can have the character of yarns spun by grizzled veterans to audiences of wide-eyed youngsters, hungry for the same outrageous experiences. In their more benign forms they present the sense of *esprit de corps*, youthful energy and exuberance that plays a key role in making participation in the jihad seem attractive to alienated, bored and directionless youth looking for adventure and companionship, and presumably they also help dispel the idea of jihad as a wholly fanatical endeavour. On the other hand, the more brutal stories serve to laugh off any potential empathy which an already radicalised online audience might be tempted to feel for the jihadis' sectarian enemies.

Even so, we believe that it is also possible to identify subversive currents in jihadi humour that may, perhaps, represent chinks in the movement's ideological armour. It seems important that some of the very same lines of attack found in anti-jihadi humour reappear as possible moments of self-doubt in this material. Jihadis, one may suppose, also worry that they have trivialised the institution of Islamic martyrdom, that they have overstepped the boundaries of what sharia can permit, that they are less united than they like to claim and, perhaps, that they are more frightened than they care to admit.

7

THE GOD OF DAESH

POPULAR AND ONLINE JIHADI JOKES

As he buzzed away with his clippers, delivering another no-frills short back and sides, the barber in the prosperous Amman neighbourhood of Shmeisani was also treating his customer to an animated disquisition on the balance between religion and freedom of expression.

'He should have known what to expect from sharing that picture', he opined. His client was nodding in agreement—as much as he was able, while still getting his hair cut. The barber went on: 'He knew that this is an Islamic country. Well, not an Islamic country—it's a secular country—but most of the people are Muslims'.

'It's like this', he continued, becoming more animated as he realised he'd hit on an inspired example. 'I travelled to Thailand. That's a Buddhist country, and you have to respect that. If you go there and insult the Buddha the ground opens up under your feet. It's the same here. I don't approve of people taking the law into their own hands but he should have known what to expect'.

The subject the barber was addressing was the recent news that writer, journalist and public intellectual Nahed Hattar had been shot dead outside of the Palace of Justice. It was 2016, and Hattar was there to stand trial for blasphemy, but the state never had the chance to deliver its verdict. Instead, a well-known Salafi with a history of militancy, employed just over the road as a maintenance engineer at the Department of Education, had taken the law into his own hands.[1]

What Hattar had done was to share a cartoon on Facebook. The cartoon in question shows a bearded man in Islamic paradise, reclining on a couch in a tent, with a virgin of paradise on either arm. God—an old man with a beard—is poking his head in to check that everything is as his guest would like it to be.

'Good day to you, Abu Saleh', the Lord of the Worlds asks. 'Do you need anything?'

> 'Yes, Lord. Get me a cup of wine from over there, and tell Gabriel to bring me some cashews. Then send me an immortal pageboy to clean the floor. And take the empty plates with you. Also, don't forget to put a door on the tent so next time you can knock before you come in, Your Immortalness'.[2]

Hattar had added his own caption when he shared the cartoon on Facebook: 'God of Daesh'. Perhaps as a result of this, there was widespread confusion about the cartoon's intention and Hattar's relationship to it. Many, perhaps especially those celebrating his death, believed that he had drawn the cartoon. Others, perhaps especially those defending him, believed that the caption was an integral part of it.

In fact, the cartoon Hattar had shared with such disastrous consequences was not originally about the Islamic State at all. It was the work of 'Musa'—a wisely anonymous Egyptian atheist cartoonist specialising in what he calls 'cartoons critical of religion'. The image in question had been drawn, he said, in response to a 'philosophical question', namely, 'what will God do after Judgement Day?'[3]

In the days following the killing, questions abounded. Angry protestors, among them Hattar's family, Jordan's Christian communities, upper-middle-class secularists and the 'Sons of the Ploughmen' (the writer's more blue collar socialist followers),[4] wanted to know why the government had drawn unnecessary attention to his case by arresting him in the first place, why it had failed to provide adequate security and why Hattar's killer was not under surveillance, even when he conspicuously hung around the Palace of Justice in the hours before the writer's appearance there.[5] Others, on the other hand, asked why the government had been so slow in arresting Hattar, forcing a hero of Jordanian people to defend their honour by taking the law into his own hands.

But there is another question also worth asking: why did Hattar do something so seemingly risky? In sharing a cartoon that depicted not the Prophet Muhammad, but Allah himself, did he really not know, as the barber of Shmeisani remarked, 'what to expect'?

Hattar was no stranger to controversy or persecution. (At the time of his death, he suffered from digestive problems that resulted from having meters of his intestines removed after security forces beat him while in police custody, having been arrested for writing critically about the Jordanian government.)[6] A well-known atheist, his aggressively secularist views contributed to his strong support for the Syrian regime in its battle against an increasingly Islamist rebel movement.[7] But it is a stretch to suppose that he shared the cartoon in the deliberate expectation of becoming a secular martyr. Rather, Hattar's unfortunate case seems to offer a stark illustration of just how polarised the Arabic internet looked in 2016. At least for people in largely secularist circles, sharing once unthinkable content had begun to seem almost normal. Anything went, it appeared, as long as it was aimed at IS.

The gradual, turbulent and, in Hattar's case, lethal process of opening up the bounds of permitted expression in the Arab info-sphere is eloquently described by another Jordanian, Isam Urayqat. As a founder of *Al-Hudood*, a satirical magazine pitched as the Arab world's answer to *The Onion*, Urayqat believes that there has been a clear evolution in the responses the outlet has received to articles touching on the subject of fundamentalist religiosity.

> I think, in the beginning, when we said anything, it was immediately just anger, threats. There was definitely no conversation, no matter how subtle we were, no matter how inoffensive we were—it was just literally [in] coming anywhere near religion, there was no conversation. [For the] first two years, I can tell you there was definitely no conversation, because people just saw it as an attack. I think one of the things was that because we were attacked all the time, people started hearing us. Whoever saw us in the beginning and was attacking us was like 'yeah, you have an agenda—you're an atheist who wants to spread the atheist thought', and then they saw us attacking that too and they're like 'what the hell are these guys doing?' Over years the comments section developed to becoming more of 'oh, don't do that' or 'it's not OK for you to say that'. Someone said to us in the beginning that defending

yourself didn't really work because it was going to lead to a more futile conversation, but with time people started replying [in ways that related to] what we like to think we were doing ... And in that way I think I can claim that it has become more of a conversation ... I think we've had a lot of very interesting conversations on the comments.[8]

In the case of *Al-Hudood*, the website has also come up with an ingenious way to deal with less constructive comments.

A year ago, we published a chatbot, which is a very interesting experiment. Most people come to us ... and it's either they want to say a good thing, a really bad thing, or want to contribute or say something and basically all these options we laid out to them. The sections are 'I want to express my love to you', and there's a section for them to fill out and the bot responds with something nice and the conversation is closed and they're happy. What I didn't expect was [what happened with] the second part: 'I want to express my hatred towards you'. I always thought that this would not really work to be handled by a bot. But because it's so predictable ... they come in and they're like 'I want to express my hatred' and their options are: I want to just attack your credibility, or I want to just swear. If you want to do that [the latter] you get the general [swear words] and then you get to [swear words about] mothers and sisters and honour, and the funny thing is, people go through the options and they're like: 'that's it'. That's them finished and we're like 'do you need anything else?' and most of them say 'no'.

The experiences of Hattar, an atheist Christian who shared what was originally at least a blasphemous, atheist cartoon, and Urayqat, a Muslim who specialises in satire but claims he tries to avoid touching on the explicitly religious (and who presently lives outside Jordan), are, thankfully, not strictly comparable. But both offer a glimpse into a rapidly changing and unstable environment where it is never entirely clear what will and won't be acceptable.

But what do 'ordinary' Arabs actually think about the limits on satirising Islamist extremism? It is a subject on which it is difficult to find systematic evidence. Sensational events, including Hattar's killing, alongside much better-known controversies in the West, such as the wave of protests and acts of violence following the 2005 controversy around *Jyllands Posten*'s Muhammad cartoons and, by tragic extension, the *Charlie Hebdo* massacre several years after, or the promulgation of the film *The Innocence of Muslims* (2012), have helped to create a popular notion that Muslim publics are constantly on a hair trigger, ready to rampage at any provocation.

But, looked at more carefully, what such events tell us is less clear. At any rate, both of the above cases started as something more complex than spontaneous, knee-jerk outrage to religious satire. In both instances, the aim, from the outset, was to provoke, and the outrage was carefully nursed and cultivated by entrepreneurs of anger on both sides.

The *Jyllands Posten*'s cartoon campaign in 2005 was initially seen as provocative, at least partially because the newspaper had a pre-existing reputation for going after Muslims. Even so, protests didn't spread beyond Denmark until a group of Danish Imams toured the Middle East with a misleading Arabic dossier, souped up with additional cartoons and images and untrue accusations about the treatment of Muslims in the country.[9] *The Innocence of Muslims* was released by anti-Islam campaigners in 2012 as a tie in with a far-right event organised by Pastor Terry Jones called 'international judge Muhammad day'. It was then picked up and partially broadcast by Egyptian TV channels eager to stoke outrage.[10]

Muslims' reactions in these cases were, of course, varied. Studying Arabic online posts in relation to the Danish cartoons, media scholar Ahmed al-Rawi found that the most common type of response was simply people defending Islam and re-asserting their commitment to the religion, although a significant number contained curses and insults, while a small number went further in calling for violence.[11] After the release of the (much more inflammatory) *Innocence of Muslims*, the reaction of Arabs on Facebook followed this pattern even more strongly. An overwhelming majority of posts were 'pro-Islamic' supplications for Allah to defend his religion, while the next most common type of posts consisted of calls for calmness.[12] Curses and insults were by no means proportionately frequent, and only a tiny proportion of posts called for a violent response. In the case of the 2015 *Charlie Hebdo* attacks, Grimm found high levels of sympathy for the victims among Muslims around the world.[13]

The production of violent outrage by Muslim audiences in response to satirical treatments of their religion is much more complex and context-dependent than popular cliché supposes. The content that seems to prompt angry reactions, for the most part, is made up more of genuine attempts to insult and provoke than blasphemies, as such. As we saw in chapters 4 and 6, Salafis and jihadis themselves sometimes crack jokes which, coming from different sources, might be seen as bordering on blasphemy. Where the understanding is that Islam is under attack, it can trigger a furious and violent 'defence' of the religion and its honour (though it is only ever a small number of people who respond thus). But not every example of humour that touches on religion or certain forms of religiosity is inevitably interpreted as an attack.

Studies of online comments are, of course, biased in favour of those who are already motivated to comment. But what can be said about Arab publics more generally? The available relevant survey data similarly paints a picture of a mixed and complex approach to religiosity and tolerance. On the one hand, there is some evidence that the Arab world, and particularly its young people, is becoming more diverse in its attitude to religion. A much-cited Gallup poll from Saudi Arabia suggested in 2012 that 19 per cent of the population described themselves as not religious, while 5 per cent were outright atheists.[14] This is not, of course, to suggest that atheism is publicly acceptable. In Saudi Arabia at least it is considered, by law, to be a form of terrorism.[15] Privately, though, it means that a significant number of even devout Saudis are likely to be personally familiar with the possibility of others choosing not to practice, or even not to believe at all. A 2015 study commissioned by the Tabah Foundation on *Muslim* [read Arab] *Millennial Attitudes on Religion and Religious Leadership*, which surveyed young people in Morocco, Egypt, Saudi Arabia, the United Arab Emirates, Bahrain, Kuwait, Jordan and Palestine, found that young people tended to see religion as a 'private, spiritual' matter, and supported government regulation to prevent incitement by religious authorities. A large majority believed that a 'renewal' was needed in the language used in Islamic sermons, while an overwhelming majority wanted to see more women as religious scholars and preachers. On the other hand, about 70 per cent agreed with the statement, 'if cultural content (movies, TV, theatre, ads, etc.) breaches the moral and ethical values of society, it should be banned'.[16] Of course, this question doesn't tell us anything specific about what kind of cultural content the respondents thought of as falling into this category.

In the absence of specific data on public attitudes to material which humorously attacks Islamist extremists such as IS and Al Qaeda, we conducted a survey of our own, designed to zoom in on the question of whether Arabs feel that humour aimed at jihadi organisations is acceptable and, if so, what they find potentially funny about it.

Conducted in 2017, prior to the liberation of the cities of Mosul and Raqqa and the effective end (for the time being) of IS's aspiration to function as a territorial state, we recognise that our survey is by no means an ideal study. Despite various attempts to disseminate it in more systematic ways, the sensitivity of the subject matter meant, not to our great surprise, that we had to fall back on a 'snowball' approach, distributing it to friends of friends via our own social networks (our immediate friends were used to pilot the survey). Apart from the fact that our own networks turned out to be, unsurprisingly, atypical of the population of the Arab world as a whole, it should be noted that those who completed it were self-selecting. This meant, in all probability, that people likely to be offended by the idea of satirising jihadi groups will have tended disproportionately to have avoided completing it.

The 642 responses we did obtain came from a group comprised overwhelmingly of young and well-educated people (just under 80 per cent of respondents were educated to undergraduate degree level or above).[17] This group was almost certainly unusually familiar with Western language and culture—57 per cent said that they consumed media from America or Europe 'often' or 'all the time', while 52 per cent said that they 'often' or 'all the time' consumed media in English. By contrast, less than 6 per cent said that they 'never' consumed media in English. Conversely, well over half said that they seldom or never consumed religious media in the form of religious television programmes or radio shows (including Quran radio). Websites were the most popular form of religious media accessed, but even these were still not widely read. This, unsurprisingly, contrasts with the broader population of the Arab world, among whom religious programming in various media is extremely popular. Fortuitously, just over half of our respondents come from Saudi Arabia. Finally, two thirds of our respondents were men—with the overrepresentation of Saudi men accounting for some of this imbalance, but by no means all of it. (Quite a significant number of Saudi women also completed the survey.)

Nonetheless, in some respects, the population of our survey is more balanced than we might have feared, particularly with regards to its religious and sectarian makeup. Overall, with 23 per cent Shia and 1.4 per cent Christian respondents, it does not look unlike the Arab world as a whole, in which Shia make up perhaps 20 per cent of the population and Christians 4 per cent, at a generous estimate. Moreover, the Saudi respondents look more similar to the rest of the respondents than we might have feared. The Saudi contingent of the survey had more Shia, who were also fairly well represented in the rest of the survey, and fewer people who claimed no religion (whatever this meant in practice) than other countries, though they were still quite plentiful among the Saudis.

The large number of apparently non-religious people among respondents (accounting for one fifth) is, at first glance, perhaps the most glaringly anomalous thing about our survey responses. Even knowing that our own circles of acquaintance were, we knew, more than usually sceptical of religion, we didn't expect anything like this proportion to answer in this way. So why did they? At the end of the survey we offered an open question in which people were invited to comment on the survey, or, if they wished, to tell us a joke relevant to our research. (We shall come back to this section later in our discussion.) In two of these responses, a respondent elaborated on why they had checked the 'no religion' option. One of these made it clear that the person in question really had left religion behind. As this person commented:

> From the point of view of anyone who has read Islamic history, he will not be amused by any joke about terrorists because what terrorists do is the same as what Islamists have done since the beginning of the age of Islam—so whoever believes in Islam and knows about Islam will not laugh but rather become angry at these jokes—because they touch on something within him. Whoever does not believe and has left Islam will probably find all Islam to be a joke.

Another, on the other hand, said:

> I chose the option that I don't consider myself to be a follower of one of the following religions because I feel that there is discrimination in this question. Why put Sunni Muslim, Shia Muslim and Muslim from another sect in the options? To discriminate among these in this way is worse by far than to tell jokes—indeed it is in itself terrorism. 'Muslim'

means that we are Muslims and people who are committed to God regardless of what sect.

At least one person, then, in choosing the no-religion option was, in fact, presumably a believing Muslim and it is therefore quite possible that others were as well. How many, we can't say. Nevertheless, as a group these ostensible non-religionists, genuinely irreligious or otherwise, did have distinctive and consistent characteristics. Relative to those who described themselves as Sunni or Shia Muslims, they were the most likely to say that they enjoyed joking about '"extremist" groups like IS or Al Qaeda', or to say that they knew somebody who did, the least likely to say that they consumed religious media, and the least likely to say that they worried that joking about extremist groups might be religiously offensive. In short, whatever their beliefs, their responses were consistent with the notion that these were people with a more or less secular mentality.

The self-identifying Sunni Muslims among those we surveyed also had a distinctive profile as a group. This was despite the fact that in most respects they looked like everyone else—their age, gender breakdown and educational attainment were similar to other respondents. They also seemed to have similar media consumption profiles. Somewhat surprisingly, they consumed nearly as much Western and English language media as people who claimed not to follow a religion, whom we might have expected to be the most Westernised group. (Shia, in fact, consumed slightly less). On the other hand, Sunnis also consumed nearly as much (though not quite as much) religious media as Shia respondents did, which isn't to say that either group averaged a great deal.

While only an extremely small number of Sunnis in our survey exhibited any actual sympathy for jihadi groups, they were, as a group, distinctly less likely to say that they enjoyed jokes about groups such as Al Qaeda or IS. Asked simply 'are you amused by jokes about "extremist" groups like IS and Al Qaeda', 59 per cent of Sunnis said they were not. On the other hand, 62 per cent of Shia and 61 per cent of people who claimed not to follow any religion said they did find such jokes amusing. Most people, regardless of religion did, however, say they knew someone who laughed at jokes on this subject. A plurality of Sunnis, in contrast to a majority of Shia and a large majority of non-religionists, strongly disagreed that joking about jihadi groups 'usually ends up insulting religion'. But over a third agreed or strongly agreed that this was the case. Moreover, although the numbers were small, Sunnis who at least 'sometimes' or 'frequently' watched religious programming were apparently more likely to agree at least 'somewhat' with this proposition.

Our survey, then, revealed a clear, if not dramatic, split between Sunni, Shia and what we can cautiously call 'secularist' respondents over the acceptability of making jokes about jihadi groups. Another relevant factor appeared to be gender, at least regarding one question in particular. While differences between women and men were not statistically significant for most of the specific questions we asked about the acceptability of humour, women turned out to be much less likely than men to agree with the idea that 'joking about these groups makes it less likely that people will want to join them'.

We also wished to explore what was seen as potentially amusing about these groups. We therefore asked a question in which we identified twelve common themes in existing anti-jihadi comedy material and asked respondents to rate how potentially funny they could be from one to five. The twelve themes were:

- Use of antiquated language
- Violent and aggressive behaviour
- Sex obsession (to avoid offence we expressed this as 'desire to marry purely for the sake of carnal enjoyment and to possess slaves')
- Hypocritical behaviours such as drinking alcohol or listening to music in secret
- Manipulation of religion to serve their ends
- The idea that they are controlled by foreign powers
- Attributes of foreign fighters, such as their accent or dress
- The gap between the groups' ambitions and the reality of their means
- Ignorance of religion
- Narrow mindedness
- Addiction to social media
- Fighters' physical appearance

The main finding from this question simply reinforced the notion that Sunni Muslims were much less enthusiastic about making jokes in relation to any aspect of jihadi groups. Compared to Shia and non-religionists, Sunnis consistently rated everything less potentially funny by nearly one point. Secularists, on the other hand, were most likely to find nearly everything funnier than the other two groups, although the difference between them and Shia respondents was very small. Drawing robust conclusions about what was considered more or less amusing turned out to be more difficult. Differences were usually small and potentially influenced by differential response rates. Some elements such as 'addiction to social media' were considered a bit obscure, meaning that people found it hard to make up their minds in order to answer the question. Nonetheless, there were some apparent differences between the groups. Sunnis appeared to find 'hypocritical behaviours', 'gap between ambition and reality' and 'physical appearance' more acceptable to laugh at than other attributes. All of these seem to be relatively safe, non-controversial topics, which don't require going into detail about what jihadi groups specifically say and do. Shia were seemingly most amused by 'narrow mindedness' and, for those that answered this question, 'addiction to social media'. Perhaps more tellingly, they were apparently least amused by sex obsession, use of old-fashioned language and violence. This seems in keeping with concerns about offence to religious morality and propriety in other senses. Secularists found sex obsession and hypocrisy most funny and were least likely to be amused (less so than Shia, for example) by the allegation that jihadis were controlled by foreign powers, or were ignorant of 'true religion'. This could reflect an anti-religious mentality whereby jihadism is seen (at least by some) as the product of traditional, unreformed understandings Islam itself rather than by outside manipulation.

In a final, open question, participants were invited either to express their views about our questionnaire, or to tell us jokes relevant to our research. Excluding responses like 'I don't know any jokes' or 'good luck with your research', sixty-three people answered this question in one way or another. The responses fell into four main categories.

First, there were responses which sought to critique the survey or the agenda that was believed to underlie it. A couple of these made comments on what the respondents saw as poor word choice in several of the questions, while another one (which we have already quoted above) complained about our decision to categorise people according to sect. The more substantive complaints, however, concerned the implicit bias seen in our decision to identify Al Qaeda and IS as examples of 'extremist' groups, without mentioning, the 'extremism' of, as these respondents suggested, Hezbollah, the Iranian Revolutionary Guard, Bashar al-Assad, the Syrian Regime or Western Coalition air strikes. Others said that our questionnaire failed to ask what they saw as the crucial question 'who do you believe is behind these groups?' (namely IS and Al Qaeda).

Comments that criticised our questionnaire directly were distinguishable from comments that expressed a more general view of the question of joking in relation to jihadi groups. These varied a good deal, from musing about why people join groups like these, to expressing contemptuous disinterest in anything to do with them. A few reflected further on the question of humour. One, for instance, expressed the interesting view that while 'satire' (*sukhriyya*) of these groups is acceptable, it is distasteful to make 'jokes' about them.

Some answers could also be categorised as recommendations or evaluations of existing comedy material deemed relevant to the subject. Only fourteen people answered in this way, but the diversity of material they brought up is interesting. One respondent discussed in some depth a poem from his city (Ha'il, Saudi Arabia), which, he noted, had historically been an independent state and which he described as a bastion against Wahhabism ever since its conquest by Saudi forces in the 1920s. The poem, he said, was a lampoon of the *Ikhwan*—the radical jihadi fighting elite of then King Abdul Aziz Al Saud as he was expanding his empire—and was traditionally recited by grandfathers to their grandchildren as a way of inoculating them against extremism. Others offered a diversity of relatively well-known satirical works, including many of those reviewed in chapter 5. Perhaps interestingly, the recommendations went beyond work that directly attacks jihadi groups, including references to comedy dealing with religious topics more generally, such as Abu al-Baraa'—a very popular spoof cleric on Facebook whom we will discuss at a later point.

Finally, there were twenty comments that provided jokes or anecdotes which, in the opinion of the teller, were in some sense humorous. The two best examples of these speak volumes regarding the blackness of humour in the war-torn countries of Syria and Iraq.

> Everything seems to me to be a silly joke since my father's cousin was martyred by them in Iraq, after they said about his work that it was

infidel work and that he was an infidel and must be killed. He worked in a travel agency for Hajj and Umra (pilgrimages).

I am one of those whom Daesh arrested because of not praying the *'asr* prayer in a mosque. They arrested me for a period of twenty-four hours and the laughable thing about the whole affair was that my mobile was with me and it had a collection of songs and films in it throughout my time in the prison. So I pulled out the external memory card that had on it a whole lot of pictures and songs and I put it in my mouth and broke it into small pieces. Then I left the prison after twenty-four hours and my punishment was forty lashes on the back.

One useful finding from our survey was that our respondents came across most of the jihadi jokes they knew online and, of the modest number of jokes they themselves submitted to us (nineteen in total, nearly all about IS), virtually all were jokes that were also circulating on the internet. As we move on from our survey to discuss online jokes and memes about IS, this gives us a certain amount of confidence that these jokes are, at least to some extent, representative of what people find amusing in 'real life' as well.

The discussion that follows is based on a collection of over three hundred images, collected by means of Arabic keyword searches,[18] which can be roughly divided into entirely or primarily textual 'jokes'; 'memes' consisting of captioned or digitally manipulated images,[19] 'screen grabs' of other media (including posts in social media accounts); and, finally, a large number of professional or professional-quality cartoons. While is overlap in the types of jokes and humour used in all these, we will for the most part exclude cartoons from our analysis for the time being, on the grounds that cartoons are typically produced by skilled professionals, often for commercial media, rather than by the 'folk humourists in whom we are mainly interested here.

In our collection, we define a 'joke', following our discussion of the same topic in chapter 3, as any short, humorous text without accompanying images, or where the accompanying images are not required for the humour. (Many of the jokes we collected in fact include images well-known from internet meme culture such as the 'trollface' character. But in these cases, the image serves only to mark the text as humorous—it isn't integral to the actual humorous content.) Some of these are very recognisable to English-speaking readers as jokes in the typical sense, with clearly identifiable set ups and punch lines. Others do not follow this structure so clearly, and have the character more of conversational witticisms, for example. Although the jokes in our collection are described, in Arabic as *nukat*(the term for 'joke' in the contemporary English sense), many have something in common with the *tara'if* we encountered in relation to 'Islamic' and jihadi humour.

The majority of the written jokes fall into three quite specific categories, namely: spoof 'Daesh fatwas', '*muhashash* jokes', and 'jokes about the afterlife'. As we shall see, the latter category also accounts for quite a lot of visual humour too.

Daesh fatwas (typically so labelled) are easily the most common type of humorous text in our collection. Some are presented as stand-alone gags. Others are delivered through the Twitter or Facebook accounts of a variety of spoof clerics (now mostly defunct) like Abu al-Iman, Abu Hukm al-Daeshi, Abu Daesh al-Jahshi and, by far the most well-known and successful, Abu al-Baraa'. These comedy social media sheikhs all follow much the same formula, mimicking the antiquated Arabic stylings of real-life scholars. Often, what is being repackaged by the person sharing the content as a 'Daeshi fatwa' seemingly originated as a parody of conservative clerics more generally. A variation of the same type of gag, usually deriving from the hashtag 'ridiculous Daeshi fatwas' misses out the name of the fake sheikh, instead opening simply with the announcement, 'Daesh has decided...'. Typically, what Daesh has decided is to kill everyone guilty of some particular (and obviously absurd) transgression.

At least some of these jokes derive from allegedly true stories about extreme or bizarre interpretations of religion. For example, Iraqi Sunni militants fighting IS in 2008 claimed that the organisation had classified cucumbers as 'male' and tomatoes as 'female' vegetables (corresponding, in fact, to their grammatical genders in Arabic as well as their suggestive shapes), and tried to ban women from buying the former in markets. They also accused IS of killing goats because their tails were upturned or because their private parts were showing.[20] Whether true or not, these claims provide copious subject matter for joking. Numerous memes poke fun at the idea of placing veils on cows' udders or camel humps, while an entire sub-genre of fatwa jokes consists of rulings about impermissible combinations of nouns of opposite grammatical gender. One says that believers may not drink water, for example, because water is masculine but the stomach is feminine. Another, rather poignant example, says that 'in the land of Daesh, it is not permissible to weep, because tears are masculine, but eye is feminine'. We shall consider further examples of the fatwa joke later on.

Unlike fatwa jokes, which inherently specialise in mocking Islamic clerical authority, whether jihadi or otherwise, *muhashash* jokes are an Arabic staple. The *muhashash* is literally a person who smokes hashish—a stoner. In practice, though, it refers to anyone who acts in a light-hearted or silly way. Probably the closest translation in English would be 'joker' with its dual sense of someone who makes jokes on purpose, and someone who acts foolishly and incompetently. Indeed, in a still broader sense, *tahshish*, the word for what a *muhashash* engages in, is a generalised term for joking, high spirits and humour. For example, many of the fatwa jokes referred to above come from a series called *tahshish fatawa Daesh*.

The *muhashash*, in Arabic jokes, is the archetypal wise fool—a latter day Juhā. In some jokes, he is simply an idiot, providing a pan-Arab equivalent for regional jokes about backward minorities such as Saidis (Upper Egyptians) in Egypt, Homsis in Syria or Khalilis (people from Hebron) in Palestine. 'A *muhashash*'s father died. At the funeral, he confided in his friend: "As if things weren't bad enough, I've just spoken to my sister, and her father has died as well."' In other jokes, though, he comes across as a rather shrewder figure.

A *muhashash* was captured and brainwashed by Daesh. 'Now that you are one of us', they said, 'you must choose for yourself a *nom de guerre*'. 'All right', said the *muhashash*. I'd like to be called 'orange'.

'That won't do', said the Daeshis. 'It has to be a *kunya*—something like Abu Baraa', Abu Qa'qa' and so on'.

'All right', said the *muhashash*, 'I'd like to be *Abū Surra*' (meaning 'navel orange' in Arabic).[21]

A *muhashash* sat down to watch a foreign film with a group of Daeshis. They came to a racy bit. The *muhashash* said, 'Let's rewind, brothers, to check up on what these unbelievers are getting up to'.[22]

A *muhashash* boarded a plane and found himself sitting next to a Daeshi. He opened his laptop. The Daeshi said, 'close that laptop if it's made in one of the countries of the unbelievers'.

'And I suppose', said the *muhashash*, 'that this plane was made by Abu Bakr al-Baghdadi?'[23]

These three jokes represent something of the range of guises the *muhashash* can adopt. In the first, he is a seemingly harmless clown; in the second, a mischief-maker; in the third, he exhibits more of a calculated, caustic wit. What the examples have in common is the way in which the protagonist is used to represent, despite his light-heartedness, a kind of earthy common sense which is naturally opposed to the rigid, puritanical attitudes supposedly characteristic of jihadi fighters.

Jokes in these first two categories target the absurdities of particular human representatives of Islam. Jokes about the afterlife, on the other hand, could be seen as more blasphemous, since they necessarily stray into matters of actual Islamic doctrine, casting paradise, angels and even Allah himself as actors on the comic stage. In reality, however, things are not so simple. In fact, as we have already seen, certain versions of jokes about the afterlife, and especially about the virgins of paradise (*hur al-'ayn*) are also told by Islamic clerics.

Daeshi jokes about the afterlife including, as we noted, many visual and text-based memes (that is, 'jokes' to us), play on the prominence of the virgins of paradise in jihadi culture and ideology. Assuming that sex is the real underlying motivation for the rush to martyrdom, the typical gag is premised on imagining ways in which the newly martyred jihadi might be disappointed. Various memes show, for example, the deceased fighter discovering that the virgins are not as conventionally beautiful as expected. Another set presents the virgins, conversely, as being physically repulsed by the unkempt jihadi. In one, titled *the suicide bomber's nightmare*, a blonde mermaid tells a fighter 'but I think of you like a brother'. In another, a singularly unattractive jihadi leers 'tomorrow, when I blow myself up, the virgins will be fighting over me'.

Other afterlife jokes present distinct variations on this theme, or sometimes altogether different concerns. In one, the jihadi suicide bomber is replaced by an old man whose truck wheel has been stolen and who goes to the sharia court run by Jabhat al-Nusra in Idlib in the hope of getting redress. The sheikh says to him that Allah will compensate him in heaven. 'That's no good to me' the man says. 'Everyone else will have a virgin of paradise, and I'll just be playing with my old wheel'.[24] Another joke, this one clearly blasphemous, dispenses with the virgins altogether. An Iraqi suicide bomber blows himself up and finds himself in a long queue. After rushing about demanding that he get priority entry, he is told to settle down and wait his turn like everyone else. 'But I am one of the martyrs of Iraq!' He insists. 'So what' says his interlocutor, 'I'm one of the martyrs of Uhud'[25] (a battle fought by the followers of Muhammad against his enemies from Mecca). Finally, we found at least one example of a joke which turns the situation around altogether.

> An old woman died and the angel of death came to her and asked her 'Who is your Lord?'
>
> She said, 'Allah is my Lord'.
>
> 'Who is your prophet?'
>
> 'Muhammad is my prophet'.
>
> 'Who is your imam?'
>
> She was silent. He asked her a second time and she was silent. She had a wise head.
>
> She said, 'what business is that of yours, Ali?'
>
> He said, 'why aren't you speaking—what's wrong with you?'
>
> 'Uncle, by Abbas, I'm thinking that you are Daesh'.

Anti-IS humour, both in our collection of memes and more generally, revolves around a number of key themes and stereotypes. Perhaps the simplest of these is what we might call the *primitive* or *wild man* motif. Here, jihadis are presented as being dirty, unkempt and animal-like. In one meme—apparently Iraqi in origin—a stick figure holds a gun to a stereotypically long haired Daeshi. 'Bathe or die', he says. 'I'll die but I won't bathe', the Daeshi replies. 'Daeshi and proud', says another meme, showing a picture of *Harry Potter's* Hagrid carrying a big, crudely hewn, stick. Another simply writes the syllable 'da' followed by a picture of a bird's nest—a visual pun on the Arabic word for nest: *'ash*. Yet another suggests that comparing IS to animals is unfair on the many animals that are celebrated in Islam for their cleverness or ethical behaviour.

Another major theme, by far the most common, in our collection concerns sex and Daeshi relations between men and women, though it is hard to draw a clear boundary between the two subjects. Many memes, along similar lines to the Daesh fatwas discussed above, present IS as absurdly prudish. Others address the idea of Daeshis as sex-obsessed. Various memes place jihadis in juxtaposition with the famously controversial Lebanese singer Haifa Wehbe or, referencing a death threat issued by IS, American-Lebanese former porn performer Mia Khalifa. Others highlight the supposed 'sex jihad', whereby young Muslim women were rumoured to be joining the group to serve as de-facto prostitutes for the fighters. This theme is also present in the numerous memes which fall into the category of 'afterlife jokes'.

Unsurprisingly, themes of violence and terror are often present in the memes, but usually they are dealt with in an oblique manner. For example, some memes use the fear provoked by Daesh as a way of expressing irritation about other topics. One meme shows a picture of a Daeshi with the caption 'if I get one more invitation to Candy Crush I'm going to blow up your house'.[26] Or, 'next week, every father will become Daesh when they see the exam results'.[27] The following joke uses IS's reputation for callous and cynical exploitation of a culture of martyrdom as a particularly artful backdrop for a gag about the transactional mentality of a tight-fisted merchant.

Abu Salih, an inhabitant of Mosul, had a shop through which he made his living. When IS entered Mosul, there was a Russian Daeshi living next to him with his wife. This Russian had learned the Iraqi habit of buying everything on debt, to the point that his debt to Abu Salih reached two million dinars. Then, before he could pay off the debt, he died.

Abu Salih knocked at his own head in grief. 'Your money has gone, Abu Salih! It's gone!'

One day, Abu Salih went to the Russian's wife, who was also Russian and was extremely beautiful (you know how beautiful these Russian women are). 'I want your dead husband's money,' he said to her.

She replied 'I don't have any money. If you like, marry me and we'll consider the debt as my bride price'.

Abu Salih rejoiced. 'I shall marry her', he said to himself, 'for a bird in the hand is worth two in the bush'.

Two days later, however, the Daeshis demanded that he divorce her.

'But she's my wife now', Abu Salih protested. 'This woman has been put down to do a suicide operation—she must go and blow herself up.'

He said to them, 'why don't you take Umm Salih [his original wife]. She prays and fasts and has even made the pilgrimage to Mecca'.[28]

Memes and, more occasionally, jokes, quite often include popular culture references which sometimes seem to derive from specific stories about IS's own engagements with modern media. Three different memes consist of reworked versions of the cover of *Grand Theft Auto*.[29] These were presumably inspired by an IS video featuring lethal real-life car chases and drive-by shootings, which itself made homage to the notoriously lawless game. Similarly, the following story, spoofing various accounts of medieval Muslim rulers, makes fun of IS members' familiarity with social media.

> One cold night, the *khalifa* (Baghdadi) emerged from his home in disguise, as was his habit, so as to find out the condition of those he was responsible for. He passed by a house and saw some of the sons sitting in the street, so he greeted them. 'What are you doing here at the end of the night? Are you hungry?' He asked them. They said to him, 'we are not hungry but the internet is cut and there isn't anything to do'. So the *khalifa* returned with tears flooding his eyes and he responded saying 'how can a Muslim sleep in my caliphate without seeing his Facebook account? By Allah, if that was my account I would struggle'. And he was unable to settle down until he had sent them a renewal of their accounts for a two-month period and paid for it from the treasury of the believers. And they thanked him and put his pictures on their profiles and lived a happy life.[30]

This story, of course, also includes another common theme in jokes about Daesh: an obsession with the medieval past which can readily be characterised as pretentious. Fatwa jokes, of course, also try to imitate the conservative linguistic style of theological announcements, while other memes make fun of the traditionalistic vestments of jihadi fighters. One, for instance, shows a picture of an umbrella bird, with its luxuriant jet-black plumage and turban-like crest, captioned:10 'Abu Bakr the Birdie'.[31]

A number of comedic stereotypes quite common elsewhere seem to be surprisingly thinly represented in our collection. The theme of IS fighters hypocritically engaging in behaviours explicitly forbidden by religious fundamentalists such as drinking alcohol, smoking or listening to music has appeared, for example in various Syrian and

Lebanese comedies. In our collection, only two memes make reference to this. One is a picture of a bottle of what looks like rum with a label in the style of the IS flag.[32] Another shows two Daeshis sitting at a keyboard.[33]

The under-representation of another theme is perhaps even more striking, namely the commonplace notion that IS and potentially other jihadi groups are puppets, created and manipulated by some foreign power, be it Israel, the US, the Syrian Regime, Turkey, Qatar or Saudi Arabia. One meme in our collection has America describing IS as its 'daughter'. Another notes IS's unwillingness to do anything about Israel bombing Gaza, though this is not quite the same as a direct accusation of collusion with the Jewish state. A third may be insinuating a link between IS and Qatar, via a reference to the formerly Qatari-sponsored Barcelona football club.[34]

This is notable as this theme is very prominent among the professional-quality cartoons which we found being shared as memes, with nearly a quarter of all the examples making some reference to IS or Al Qaeda being the work of America and Israel (usually together), Saudi Arabia or the Syrian Regime. Presumably this is because cartoonists, who are often publishing openly in media that are subject to state censorship (and the scruples of the general public) are more likely to present views that are convenient to government interests, and unlikely to offend religious sentiments in the wider population. Indeed, the proportion of cartoons advancing the conspiracy narrative is further increased if we choose to focus only on those cartoons where the cartoonist's identity is known. This is because quite a number of cartoons in our collection are the work of anonymous Arabic cartoonists whose work directly attacks Islam itself.

We might be tempted to take the view that our memes (that is, the text-based jokes and captioned images) reflect views put forward by self-selecting individuals whereas cartoons reflect those of more public facing institutions, except that the cartoons, regardless of who originally drew them, were also shared by individuals online, who presumably did so in most cases because they resonated with their own attitudes. Another possibility is that cartoons are simply better at reflecting certain particular ideas. Conspiratorial cartoons, in contrast to most of our other memes, are examples of satire, but generally not of humour as such. And while they synthesise an explicitly political message, most of the memes present IS in a depoliticised manner, reducing them to one-dimensional objects of fun.

This is not to say that it is simple to unpack fun of this sort.

> Some Daeshis captured Haifa Wehbi. After interrogating her for two hours, their commander asked her 'How did you get your chest so big, you slut?' She said *takbir*. And the Daeshis all said '*Allahu akbar*'.[35]

This joke relies on a classic humour mechanism: the pun. In Arabic, the word *takbir* has two distinct meanings. In a religious context, it specifically refers to the practice of saying '*Allahu akbar*' (God is the greatest). But grammatically speaking, the word simply refers to making anything bigger, which means that in other cases it simply means 'enlargement'.

The joke here fits well with the semantic script theory proposed by Victor Raskin and developed by Salvatore Attardo. As previously alluded to, this account of verbal humour assumes that jokes work through the incongruous juxtaposition of two different and conflicting cultural 'scripts'.[36] For example, in the joke above, the script represented by Wehbi relates to what in Arabic might judgementally be called *fahishat* (indecent)—but glamorous and entertaining—sexual allurement. By contrast, the Daeshis ostensibly stand for *tashaddud* (excessive, inflexible strictness in matters of religious purity). What transforms this encounter into a joke is the presence of a mechanism which serves simultaneously to link these two scripts, but also to preserve the distance between them. The pun on the word *takbir* links the sacred utterance '*Allahu akbar*' with the profane practice of breast enlargement surgery. But because it is a pun—that is, a confusion between two distinct meanings—it provides an out. It's not as if piety is *really* being confused with sexual allurement. The resemblance is a 'mistake'.

Punch lines of this sort are of more than just linguistic interest. Because it is their job to hook on to and resolve the tension between the underlying cultural frames ('frame' Attardo says, is synonymous with 'script') that are in conflict in a joke, they provide a useful way of interrogating what these clashing scripts, sitting like icebergs beneath the visible peaks of language, are actually supposed to be. Take, for example the following comedy fatwa:

It is impermissible to use the *i'jab*, because the *i'jab* is from love, and love is *haram*. Instead, you should say *ma sha' Allah*.[37]

This joke (which does not translate in English) relies on what is arguably a three-way pun. *I'jab* in the first sense means 'exclamation mark'. Here, it is a term belonging to the technical, educated register of Modern Standard Arabic (particularly so, perhaps, since punctuation marks of this kind are originally Western imports into Arabic script).[38] On the other hand, in classical Arabic, *i'jab* has the more general meaning of 'admiration'. Thirdly, however, and particularly in contemporary colloquial Arabic, it also has connotations of 'fancying' or 'having a crush on' someone. Like many fatwa jokes, the incongruity is dependent on assuming two contrasting sources of authority: the traditional religious authority of the *mufti* and the allegedly contrasting authority of 'modern' technical forms of learning. But here, this conflict is also directly reflected in a play on words which draws on the contrasting authority of different registers of Arabic: modern standard Arabic for the technical practice of writing in printed characters, classical Arabic for the linguistic inferences necessary for Islamic jurisprudence, and colloquial Arabic for online flirting.

An interesting point is that cross-register punning of this kind is quite often subjectively dependent on how far the reader sees these registers as genuinely distinct. In this case there is a true pun in the contrasting senses of 'exclamation mark' and 'admiration' (even though both are different meanings of the same word, rather than homonyms). But the sense of a pun between the classical and colloquial senses is less firm. We can see this even more clearly in a joke such as this one:

It is forbidden to work as a *muhāsib* [accountant], because Allah alone is the *muhāsib* [reckoner] of all things.[39]

What we have here are two different usages of the same word, but it is perhaps somewhat moot as to whether they are really two distinct meanings. And while there is no reason to think that any Islamic scholar would actually condemn accountancy on these grounds, the general idea that, from certain cultural standpoints, it might seem to be a blasphemous and shameful usurpation of God's authority to count and reckon up even the tiniest incomings and outgoings is not entirely farfetched. Indeed, we can take this line of thought even further:

It is forbidden to install brakes in a car, because it violates of the principle of divine preordination [*qadr*].[40]

The obviously absurd recommendation that this spoof fatwa refers to is in fact intended to lampoon a very particular belief that is actually quite widespread in the Arab world, namely, that it is wrong to wear a seatbelt for this very same reason. Indeed, it is not really a joke at all, so much as an attempt to use the technique of *reductio ad absurdum* against this view. If wearing a seatbelt is an attempt to cheat God, why not simply go the whole way?

Humour, contrary to what script theory seemingly claims, is never objectively present in a text. In general, jokes are only funny to some people in some contexts. Nevertheless, an interesting feature of jokes such as those discussed above is that the success of what may normally be considered the most stable part of a joke—the basic linguistic mechanism linking the two scripts—can hinge on an ideological judgement about the relatedness of senses of words. A person who sees the Arabic terminology used in religious fatwas or in the Quran as divorced from the Arabic terminology used to regulate modern life will likely perceive a pun between two senses of *muhāsib*. A person who sees religion as suffusing everyday life may not—or at least not to quite the same extent.

In another sense, the creative application of religious terminology to quotidian or profane matters is by no means restricted to clashes between notions of religion and modernity. It could be argued that these jokes, knowingly or otherwise, are part of an old tradition of Arabic humour, premised specifically on quoting the Quran out of context. This dates back at least to the seventh century, when Abu Sa'd Mansur al-Abi recorded the joking practices of the *tufaylīs* of his day (semi-professional wits who would show up uninvited to dinner parties and tell jokes in exchange for food). In one virtuoso performance, a *tufaylī* called Bunān quoted passages of the Quran containing the numbers one to twelve in consecutive order in exchange for an equivalent number of sweets. Interestingly, a very similar joke is still being circulated today.[41]

A Syrian, a Kuwaiti, an Emirati and a Saudi bought a chicken, which they slaughtered and began to cook. They agreed that whoever had memorised a verse of the Quran which contained the name of a part of a chicken should get that part.

The Saudi recited: 'and lower to them the wing of humility' [Al Isra': 24].

And thus his share was the wings.

The Kuwaiti recited: 'And the leg is wound about the leg' [Al-Qiyama: 29].

So he was to have the legs.

The Emirati said: 'Did we not expand, for you, your breast?' [Al-Sharh: 1].

So his was the breast.

Well, the Syrian couldn't recall any verse which would enable him to obtain a part of the chicken. And while he was thinking, the rest of the group fell asleep, waiting for the chicken to finish cooking. So he seized his chance without delay. He ate the chicken, and hid its bones.

When the group woke up they asked him light heartedly where the chicken had got to.

Without hesitation, he replied to them: 'and so there came upon the garden an affliction from your Lord while they were asleep' [Al-Qalam: 19].[42]

The difference is that, in the IS jokes, the situation is reversed. Instead of the joker engaging in mischievous misapplication of the Quran in a self-interested but essentially harmless manner, the butt of the joke here is whoever is doing the misquoting, typically for similarly self-interested but often more harmful purposes.

8

INFIDELS OF IDEOLOGY

FINAL THOUGHTS AND FUTURE DIRECTIONS

When IS declared their caliphate and raised up their flag across Iraq and Syria, 'Ahmad' was enthusiastically cheering them on, eagerly seizing on every scrap of news about each victory or advance, and becoming enraged whenever he heard of efforts to thwart them by their rivals and opponents. In the past, back home in the Middle Eastern country in which he grew up, he had thought seriously about abandoning his studies and joining the jihad. Now, as a postgraduate student in Western Europe, he tended to joke about the subject. 'If I could just get myself one of these blonde girls', he would quip to friends, 'that would be enough for me in this life. Then I could go to jihad'.

Such jokes were rarities, though. A dour man from a strict Bedouin background, he usually had little time for the trivial or the frivolous. But, as he used to admit, it isn't possible to be serious all the time. And he did have a soft spot for Syrian comedy—particularly the series *The Lost Village* (an absurd show about a group of country bumpkins) and *Tash Ma Tash*.

Aware of this, a friend one day suggested that he watch *Spotlight*, specifically the episode 'The Safe Road', which is among those we discussed in chapter 5. 'I know that this might not be very funny to you', the friend admitted, 'It's kind of mocking clerics. But I like it, and I

195

want to see what your reaction will be,' he continued, adding hopefully, 'It's got Bassem Yakhour in it' (Bassem Yakhour, also stars in *The Lost Village*).

Ahmad was uneasy when he began to watch the episode, but he persisted, perhaps for the sake of politeness. At the point at which Yakhour, dressed as an ultra-religious sheikh, self-righteously slaps the jihadi checkpoint commander, he burst into laughter.

This isn't a conversion narrative. Ahmad has returned to his home country, where he now holds a respectable job as a university lecturer in a science-related subject. His views have not fundamentally changed. Despite everything, he still basically believes in the Islamic State cause. However, some of the rigidity that once accompanied this has gone. Watching people making fun of jihadis and religious people no longer outrages him the way it once did. Indeed, in his serious, cerebral way, he has become something of an amateur theorist of comedy. As he puts it, 'comedy helps you to accept criticism with a welcoming heart'.

While the name and some key identifying features in this account have been changed, this true account may be applicable to a number of other young Arabs. It any case, it serves to crystallise the main themes of this book. Comedy is by no means a magic bullet against jihadism in particular, or by extension 'violent extremism' in general. To suppose this is not just to overrate the power of comedy, but also to underrate the subtlety and complexity of people who are drawn to extremism. At the same time, it would be unduly pessimistic to suppose that comedy cannot change anything. Its effects are subtle, complex and difficult to measure scientifically—but that doesn't mean that they don't exist.

In this book we have attempted to tease apart the key elements of joking on the subject of Islamist extremism, setting this in the context of the jokes told by the 'extremists' themselves. In this final chapter, it falls to us to offer some sort of final assessment—to make an attempt, however tentative, at evaluating the significance of the examples examined so far.

This requires a framework. In chapter 2, we outlined a tentative set of labels that apply, very much for our own purposes, to various distinct pathways by which humour might bring about social or political change. Humour is, of course, already well served with theories addressing the many aspects, forms and levels of analysis on which it can be understood. There is always the risk, then, that we are reinventing the wheel (or maybe even doing something less practical). Our hope is that we have found some middle ground between the set of binary options we found to be present in the literature:

1. Treating humour as a set of techniques (as tends to be the case in rhetoric or politics) as opposed to examining fundamental questions about what it ultimately is and why things are perceived to be humorous in the first place (as is typically done in philosophy, psychology and so on).
2. Treating humour as something that exists within the text itself (as is often the case in linguistics or literary criticism) as opposed to something that exists only in an interactive context (an approach often seen in anthropology and sometimes in psychology).
3. Treating humour as something inherently liberating and praiseworthy (seen in some philosophical and political approaches) as opposed to focusing instead on critique of inappropriate humour (as in cultural and critical studies).

In offering the categories of 'travesty', 'pillory', 'raillery' and 'coxcombry' as ideal types, our aim was not to be fully systematic or comprehensive. Nevertheless, since it is almost impossible to resist further schematising, we note that in our typology travesty and coxcombry seem to form a complementary pair, as do pillory and raillery.

Travesty and coxcombry both concern the question of where the joke is. In travesty, the joke is on the inside, gradually emerging from what might at first glance be mistaken for seriousness. In coxcombry, by contrast, the joke is on the outside, wrapped around the serious message that the comedian ultimately hopes to communicate. In travesty, the aim is to begin with something portentous and offer the audience a 'get out', demonstrating that humour (as opposed to fear, outrage or shock) is a possible interpretation of the original object of travesty: 'fight or flight—or laughter' as John Morreall puts it.[1] In coxcombry, the aim is to use the special licence granted to comic speech to say something that it would be difficult to get away with saying otherwise.

Pillory and raillery, on the other hand, are concerned as categories with who is in on the joke. In pillory, the butt is outside the group, and the jokes serve to reinforce this fact. In essence, the attacks on the object of pillory are, themselves, the joke. This is why pillory can consist of straightforward insults or even violent assaults that produce gleeful laughter among the in-group, even when there is nothing remotely resembling an incongruity or a punch line present. In raillery, the opposite is true. The playful attack serves to collapse the distinction between in-group and outsider, rendering the formerly threatening alien a potential participant in fun. Raillery, can, at times, contain elements that appear to an outsider like a gross insult. A.R. Radcliffe-Brown, in his seminal paper introducing the anthropological concept of the joking relationship, notes that the 'jokes' through which this dynamic is maintained include 'the most vulgar accusations'.[2] Nevertheless, this sort of thing can happen only within the context of a very clear set of social rules protecting and prescribing this sort of conduct. When the aim of raillery is instead to bring someone into the realm of play, stronger and more obvious symbols of playfulness are likely necessary.

Travesty appears, on the face of it, to be a promising means of satirising jihadis. As we observed in chapter 1, a key function of comedy, at least according to Western-backed practitioners, is to deprive 'terrorists' of their ability to inspire terror. As we suggested in chapter 2, jihadis, particularly IS, don't indiscriminately use lethal force to inspire fear alone. It seems that their most shocking material is capable of prompting something deeper—a dizzying, dislocating moral dread that results from the way in which they violate common assumptions about religious values and norms. Søren Kierkegaard, who himself once approvingly described the prophet Muhammad as a 'humourist',[3] saw the cultivation of a special kind of deep, dark ironic humour as a spiritual response to notions of dread, writing that 'when sin is drawn into aesthetics the mood becomes either frivolous or melancholy; for the category under which sin lies is contradiction, and this is either comic or tragic'.[4]

Even so, it seems that Arab humourists have often struggled to effectively travesty jihadis. As we saw in chapter 3, *The Terrorist* and early episodes of *Tash Ma Tash* that engaged the subject of terrorism and religious extremism portrayed these individuals with great seriousness, allowing comedy to enter only when represented by ordinary people. Although this taboo would later be broken, with IS in particular inspiring numerous portrayals attempting to reimagine the group in a comical light, these frequently have a stilted quality, falling back on the same tried and tested motifs—false beards, incompetent, buffoonish henchmen and cheerfully hypocritical caliphs.

The difficulty of effectively travestying jihadis is not hard to pinpoint. It goes without saying that their core business (brutal violence) is not in itself appropriate material for travesty. Even if people do find ways to laugh at the most horrible things amidst the brutal realities of war, it is not at all the same thing to create material that encourages others to make light of such matters. Therefore, travestying jihadis must take aim at their superficial style, not the gory substance of their actions. But the key elements of jihadi style are, of course, almost exclusively a collage of symbols and slogans popularly recognised as 'Islamic'. Although this no longer shields jihadis from travesty, it does mean that attempts must be careful to follow a tight formula, cleaving always to an authorised caricature. An additional issue—both an asset and a liability—is that this caricature bears a close, if parodic, resemblance to a pre-existing set of visual motifs found in Arabic-language period dramas set around the time of the coming of Islam. As such, the parody jihadis present in shows like *Spotlight* or *Kteer Selbi* often appear less as direct parodies, and more like attempts to show jihadis as people who are themselves parodying historical television shows.

This seems to offer the key to truly effective travesty of jihadis: focusing not on the superficial appearance of the fighters, but rather the obsessive focus on media manipulation that lies behind the construction of this façade. As noted, this general point has previously been made by others, including, in specific relation to anti-IS comedy, Greenberg and Kraidy, who argue that the key to IS propaganda lies in its postmodern concern with aesthetics and spectacle over underlying reality.[5]

However, travestying something as elusive and intangible as this in practice is not always an easy matter. Part of the problem is that jihadi propaganda often seems to be a step ahead of those trying to parody it—slicker and perhaps even more self-aware. For example, one of Dayaaltaseh's attempts to satirise IS's social media obsession is a characteristically surreal video in which an IS fighter kills a blue bird representing the Twitter logo. The problem, to our mind, with this sketch is that it implies that thuggish IS are too stupid and backwards to 'get' Twitter. As there isn't a grain of truth to this accusation, it lacks the basic verisimilitude that satire normally requires. Another joke that has appeared as the basis of at least two different sketches (and which plays a supporting role in numerous other lampoons) addresses the highly staged quality of IS execution videos (apparently the grisly result of the fact that IS actually used to rehearse these videos with captives, who were not told that they were not participating in another dry run). A widely shared video features an inept IS camera crew going through unsuccessful take after unsuccessful take, eventually ending with the hostage making a run for it. In the animated series *The Bigh Daddy Show*, an episode based on the same conceit shows an IS video directed by an exasperated director called 'Farantino', in which the hostage ends up helping the fighters out with their poor Arabic grammar.

A particularly inspired travesty of IS propaganda techniques can be found in the conclusion of the same show's second season, with an entire episode devoted to spoofing a single IS video: 'The Structure of the Caliphate'. At the heart of the humour in this animation is it mimicry and exaggeration of specific signature elements of the camerawork in IS propaganda videos, as well as the exact replication of the computer graphics which, in the original, are used to illustrate IS's supposed organisational structure. In IS propaganda, long camera sweeps and the extensive use of drone footage create an atmosphere of intangible gravity and significance, which casts a numinous patina over the mundane or grisly material in the video. By unmasking and showing how easily replicable the techniques behind IS's self-documentation are, it could make it more difficult for IS videos to cast the same cinematic spell on subsequent viewings.

Coxcombry has traditionally been an important element of Arab comedy. Comedians have very much played the role of the court jester to the absolute power of kings, both metaphorical and real, saying things indirectly that could not be expressed in the open. The Jordanian cartoonist Emad Hajjaj—the creator of the everyman character Abu Mahjoub, who has become a mirror of the country's travails—described to us he sees his responsibilities:

> The *sha'b*—the people—have their own ideas or thoughts that nobody [has yet] grabbed. I'm not a politics man, and when I talk to people I don't put [out] a table and [have them] sit on chairs and listen to me. I go among the ordinary people and they talk to me. Most of the people... do not know my face. They do not know that I am Abu Mahjoub.[6]

This traditionally sanctioned role has been a mixed blessing in taking on jihadis. On the one hand, comedy functions as a platform for content directed towards them; but it is telling that so much material contains little obvious mirth. This, in a sense, is coxcombry taken to an extreme—almost entirely serious content with just a hint of the mirthful entertainment expected by viewers. On the other hand, as this absence of joking suggests, a sense of responsibility towards the collective sensitivities of an idealised *sha'b* can constrain what comics feel able to address in practice.

One obvious problem is that coxcombry is, prototypically, a way of speaking truth to power. And yet with the partial exception of IS between roughly 2014 and 2016 and some more limited cases of groups carving out temporary emirates in the context of civil war, jihadi groups have rarely been in power in a meaningful sense. The same is broadly true of Islamists generally. On the other hand—to repeat the obvious—the social licence granted to comics to address anything pertaining to religion is very limited. Far from being at greater liberty to address the subject of religious extremism, comedians are often more constrained than those using other approaches.

Finally, there is the issue of what serious content can be effectively conveyed using humorous means. Coxcombry requires that the 'coxcomb' be able to express something more complex than antipathy. Since this will be done in a more or less indirect manner, the message to which a voice is being given is typically not in fact new, but rather represents something widely recognised as a hitherto unspoken truth. But it is not obvious that there are many widely recognised truths about jihadis that are not already openly and frequently expressed.

In another sense, though, the urgency that has led embattled Arab regimes to favour the use of cultural tools, including comedy, against jihadis has offered cover for comedians to say other things. One example is the way in which jihadism can serve as a proxy for the expression of views about the relationship between religion and society that might otherwise be too controversial to put forward. We previously touched on how some contemporary Egyptian comedians do just this—using cartoonish portrayals of jihadis as a pretext for commenting on more moderate Islamists. We also considered how the radicalisation of the Syrian Civil War opened up a space for *Spotlight* to produce material that at its best, whatever its ultimate political purpose and affiliation, we see as some of the most subtle and thoughtful commentary yet made on the crisis of religious identity in Syria and the wider region.

Some material that ostensibly targets jihadis also seems to contain subtext apparently relating to other, perhaps riskier targets as well. As Hajjaj points out, the totalitarian ideology of jihadi groups can bear more than a passing resemblance to other systems of domination, all of which, he believes, satirists are bound to oppose.

> The idea of totalitarianism—it's all about the stupid [notion] that you can … build the perfect idea that applies to everyone, everywhere, every time, which I think is not true. It's about laws, it's about rules— and humour—the concept of that is about manipulating the rules, it's about … it's all about collapsing these rules. Religious or ideological people have a specific way of looking at the world. The way they live is that there is only one way to look at the world, which is not true. In the cartoonist's eye, they look funny because they are trying to make a very perfect model but they cannot because ideals—when you implement them in reality there will always be a conflict and there will always be cartoons. If you look at the Soviet era or at the socialist era, ironically one of the biggest human experiments in implementing a totalitarian system, at the same time you still find very good cartoons coming out of these Soviet guys who lived there, and you can easily find how stupid this idea was when it's implemented in reality. When we talk about Daesh or we talk about Communism or we talk about Arab Nationalism it's the same. What they don't like about cartoons is that cartoonists don't recognise or admit their rules—they don't take their bibles for granted. We are like the infidels of ideology.[7]

We noted how *Dawlat al-Khurafa* took a swipe at Saudi Arabia (as well as, in its original opening credits, Qatar, Israel and America). *Mini Daesh* took aim not at IS, but at Egyptian celebrities. In its final two episodes *The Bigh Daddy Show* took a surreal turn, interposing the CG animated Daeshis—now defeated and in hiding—with live footage featuring actors from the sketch show *Melon City*, who play corrupt and self-serving Iraqi politicians scrambling to profit from the group's demise (while gratuitously flattening Mosul to emphasise their own power and importance). The ultimate joke, as these episodes suggest, is that IS was itself never more than an absurd cartoon behind which lay the same cynical unchanging political power plays that continue on past its present decline.

Another place where comic license may be important as a tool of critique is within jihadi organisations themselves. While there are few robust comic institutions in these movements, we have seen how cultural practices such as *nashid* singing and storytelling can apparently provide opportunities for subtly dissenting narratives. It is, of course, very much a moot point whether jihadi humour serves to undermine these groups or to strengthen their appeal. But in a sense, this debate misses the point—given that a key attribute of humour is its ambivalence, it doesn't make sense to assume a single answer to this question. Both can be possible at one and the same time. But this is not to evade the issue entirely. Above all, what jihadi humour helps point to is a capacity for reflexivity. Even the least reflexive of jihadi stories—those which mock the religion of Shia and Alawites before condemning them to death—also seem to contain a deep disquiet about where the boundaries really lie between insider and outsider. Jihadis' capacity to entertain grains of doubt, to stand outside themselves and imagine how they look to outsiders and perhaps to question the rightness of their cause need not weaken their commitment to the cause. Conceivably, it may at times strengthen it. But it at least helps to show where room for change, whether individual or collective, might exist among such supposedly 'incorrigible' terrorists. It also points to a paradox that has been observed for some time in the relationship between jihadi leaders and new media. While jihadi groups are portrayed as maintaining smoothly functioning propaganda machines, in which every slickly edited new release and every move into a new platform is presented as part of a carefully worked out and coordinated plan, jihadi leaders face the same challenges as heads of other political movements when it comes to balancing between the benefits of openness and generativity and the risk of losing message control. The more creativity jihadi 'fans' pour into making their own popular culture, the more risk there is that this will end up fracturing and distracting them—providing them with sources of cultural capital that may offer an alternative to the formula of jihad or martyrdom.

Whatever doubts they may conceal, however, stories about toying with and killing members of 'heretic' sects are still humour at its very darkest and most aggressive—examples of pillory having reached its logical conclusion, and the boundaries of group membership having

been drawn with lines of blood and laughter. And yet, such elimination-
ist language is not restricted to jihadis, and it is important to be mindful of this in reading the more aggressive examples of anti-jihadi
humour. Among the collection of memes we analysed in the previous
chapter were images of the Shia militiaman known as Abu Azrael—an
axe wielding, body building fighter who released videos in which he
mockingly defiled the corpses of dead IS fighters.[8] While it is not difficult to see this as 'problematic' (or disgusting and immoral), similar
basic attitudes are expressed in Iraqi government-sanctioned cartoons,
for example, such as one in which IS fighters are depicted as cartoon
rat-people scurrying about to the tune of an old Fairuz children's song,
who rapidly disappear into their holes when a bold soldier from the
Iraqi military army appears. The soldier, in jarring contrast, is presented in a naturalistic, if idealised, drawing style entirely different
from that used for the Daeshis, with the Iraq flag, complete with the
takbir, prominent on his armband.[9] Even secular 'liberals' can engage
in what looks like aggressive sectarian humour. The authors have
encountered isolated examples of Arab women who laugh and celebrate news stories about the abuse of veiled Muslim women in
European countries, seeing it as payback for what they see as their own
oppression. There is also material that uses apparently anti-Shia sectarian motifs to poke fun at Sunni jihadis. In one *Melon City* sketch, jihadis
bewail their slain commander by slapping themselves in a parody of
Shia *'ashura* mourning rituals.[10]

But it is too simple to suggest that pillory is universally undesirable.
Like all humour, it is ambivalent. Its significance shifts rapidly according to vagaries of context, circumstance and interpretation. An Iraqi
meme which, typically of such material, is both blatant and cryptic,
depicts a cat singing 'Dirty Daesh, pass the soap'. This neatly encapsulates the ambiguous nature of pillory and expresses what can literally
be read as a 'toxifying' belief about IS fighters, many of whom are
essentially ordinary Sunni Iraqis who, whatever their deeds may have
been, would in many cases go on to pay a terrible price for them.[11] At
the same time, such jokes also express a spirit of defiance against what
was seen as a genuinely terrifying threat, and played their part in a
culture of resistance that also encompassed Sunni Muslims living in
Iraq and Syria under IS domination.

What we call raillery is the humorous ideal from a liberal stand-point, and it is perhaps the most complex and difficult concept to grapple with when it comes to dealing with people who are already far beyond the pale of liberal values. In chapter 2, we spoke about this term in two related senses. One refers to the ideal of the sense of humour as a democratic virtue, underpinning an idealised, egalitarian culture in which all have the right to laugh at one another without treating the matter as a deadly affront. The other refers to joking that does not necessarily set out to engage targets in this way, but which has the effect of humanising rather than excluding them, presenting the butts of jokes not as rats whose demise is funny in its own right, but as flawed and misled individuals who are, implicitly at least, candidates for rehabilitation into society.

Understood in the latter sense, a good deal of Arab comedy about jihadis is, or can be understood as, humanising in a sense. This is perhaps a surprising observation, given that portrayals of jihadis in Arabic comedy are, in most cases, scarcely sympathetic and rarely subtle.

One thing that seems to have driven humanising portrayals of jihadis where they have occurred has been the need for Arab countries to grapple with the issue of radicalisation. Interestingly, it seems that some places have handled this better than others. Although recruiters are still typically presented as shadowy evil forces, Saudi material has for a long time found dramatic and sometimes even comic potential in the idea that recruits to terrorist organisations can be ordinary people with sincere religious motivations. The drama of Hassan Sabaileh explores a similar premise. On the other hand, while *Spotlight* has sometimes approached these issues, its characteristic depiction of jihadis in Syria emphasises their foreignness, while Egyptian comedies, especially recent films dealing with IS, tend to present the protagonist as falling into the group in a casual or even accidental manner, leaving his officially authorised Egyptian-ness intact.

Curiously, there is something humanising in the common portrayal of jihadis as simple-minded, licentious buffoons, motivated by worldly appetites for sex, money and status. Even though the stereotype that this humour seeks to construct is coarse and demeaning, intended to strip jihadis of their dignity and intimidating reputation, the effect can invest them with a sort of raucous, carnivalistic charm, especially when accompanied, as is often the case, with an innocent, troglodyte stupidity. This characteristic is necessarily removed from the sense of laddish exuberance that jihadis themselves have at times sought to project. It is precisely this unruly spirit, acceptably filtered through the comic lens, that seemingly powered the controversial humour of *Mini Daesh*.

However, as we argued in chapter 2, it is not possible to separate these two senses of raillery. To mock someone in a way that humanises them and presents them as potentially admissible to the circle of play is to present an open invitation for a sort of dialogue, whether one likes it or not. As we noted, there have been occasions of direct joking between jihadis and their opponents in the form of the *nashid* battles between Saudi IS members and loyalists. This occurrence, although here it was underpinned as much by domestic Saudi and tribal politics, and the ancient idiom of Arabic Bedouin poetry, is also very much a story about the oddly contradictory nature of digital media, which simultaneously polarises people into ever more fractious micro-groups, while also making possible dialogues where they might not otherwise have seemed possible.

Reflecting on the character Abu Mahjoub with whom his work has become synonymous, Emad Hajjaj mused about what sort of everyman character he might create if he were starting out on his career today.

> If I were to create another character something like Abu Mahjoub I would make him a pan Arab guy—something for an Arab audience, not only Jordan. I might make him younger … he wouldn't be using his real name, he would be using a nickname on Facebook and he would be very aggressive in talking about everything. I would create a character like this: a guy in a coffee shop in some place in Baghdad or Beirut—an angry guy who's practising some kind of free speech but in an odd way.[12]

This statement will surely resonate with any interested observers of the Middle East over the past decade or so. And yet the situation Hajjaj describes is hardly a uniquely Arab issue. All over the world, the same two complementary but apparently opposite trends seem to be accelerating: the sense of a global village, in which geographical boundaries seem less and less important and, at the same time, the sense of fragmentation, as what once seemed coherent masses of people splinter into small and mutually polarised communities. In the supposedly liberal West today, the rise of phenomena such as the alt-right, with their characteristic use of satire, in-jokes and ambiguity,[13] has deeply shaken the idea that humour belongs in any special sense to the culture of liberalism.

In a world in which even Nazi websites pride themselves on their ability to use comedy as a way of attracting new recruits and creating a sense of shared identity among existing members, we should not be surprised to find that there are online communities of apparent jihadis who seem to operate in a similar way.[14]

Despite all this, one of the real lessons emerging from the cultural inferno that has blazed alongside the sectarian carnage often seen in the Middle East since 2003, and more still since 2011, is a more heartening one. As media literacy increases within new generations of Arabs and despite their differences, it seems that the increasingly routine acceptance of comedy by liberals and Islamists alike is beginning to make room for some unlikely conversations.

Isam Urayqat of satirical newspaper *Al-Hudood* claims that for a time, one of his best writers was a Moroccan Salafi whose satirical career was cut short when he was thrown into jail. 'He would write about anything—he would even go after Saudi Arabia'.[15] What is worthy of note here is less the existence of a Salafi satirist, so much as the existence of one who was happy to write for a website notorious for its willingness to poke fun at religiosity.

On the other hand, in 2017, satirist Youssef Hussein hosted the Jordanian comic Ahmed Massad on his television comedy *Joe Show*, airing on Al-Jazeera's youth-oriented channel Al-Arabi. The episode isn't, in itself, very remarkable—Massad, a comedian with an unpredictable, madcap persona whose trademarks are making his face up like Heath Ledger's version of the Joker and making a maddening pig-like snort, was on subdued form, chatting about his desire to work with children before strumming out a version of the soundtrack to the nostalgic cartoon favourite *Mowgli*.[16] But the fact the two men appeared on the same show is significant in itself. Hussein, we will recall, started his career by poking fun at Egyptian liberals for their ignorance of religion and pixelating out images of unveiled women. Massad, by contrast, is famous for making videos in which he deliberately baits popular pious sensitivities, laughing at tall tales or pseudo-scientific claims propagated by famous sheikhs.[17]

At the time of writing, Massad is, in fact, one of the few liberal comedians that are still actively engaged in satirising religious topics. As the immediate threat from IS has receded, the relevance of this topic has diminished, at least for now. Other subjects, unsurprisingly, have acquired greater urgency: the war in Yemen, the autocracy of Sisi, the megalomania of Mohammed bin Salman and the desperate economic situation almost everywhere.

Curiously, when it comes to mocking the clergy, the mantle seems to have been passed on to Islamist-leaning comedians—Hussein foremost among them. Unlike Massad, whose criticism focuses on simple-minded piety, or the anti-jihadi humour of the comedians we have focused on in this book, Hussein's mockery is in principle aimed at the so-called 'fat-free' Islam,[18] which Islamists disparagingly ascribe to the form of the religion promoted by politically quiescent, pro-regime scholars, as well as the Salafi Nour Party in Egypt, which chose to back the military overthrow of Islamist Mohamed Morsi's presidency. And yet, by daring to laugh at these symbols of sacred authority, Hussein and others like him are demonstrating just how far Arab comedians have managed to roll back the boundaries of social acceptability. Whereas in the past, established religious institutions such as Al-Azhar in Egypt would have been widely regarded as too sacred and venerable to be the objects of overt mockery, these taboos have begun to slip. In one clip, for example, wearing the white and red turban unique to Al-Azhar clerics, Hussein joked about how the sheikhs issued a fatwa on the chest hair of Egyptian footballer and national hero Muhammad Salah.[19] In another episode, he ridiculed the grand mufti of Saudi Arabia's style of speaking, questioning his competence to issue fatwas.[20] Even Abdul Rahman Al-Sudais, the venerated imam of the Great Mosque of Mecca and a beloved Quran reciter, was presented, with the help of some digital manipulation, as coming out of the pocket of the crown prince Muhammad bin Salman.[21] It is hard to imagine that such harsh mockery would have been accepted from a secular comedian. Hussein got away with it because of his reputation as an Islamist sympathiser in a fight so fierce that any weapon was now perceived as halal. In a supreme irony, Hussein, who had started his career fighting back against perceived attacks on religion by the liberal comedian Bassem Youssef, was now partially filling the niche that Youssef's exile to the United States had left vacant.

There is something extraordinary about the moment close to the beginning of *The Terrorist* when Adel Imam's jihadi character Ali smashes up and torches a video shop. It represents a sort of auto-iconoclasm, since at the time the film was released, Imam's face would have been among the most commonly displayed on the covers of the VHS tapes sold in places like this. It powerfully conveys an intense and violent clash, supposedly between religious backwardness and technological modernity. And yet at one and the same time, it also seems to portray a new iteration of an ancient equilibrium: the back-and-forth struggle of the forces of sacred purity and necessary profanity, now represented by the entertainment media as they once were by shadow plays and carnival festivities. Looking back at this in the present day, however, the moment seems to take on a new and still more ironic import. In a world of playful jihadis and Islamist satirists, of militant atheist cartoonists and anti-clerical memes, the sight of this ageing giant of the old-media and the *ancien régime* rampaging over his own back catalogue begins to look more and more like a joke at his own expense.

The new laughter of the Arab world can be a frightening thing: at times inconceivably dark and cynical, at others simply a hysterical yelp before an awful, gory shock. In this book we have tried hard to avoid mythologising laughter, to relentlessly argue against the sunny belief that there is something within it that is beyond taint—some glimpse via the path of paradox of something divine. And yet in writing our concluding words, it seems that try as we may, laughter will not be altogether repressed by sombre analysis. On its own, comedy will, of course, not defeat religious extremism. But contemporary Arab comedy has played a role in shattering once seemingly inviolable taboos, transgressing the boundaries of consensus while somehow also enabling conversations where they once seemed impossible. A final irony, perhaps, is that the idea of humour as a way of opening up a space for raucous dialogue is taking a firmer hold in the Arab world while it seems increasingly like a naïve fantasy in the West. At the time of writing, Sacha Baron Cohen had recently come out with a new show *Who Is America* which tries to straddle the growing political divide in American society. The effort has received mixed reviews. [22] Perhaps he could learn a thing or two from a Middle Eastern deployment?

NOTES

INTRODUCTION

1. Jihad literally means 'struggle' and has a religious meaning that traditionally encompasses both military struggle and spiritual struggle against sinful desires. For a detailed investigation see, Michael Bonner, *Jihad in Islamic History: Doctrines and Practice*, Princeton: Princeton University Press, 2008.

1. BONO LOSES THE PLOT: COMEDY AND COUNTERTERRORISM

1. The original video can be seen here https://www.c-span.org/video/? 4080281/bonos-testimony-foreign-aid-combating-violent-extremism (accessed 12 Dec. 2017).
2. https://archive.org/details/FOXNEWSW_20160414_070000_Red_ Eye
3. R. LeDonne, 'Bono's Plan to Combat ISIS with Comedians Suggests He's Lost the Plot', *Guardian*, 22 Feb. 2017.
4. See, for example, D. Byman, *The Five Front War: The Better Way to Fight Global Jihad*, Hoboken: Wiley, 2008, p. 173.
5. See, for example, J. Nye, *Soft Power: The Means to Success in World Politics*, New York: Public Affairs Press, 2005.
6. The 9/11 plot was premised on the ease with which a group of Saudis could enrol to study in US flight schools.
7. See, for example, the notorious Sageman/Hoffman debate in the importance of hierarchical structures in Al Qaeda.
8. Quoted by D. Byman, op. cit., p. 174.
9. D. Casciani, 'The Islamic State's Social Media Machine' *BBC World Service*, 5 May 2015, https://www.bbc.co.uk/programmes/p02q5dpp

10. J.P. Farwell, 'Jihadi Video in the War of Ideas', *Survival: Global Politics and Strategy*, vol. 52, no. 6, 2010, pp. 127–150.

11. 'Prof. J. Michael Waller', https://www.wikistrat.com/experts/prof-j-michael-waller/ (accessed 10 Nov. 2018).

12. J.M. Waller, *Fighting the War of Ideas like a Real War*, Washington: Institute of World Politics Press, 2007.

13. Ibid., p. 15.

14. Ibid., p. 94.

15. 'Text: Bin Laden Tape,' *BBC*, 19 Jan. 2006, http://news.bbc.co.uk/1/hi/world/middle_east/4628932.stm (accessed 14 Mar. 2018).

16. D. Byman & C. Fair, 'The Case for Calling Them Nitwits', *Atlantic*, July, 2010, https://www.theatlantic.com/magazine/archive/2010/07/the-case-for-calling-them-nitwits/308130/ (accessed 20 Sept. 2017).

17. J. Brachman, 'Fight Fire with Funny', *Newsweek*, 30 Aug. 2010.

18. A. Al-Zawahiri 'Days with the Imam', n.d.

19. J. Brachman, 'Ansarnet's Jihobbyist Orcs are at it Again', *Free Republic*, 22 Nov. 2009, http://www.freerepublic.com/focus/f-bloggers/2393224/posts

20. H. Goodall, P. Cheong, K. Fleischer and S. Corman, 'Rhetorical Charms: The Promises and Pitfalls of Humor and Ridicule as Strategies to Counter Extremist Narratives', *Perspectives on Terrorism*, vol. 6, no. 1, 2012.

21. The Global Coalition Against Daesh, http://theglobalcoalition.org/en/home/ (accessed 10 Nov. 2018).

22. G. Hussein and E.M. Saltman, 'Jihad Trending: A Comprehensive Analysis of Online Extremism, and How to Counter It', Quilliam Foundation, 13 May 2014, https://www.quilliaminternational.com/jihad-trending-a-comprehensive-analysis-of-online-extremism-and-how-to-counter-it-executive-summary/ (accessed 20 Dec. 2017).

23. L. Elsayed, T. Faris and S. Zeiger, 'Undermining Violent Extremist Narratives in the Middle East and North Africa: A How-To Guide', Hedayah Institute, 2017.

24. Institute for Strategic Dialogue and Radicalisation Awareness Network Centre of Excellence, 'Counter Narratives and Alternative Narratives', RAN Issue Paper, 1 Oct. 2015.

25. J. Bartlett and A. Krasodomski-Jones, 'Counter-Speech on Facebook', Demos, Sept. 2016, https://www.demos.co.uk/wp-content/uploads/2016/09/Counter-speech-on-facebook-report.pdf (accessed 20 Dec. 2017).

26. N. Greenberg, 'Mythical State: The Aesthetics and Counter-Aesthetics of the Islamic State in Iraq and Syria', *Middle East Journal of Culture and Communication*, vol. 10, nos. 2–3, 2017.

27. M. Kraidy, 'Fun Against Fear in the Caliphate: Islamic State's Spectacle and Counter-Spectacle', *Critical Studies in Media Communication*, vol. 35, no. 1, 2017, pp. 40–56.
28. Waller, 2007 op. cit., p. 108.
29. 'US State Department Releases "Think Again Turn Away" Campaign to Discourage Recruits from Joining IS', News.com.au, 10 Sept. 2014, https://www.news.com.au/world/north-america/us-state-department-releases-think-again-turn-away-campaign-to-discourage-foreign-recruits-from-joining-is/news-story/f4b4f93e27a6d1255b3bdbb2b696a9d0 (accessed 14 Nov. 2018). Original video embedded with story.
30. Ibid.
31. See, for example, G. Miller and S. Higham, 'In a Propaganda War Against ISIS, the US Tried to Play by the Enemy's Rules', *Washington Post*, 8 May 2015, https://www.washingtonpost.com/world/national-security/in-a-propaganda-war-us-tried-to-play-by-the-enemys-rules/2015/05/08/6eb6b732-e52f-11e4-81ea-0649268f729e_story.html?noredirect=on&utm_term=.12de4e00425a (accessed 14 Nov. 2018).
32. 'US Digital Outreach Team', Facebook, page https://www.facebook.com/DigitalOutreachTeam/?ref=search&__tn__=%2Cd%2CP-R&eid=ARAMO5FeKKzp_Sh_D8bLxxWuP8CxjkQ51N5Sbs6Ro12k_cuSNXl9Sjl3jhMWBdPrvhi_wdqAhPPaks97 (accessed 12 Aug. 2018).
33. Goodall et al., 2012, op. cit.
34. Waller, op. cit., pp. 106 ff.
35. 'The Truth About Life Under Daesh in Raqqa: Five Things You Need to Know About Life in Raqqa Under Daesh', The Global Coalition, https://theglobalcoalition.org/en/5-things-life-under-daesh-raqqa/ (accessed 14 Nov. 2018).
36. Goodall et al., 2012, op. cit.
37. A. Speckhard and A. Shajkovci, 'Perspective: Debating the Use of ISIS Counter-Narratives in the Heart of Europe', *Homeland Security Today*, 4 Dec. 2018.
38. 'Priyank Mathur', https://www.linkedin.com/in/priyank-mathur-89818923/ (accessed 14 Nov. 2018)
39. W. Bruer, 'India: Laughing at ISIS to Defeat Them', 21 July 2017 https://pulitzercenter.org/reporting/india-laughing-isis-defeat-them (accessed 14 Nov. 2018).
40. For a general discussion of this, see J. Shapiro, *The Terrorist's Dilemma: Managing Violent Covert Organizations*, New Haven: Princeton University Press, 2015. This specific claim was made to the author in conversation with a journalist embedded with the YPG.
41. UK Home Office official, interviewed by Gilbert Ramsay, 16 Aug. 2018, via Skype.

42. Former senior British Foreign Office official, interviewed by Gilbert Ramsay, 2 Nov. 2017, via Skype.

43. I. Cobain, A. Ross, R. Evans and M. Mahmood, 'Help for Syria: The Aid Campaign Secretly Run by the UK Government' *Guardian*, 3 May 2016, https://www.theguardian.com/world/2016/may/03/help-for-syria-aid-campaign-secretly-run-by-uk-government; see also 'Inside RICU the Shadowy Propaganda Unit Inspired by the Cold War', 2 May 2016, https://www.theguardian.com/politics/2016/may/02/inside-ricu-the-shadowy-propaganda-unit-inspired-by-the-cold-war (accessed 14 Nov. 2018).

44. B. Hayes and A. Qureshi, 'Going Global: The UK Government's CVE Agenda and Covert Propaganda', *OpenDemocracy*, 4 May 2016, https://www.opendemocracy.net/ben-hayes-asim-qureshi/going-global-uk-government-s-propaganda-and-censorship-silicon-valley-and-cve (accessed 14 Nov. 2018).

45. Interview, British Foreign Office official, 2 Nov. 2017, op. cit.

46. See, for example, J. Braude, *Broadcasting Change: Arabic Media as a Catalyst for Liberalism*, New York: Rowman and Littlefield, 2017.

47. These conversations took place in Amman, Jordan, over the summer of 2016.

48. 'Real Housewives of ISIS', from *Revolting* episode 1, BBC 2, originally aired 3 Jan. 2017.

49. 'Real Housewives of ISIS (Parody)', Human Rights Network, 22 Jan. 2017, https://www.youtube.com/watch?v=XPxs9WQ6ZW8 (accessed 15 Nov. 2018).

50. https://rightweb.irc-online.org/profile/waller_michael/

51. Interview, UK Home Office official, 16 Aug. 2018, op cit.

52. Presentation delivered at 'Dialogue for a Better Future: Countering Violent Extremism in Europe and the WANA Region', West Asia and North Africa Institute, Amman, Jordan, 16–17 Nov. 2016.

53. Counterextremism practitioner, interviewed by Gilbert Ramsay 16 Aug. 2018, via Skype.

54. The idea derives from the work of John Arquilla and David Ronfeldt for RAND Corporation, for example, J. Arquilla and D. Ronfeldt, eds., *Networks and Netwars: The Future of Terrorism, Crime and Militancy*, Santa Monica: RAND, 1999.

55. S. Parkin, 'Operation Troll ISIS: Inside Anonymous' War to Take Down ISIS', *Wired*, 6 Oct. 2016, https://www.wired.co.uk/article/anonymous-war-to-undermine-daesh (accessed 21 Nov. 2018).

56. T. Dowling, 'ISIS Karaoke: Satire's Answer to Hate Preachers with Microphones', *Guardian*. https://www.theguardian.com/global/2015/aug/31/isis-karaoke-satires-answer-to-hate-preachers-with-microphones, 31 Aug. 2015 (accessed 21 Nov. 2018).

57. A. Johansson, 'ISIS-Chan: The Meanings of the Manga Girl in Image Warfare Against the Islamic State', *Critical Studies on Terrorism*, vol. 11, no. 1, 2018, pp. 1–25.

58. J. Pieslak, 'A Musicological Perspective on Jihadi *Anashid*' in T. Hegghammer, ed., *Jihadi Culture: The Art and Social Practices of Militant Islamists*, Cambridge: Cambridge University Press, 2017.

59. While the channel In Jihad We Rock has since been shut down, ironically (according to its anonymous owner) for violation of YouTube's community standards, some of its content has since been reposted, see 'Soon, Soon', https://www.youtube.com/watch?v=JzBo-D5UirY, 1 Sept. 2017 (accessed 20 Dec. 2018).

60. Email correspondence between Marko Papic and Fred Burton of STRATFOR, 2 Feb. 2010, published by Wikileaks concerning the Serbian activism training. centre CANVAS, https://search.wikileaks.org/gifiles/?viewemailid=1729054 (accessed 20 Dec. 2018).

61. South Asian comedian, interviewed by Gilbert Ramsay 11 Sept. 2018, via Skype.

62. Priyank Mathur, personal correspondence with Gilbert Ramsay, 26 Nov. 2018.

63. Interview, British Foreign Office official, 2 Nov. 2017, op. cit.

2. LAUGHTER AND SLAUGHTER: USES AND ABUSES OF HUMOUR IN THEORY AND PRACTICE

1. C. Gruner, 'Wit and Humor in Mass Communications' in A. Chapman and H. Foot, ed. *Humour and Laughter: Theory, Research and Applications*, New York: Transaction, 1995.

2. M. Weinberger and C. Sulas, 'The Impact of Humor in Advertising: A Review', *Journal of Advertising*, vol. 21, no. 4, 1992, pp. 35–59.

3. M. Eisend, 'A Meta-Analysis of Humor in Advertising', *Journal of the Academy of Marketing Science*, vol. 37, no. 2, 2009, pp. 191–203.

4. P. Simpson, *On The Discourse of Satire, Towards a Stylistic Model of Satirical Humour*, Amsterdam: John Benjamins, 2003, p. ix.

5. Cicero, *De Oratore II: LXXI*.

6. C. Perelman and L. Olbrechts-Tyteca, *The New Rhetoric: A Treatise on Argumentation*, trans. J. Wilkinson, Notre Dame, IN: University of Notre Dame Press, 1973; also, for a discussion of the place of 'the comic' in this work, see D.A. Frank and M. Bolduc, 'Lucie Olbrechts-Tyteca's New Rhetoric', *Quarterly Journal of Speech*, vol. 96, no. 2, 2010, pp. 141–163.

7. Simpson, 2003, op. cit., p. xvii.

8. Ibid. pp. 8–10.

9. M. Hodgart, *Satire*, London: Weidenfeld and Nicolson, 1959, p. 12.

10. B. Innocenti and E. Miller, 'The Persuasive Force of Political Humor', *Journal of Communication*, vol. 66, 2016, pp. 366–385.

11. R. Lance Holbert, J. Hmielowski and P. Jain, 'Adding Nuance to the Study of Political Humor Effects: Experimental Research on Juvenalian Satire Versus Horatian Satire', *American Behavioral Scientist*, vol. 55, no. 3, 2011, pp. 187–211.

12. S. Alinsky, *Rules for Radicals: A Pragmatic Primer for Realistic Radicals*, New York: Vintage Books, 1989, p. 132

13. Ibid.

14. S. Popovic, *Blueprint for Revolution: How to Use Rice Pudding, Lego Men and Other Non-Violent Techniques to Galvanise Communities, Overthrow Dictators or Simply Change the World*, Melbourne and London: Scribe, 2015, Amazon Kindle edition, location 1166.

15. Ibid., loc. 219.

16. J. Sombatpoonsiri, *Humour and Nonviolent Struggle in Serbia*, New York: Syracuse University Press, 2015, p. 106.

17. Popovic, 2015, op. cit., loc. 1317.

18. E-mail correspondence between Marko Papic and Fred Burton, op. cit.

19. *Blueprint for Revolution*, loc. 159.

20. M. Sørensen, *Humorous Political Stunts: Speaking the Truth to Power*, Sparsnäs, Sweden: Irene Publishing, 2015.

21. Sombatpoonsiri, 2015, op. cit. p. 2.

22. C. Tilly, *From Mobilization to Revolution*, New York: Random House, 1973.

23. Interview, 26 Apr. 2018, via Skype.

24. Sørensen, 2015, op. cit., p. 59.

25. Ibid., p. 55.

26. S. Attardo, *Humorous Texts: A Semantic and Pragmatic Analysis*, Berlin: De Gruyter, 2001, p. 17.

27. V. Raskin, *Semantic Mechanisms of Humour*, New York: Springer, 1984.

28. A. Kozintsev, *The Mirror of Laughter*, trans. R.P. Martin, New Brunswick, NJ: Transaction, 2012, p. 4.

29. Ibid., p. 5.

30. Alinsky, 1989, op. cit., p. 84.

31. D. Wickberg, *The Senses of Humor: Self and Laughter in Modern America*, Ithaca, NY: Cornell University Press, 1998.

32. Ibid., p. 204.

33. See R. Scruton, 'Laughter' in *The Philosophy of Laughter and Humor*, ed. J. Morreal, Albany: State University of New York Press, 1985, p. 181.

34. For a review of the approach see A. Krikmann, 'Linguistic Theories of Humour', *Folklore*, vol. 33, 2014.

35. J. Morreall, *Comedy, Tragedy and Religion*, Albany: State University of New York, 1999.
36. See S. Lockyer and M. Pickering, *Beyond a Joke: the Limits of Humour*, New York: Palgrave Macmillan, 2005.
37. M. Billig, *Laughter and Ridicule: Towards a Social Critique of Humour*, Thousand Oaks: SAGE, 2005.
38. M. Mulkay, *On Laughter: Its Nature and Place in Modern Society*, Cambridge: Polity, 1989.
39. J. Haidt, *The Righteous Mind: Why Good People are Divided by Politics and Religion*, New York: Penguin, 2012.
40. N. Kuiper, S. Kazarian, J. Sineand M. Bassil, 'The Impact of Humor in North American versus Middle Eastern Cultures', *Europe's Journal of Psychology*, vol. 6, no. 3, 2010.
41. R. Martin et al., 'Individual Differences in Uses of Humor and their Relation to Psychological Well-Being: Development of the Humor Styles Questionnaire', *Journal of Research in Personality*, vol. 37, no. 1, 2003, pp. 48–75.
42. X. Yue, F. Jiang, S. Lu & N. Hiranandani, 'To Be or Not To Be Humorous? Cross Cultural Perspectives on Humor', *Frontiers in Psychology*, vol. 7, article 1495, 2016.
43. J. Morreall, 'The Rejection of Humor in Western Thought', *Philosophy East and West*, vol. 39, no. 3, 1989, pp. 243–265.
44. AFP News Agency YouTube Channel, https://www.youtube.com/watch?v=TxNprnas7i8 (accessed 31 Oct. 2018); 'George W. Bush Ducks as Shoes Thrown by Iraqi Journalist', 12 Oct. 2009, http://www.news.com.au/news/dog-bush-ducks-shoe-attack/news-story/644c4c6461431d16738091b25475c9f0
45. Yue, et. al., 2016, op. cit.
46. Al Jazeera interview with Muntadhar al-Zaidi, 30 Sept. 2009, https://www.youtube.com/watch?v=GcvdQvHcFbM (accessed 31 Oct. 2018).
47. M. Bakhtin, *Rabelais and His World*, trans. Hélène Iswolsky, Bloomington, IN: Indiana University Press, 1984, p. 66.
48. Ibid.
49. Ibid., p. 71.
50. Ibid., p. 23.
51. Ibid., p. 90.
52. See, for example, P. Greenhill, *Make the Night Hideous: Four English-Canadian Charivaris, 1881–1940*, Toronto: University of Toronto Press, 2010.
53. R. Darnton, *The Great Cat Massacre and Other Episodes in French Cultural History*, New York: Basic Books, 2009, second edition, Amazon Kindle version, loc. 88.

54. 'Text: The Bin Laden Tape', *BBC News*, 19 Jan. 2006, http://news.bbc.co.uk/1/hi/world/middle_east/4628932.stm (accessed 18 Dec. 2018).

55. A. Ojeda, 'Confessions of a Guantanamo Guard', *Independent*, http://www.independent.co.uk/news/world/americas/confessions-of-a-guantanamo-guard-1624749.html

56. 'Abu Ghraib Inmates Recall Torture', *BBC News*, 1 Dec. 2005, http://news.bbc.co.uk/1/hi/world/americas/4165627.stm

57. S. Critchley, *On Humour*, London: Routledge, 2002, p. 10.

58. D. Grossman, *On Killing: The Psychological Cost of Learning to Kill in War and Society*, revised edition, New York: E-Rights/E-Reads Ltd, 2009, location 1214.

59. Ganser syndrome seems to be 'an unusual hysterical confusional state' in which individuals exhibit symptoms of mental illness for brief periods of time. See F.A. Whitlock, 'The Ganser Syndrome', *The British Journal of Psychiatry*, vol. 113, pp. 19–29.

60. S. Neitzel and H. Welzer, *Soldaten—On Fighting, Killing and Dying: The Secret World War Tapes of German POWs*, London: Simon and Schuster UK, 2013.

61. P. Gourevitsh, *We Wish to Inform You That Tomorrow We Will Be Killed With Our Families*, London: Picador, 2000, p. 202.

62. Kozintsev, 2012, op. cit., p. 50.

63. D. Horowitz, *The Deadly Ethnic Riot*, Oakland: University of California Press, 2001, p. 115.

64. Ibid., p. 114.

65. T. Hobbes, *Leviathan*, edited with and introduction and notes by J.C.A Gaskin, Oxford: Oxford University Press, 2008, p. 52.

66. R.E. Ewin, 'Hobbes on Laughter', *Philosophical Quarterly*, vol. 51, no. 202, 2001, pp. 29–40.

67. A. Rapp, *Origins of Wit and Humor*, New York: EP Dutton & Company, 1951.

68. Ibid., p. 22.

69. As set out in N. Elias, *The Civilizing Process: The History of Manners, and State Formation, and Civilization*, trans. Edmund Jephcott, Oxford: Blackwell, 1994.

70. S. Freud, *The Joke and Its Relation to the Unconscious*, trans. J. Crick, London: Penguin, 2002.

71. F. Fanon, *The Wretched of the Earth*, trans. R. Philcox, New York: Grove Press, 2004, p. 33.

72. P. Berger, *Redeeming Laughter: The Comic Dimension of Human Experience*, second edition, Berlin: De Gruyter, 2014, p. 183.

73. Billig, 2005, op. cit., p. 180.

74. See, for example, M. Davila Ross, J. Owren and E. Zimmerman, 'Reconstructing the Evolution of Laughter in Great Apes and Humans', *Current Biology*, vol. 19, no. 13, 2009, pp. 1106–1111.
75. J. Panskepp, 'Neuroevolutionary Sources of Laughter and Social Joy: Modelling Primal Human Laughter in Laboratory Rats', *Behavioural Brain Research*, vol. 182, no. 2, 2007, pp. 231–244.
76. J. Panskepp, 'Beyond a Joke: From Animal Laughter to Human Joy', *Science*, vol. 308, no. 5718, 2005, pp. 62–63.
77. O. Aldis, *Play Fighting*, Cambridge, MA: Academic Press, 2013.
78. N. N. Holland, 'Tickled Rats and Human Laughter', *Neuropsychanalysis*, vol. 9, no. 1, 2007, pp. 41–57.
79. T. Matsusaka, 'When Does Play Panting Occur during Social Play in Wild Chimpanzees?' *Primates*, vol. 4 (October) no. 5, 2004, pp. 221–229.
80. Aldis, 2013, op. cit.
81. P. Bateson and P. Martin, *Play, Playfulness, Creativity and Innovation*, Cambridge: Cambridge University Press, 2013, p. 26.
82. M. Potegal and D. Einon, 'Aggressive Behaviors in Adult Rats Deprived of Playfighting Experience as Juveniles', *Developmental Psychobiology*, vol. 22, pp. 159–172.
83. Bateson and Martin, 2013, op. cit, p. 14.
84. Kozintsev, 2012, op. cit., p. 107.
85. A. Kozintsev, 'War Propaganda and Humour: World War 2 German, British and Soviet Cartoons', 2015, https://www.academia.edu/7800182/ (accessed 18 Dec. 2018).
86. Hodgart, 1959, op. cit., p. 10.
87. Ibid., pp. 20 ff.
88. J.L. Campbell and F. Collinson, *Hebridean Folksongs Volume 2: Waulking Songs from Barra, South Uist, Eriskay and Benbecula*, Oxford: Clarendon Press, 1977, pp. 113–121.
89. M.V. MacDonald, 'Orally Transmitted Poetry in Pre-Islamic Arabia and Other Pre-Literate Societies', *Journal of Arabic Literature*, vol. 9, 1978, pp. 14–31.
90. A. Al-Awlaqi, 'The Dust Will Never Settle Down', 2008.
91. T. Proulx, S. Heine and K. Vohs, 'When is the Unfamiliar the Uncanny? Meaning Affirmation After Exposure to Absurdist Literature, Humor and Art', *Personality and Social Psychology Bulletin*, vol. 36, no. 6, 2010, pp. 817–829.
92. S. Heine, T. Proulx and K. Vohs, 'The Meaning Maintenance Model: On the Coherence of Social Motivations', *Personality and Social Psychology Review*, vol. 10, no. 2, 2006, pp. 88–110.
93. Bakhtin, 1984, op. cit., chapter 5.

94. C. Morris, *Four Lions*, UK, Film Four, 2010.

95. UK Home Office official, interviewed by Gilbert Ramsay, 16 Aug. 2018, via Skype.

96. R. Jenkins, *Subversive Laughter: The Liberating Power of Comedy*, New York: The Free Press, 1994.

3. 'LET HIM WEAR IT HIMSELF!' HOW ISLAMISTS BECAME LAUGHABLE

1. 'Rare Video of Abdel Nasser: "The Supreme Guide of the Muslim Brotherhood isn't able to get his daughter to wear a headscarf, and he wants me to get ten million people to wear it"', *Al Watan Voice*, 27 Dec. 2011, https://www.alwatanvoice.com/arabic/news/2011/12/27/232261.html (accessed 17 Nov. 2019).

2. Egyptian comedian, interviewed by Gilbert Ramsay, Cairo, 2 May 2018.

3. In the election, the Muslim Brotherhood's Freedom and Justice Party won 47 per cent of the seats in the People's Assembly, while the Salafi Nour Party (Party of Light) won 24 per cent. See https://carnegieendowment.org/2015/01/22/2012-egyptian-parliamentary-elections-pub-58800

4. S. Al-Qaranshawi, 'Actor Adel Imam Sentenced to Imprisonment for Three Months on Charges of "Insulting Religion"', *Al-Masry Al-Youm* [Arabic], 1 Feb. 2012, http://www.almasryalyoum.com/news/details/148570

5. Sky News Arabic, 'Rejection of "Insulting Religion" Charges Against Adel Imam', https://www.skynewsarabia.com/varieties/

6. Sky News Arabic, 'Adel Imam Faces Prison on Charges of "Insulting Religion"', 5 Feb. 2012, https://www.skynewsarabia.com/varieties

7. In fact, Adel Imam's clout within the Egyptian film industry and status as a prominent pro-Mubarak mogul means that the prosecution makes more sense—at least from the point of view of Imam's opponents—than might first appear. Imam is believed to have personally financed the film *The Islamist*, which we discuss below, according to Walter Armbrust, an opinion we also heard during fieldwork in Egypt.

8. It is perhaps notable that Sayyid Qutb, one of the most influential leaders and intellectuals of the Muslim Brotherhood was hanged in 1966 after a lengthy imprisonment—the same year that Nasser delivered the speech quoted above.

9. As, for example, in 1982, when Syrian President Hafez al-Assad used aerial bombardment to end a Muslim Brotherhood-led uprising in the city of Hama, killing as many as 17,000 people. See R. Ziadeh, 'Revolution in Syria: The Struggle for Freedom in a Regional Battle' in

The Arab Spring and the Arab Thaw: Unfinished Revolutions and the Quest for Democracy, second edition, ed. J. Davis, London: Routledge, 2016.

10. The word secularist is a singularly unhelpful term, since very few of the many people in Arabic-speaking countries who support the separation of religion and politics would actually use it, as it is seen as largely pejorative. We use it for want of a better word to refer to this diverse grouping.

11. The questions of what 'Islamism' really is, how best to label its numerous forms, subcategories and allied phenomena, and its relationship to 'modernity' are the subject of a voluminous literature to which we cannot begin to give adequate attention here. An excellent review of various disciplinary perspectives on the subject is to be found in Frederic Volpi's *Political Islam Observed*, London: Hurst, 2010.

12. See, for example, A. Rowell, 'Introduction' in *Vintage Humour: The Islamic Wine Poetry of Abu Nuwas*, trans. A. Rowell, London: Hurst, 2018.

13. S. Stroumsa, *Freethinkers of Medieval Islam*, Leiden: Brill, 2016, p. 16.

14. In several places, *Al-Baqara: 23*, for example, the Quran challenges mankind to 'produce a sura the like thereof'. Muslims have understood this to entail that the Quran is a linguistic miracle, inimitable by human intellect.

15. 'Jihadists Behead Statue of Syrian Poet Abul Ala al-Maari', *Observers*, http://observers.france24.com/en/20130214-jihadists-behead-statue-syrian-poet-abul-ala-al-maari. It is worth noting that, as this source points out, the attack may have been motivated by the jihadis either mistakenly believing the statue to have been of a Shia, or by simply a religious aversion to statues in general rather than to Ma'arri himself, whose works remained untouched in the neighbouring Al-Ma'ara Museum. If the intention was simply to break a statue, however, it is notable that the statue was beheaded, not toppled altogether.

16. A. Rowell, *Vintage Humour: The Islamic Wine Poetry of Abu Nuwas*, pp. lvii–lviii.

17. For example, Egyptian writer Yusuf Idris based his play *Farafir* on the second shadow play in Ibn Daniyal's trilogy, *The Amazing Preacher and the Strange*. See M.M. Badawi, 'The Plays of Yusuf Idris' in *Critical Perspectives on Yusuf Idris*, ed. R. Allen, Washington, D.C.: Three Continents Press, 1992.

18. See, for example, M. Al-Faruque, 'The Mongol Conquest of Baghdad: Medieval Accounts and their Modern Assessments', *Islamic Quarterly*, vol. 32, no. 4, pp. 194–206.

19. S. Mahfouz and M. Carlson, 'Introduction' in *Theater from Medieval Cairo: The Ibn Daniyal Trilogy*, New York: Martin E. Segal Theater Center, 2013.

20. See R. Amitai-Preiss, *Mongols and Mamluks: The Mamluk-Ilkhanid War*, Cambridge: Cambridge University Press, p. 47.

21. L. Guo, 'Paradise Lost: Ibn Daniyal's Response to Baybars' Campaign against Vice in Cairo', *Journal of the American Oriental Society*, vol. 121, no. 2, 2001, pp. 219–235.

22. Ibid.

23. M.M. Badawi, 'Medieval Arabic Drama: Ibn Daniyal', *Journal of Arabic Literature*, Vol. 13, pp. 83–107.

24. L. Guo, 'The Devil's Advocate: Ibn Daniyal's Art of Parody in His Qasidah No. 71', 2003, *Mamluk Studies Review*.

25. Ibid.

26. M. Carlson, 'The Arab Aristophanes', *Comparative Drama*, vol. 47, no. 2, 2013, pp. 151–66.

27. See A.L. Al-Sayyid Marsot, *Egypt in the Reign of Muhammad Ali*, Cambridge: Cambridge University Press, 1984.

28. L. El-Ramly, 'The Comedy of the East, or, The Art of Cunning: A Testimony', trans. Hazem Azmy, *Ecumenica: Journal of Theater and Performance*, vol. 1.2. Autumn, 2008, pp. 75–86.

29. K. Kishtainy, *Arab Political Humour*, London: Quartet Books, 1985, p. 123.

30. See E. Kedourie, *Afghani and Abduh: An Essay on Religious Unbelief and Political Activism in Modern Islam*, London: Cass, 1966.

31. P.C. Sadgrove, *The Egyptian Theatre in the Nineteenth Century*, New York: Ithaca Press, 2007, p. 96.

32. A. Fu'ad, *Censorship: The Expressive Dilemma Between Writer and Producer* [Arabic], Cairo: Arab Press Agency (Nashiroon), 2018, pp. 52–57.

33. R. Sami, 'Art after the 23rd of July, by Direct Command', [Arabic], *Fakartany*, 24 July 2017, http://fakartany.com/a/44142332125343dd8e5b4072f0754baf

34. I. Hamam, 'Disarticulating Arab Popular Culture: The Case of Egyptian Comedies' in *Arab Cultural Studies: Mapping the Field*, ed. T. Sabry, London: IB Tauris, 2012.

35. See D. Boyd, 'Egyptian Radio: Tool of Political and National Development', *Journalism Monographs*, No. 48, Association for Education in Journalism, February 1977, http://files.eric.ed.gov/fulltext/ED137821.pdf

36. See M. Kraidy and J. Khalil, *Arab Television Industries*, London: British Film Institute, 2009, p. 2; N. Sakr, *Satellite Realms: Globalisation, Transnational Television and the Middle East*, London: I.B. Tauris, 2002.

37. R.M. Abdulla, *The Internet in the Arab World: Egypt and Beyond*, Oxford: Peter Lang, 2007.

38. For a detailed mapping of the relationship between private capital and

an Arab state (Saudi Arabia) see A. Hammond, 'Maintaining Saudi Arabia's *Cordon Sanitaire* in the Arab Media' in R. Rasheed, *Kingdom Without Borders: Saudi Arabia's Political, Religious and Media Frontiers*, London: Hurst, 2008; for a more general discussion see Kraidy and Khalil, 2009, op. cit.

39. See A. Nasr, 'An Historical Perspective on Fundamentalist Media: The Case of Al Manar Television', *Global Media Journal*, vol. 6, no. 11, 2007.

40. Both of these scholars have written extensively on this topic. See L. Abu Lughod, *Dramas of Nationhood: The Politics of Television in Egypt*, Chicago: University of Chicago Press, 2004; W. Armbrust, 'Islamically Marked Bodies and Urban Space in Two Egyptian Films' in *Islamism and Cultural Expression in the Arab World*, eds A. Hamdar and L. Moore, London: Routledge, 2015.

41. H. Darwish, 'Egyptian Cinema and Terrorism', [Arabic] in *Terrorism and Cinema: Controversies of the Relationship and Possibilities for Employment*, eds Rima al-Mismar and Ahmad Zu'bi [Arabic], Beirut: Madarek, 2010, pp. 27–105.

42. A. Salem, *The Image of Islamists on the Screen* [Arabic], Beirut: Nama Centre for Research, 2014, p. 185.

43. Fu'ad, 2018, op. cit., p. 65.

44. Salem, 2014, op. cit., p. 189.

45. Ibid., p. 190.

46. Darwish, 2010, op. cit.

47. L. Abu Lughod, 'Movie Stars and Islamic Morality in Egypt', *Social Text*, no. 42, Spring 1995, pp. 53–67.

48. S. Gauch, 'Egypt's Media Target Islam', *Christian Science Monitor*, 2 Sept. 1992, https://www.csmonitor.com/1992/0902/02141.html

49. W. Armbrust, 'Islamists in Egyptian Cinema', *American Anthropologist*, vol. 104, no. 3, 2002, pp. 922–931.

50. V. Shafik, *Popular Egyptian Cinema: Gender, Class and Nation*, Cairo: American University in Cairo Press, 2007.

51. L. Khatib, 'Arab Film and Islamic Fundamentalism' in *Media and Society*, ed. J.L. Curran, London: Bloomsbury, 2010.

52. A. Hammond, *Pop Culture in North Africa and the Middle East*, Santa Barbara, Ca: ABC-Clio, 2017, p. 92.

53. R. Baker, 'Combative Cultural Politics: Film Art and Political Spaces in Egypt', *Alif: Journal of Comparative Poetics*, no. 15, Arab Cinematics: Toward the New and the Alternative, 1995, pp. 6–38.

54. I. Allagui and A. Najjar, 'Framing Political Islam in Popular Egyptian Cinema', *Middle East Journal of Culture and Communication*, vol. 4, no. 2, 2011, pp. 203–224.

55. O. Leaman, ed., *Companion Encyclopedia of Middle Eastern and North African Film*.

56. Salem, 2014, op. cit., pp. 190–213.

57. U. Lindsey, 'The Egyptian Comic Convicted of "Insulting Islam"', *National*, 5 May 2012, https://www.thenational.ae/arts-culture/the-egyptian-comic-convicted-of-insulting-islam-1.361908

58. Hazem Azmy, interviewed by Gilbert Ramsay, Cairo, 1 May 2018.

59. C. Hedges, 'Cairo Journal: Battling the Religious Right: The Celluloid Front', *The New York Times*, 18 Apr. 1994, https://www.nytimes.com/1994/04/18/world/cairo-journal-battling-the-religious-right-the-celluloid-front.html (accessed 29 Dec. 2018).

60. Billig, 2005, op. cit., pp. 175 ff.

61. Armbrust, 2002, op. cit., observes that Ali reads the popular religious work *The Torment of the Grave*, rocking incongruously back and forth in the same style as a student learning to recite Quran at a traditional Islamic school.

62. 'Imam and Gindy [another Egyptian star] played supposedly attractive thirty-somethings well into the 1990s, when they were in fact sixty-somethings, but pulled it off with a degree of success.' A. Hammond, *Popular Culture in the Arab World*, Cairo: American University of Cairo Press, 2007, p. 124.

63. In English, the progress from the medieval idea of the physical humour to the psychological notion of a sense of humour began with the Jacobean comic device of 'every man out of his humour'[0]. See Wickberg, 2015, op. cit.

64. A.A. Berger, *An Anatomy of Humor*, New Brunswick, NJ: Transaction Publishers, 1993, p. 10.

65. Armbrust, 2002, op. cit.

66. N. Galal, *Hello America*, Cairo, Al-Nasr Films, 2000.

67. A. Arafa, *The Embassy in the Building*, Cairo, Essam-Imam Productions, 2005.

68. M. Yassine, *The Gazelle's Blood*, Cairo, El Arabia, 2005.

69. M. Hamed, *The Yacoubian Building*, Cairo, Good News, 2006.

70. Salem, 2014, op. cit., p. 195.

71. A. Idris, *Al Thalatha Yashtaghalonaha [Three Men Deceive Her]*, Cairo, Arabica Movies, 2010.

72. L. Wedeen, *Ambiguities of Domination: Politics, Rhetoric and Symbols in Contemporary Syria*, Chicago: University of Chicago Press, 2015, p. 89.

73. S. Haugbolle, 'That Joke Isn't Funny Anymore: Bass Mat Watan's Nasrallah Skit and the Limits of Laughter in Lebanon', *Arab Culture and Society*, 1 Oct. 2008, https://www.arabmediasociety.com/that-joke-isnt-funny-anymore-bass-mat-watans-nasrallah-skit-and-the-limits-of-laughter-in-lebanon/ (accessed 12 Nov. 2019).

74. J. Tarabay, 'Popular Iraqi TV Comedian Killed; Ministers Attacked',

National Public Radio, 20 Nov. 2006, https://www.npr.org/templates/story/story.php?storyId=6515072

75. For a detailed account of the events of the siege, see Y. Trofimov, *The Siege of Mecca: The Forgotten Uprising in Islam's Holiest Shrine*, London: Penguin, 2008.

76. S. Lacroix, *Awakening Islam: Religious Dissent in Contemporary Saudi Arabia*, Cambridge, MA: Harvard University Press, 2011.

77. For an account of this bombing campaign, see T. Hegghammer, *Jihad in Saudi Arabia: Violence and Pan-Islamism since 1979*, Cambridge: Cambridge University Press, 2010.

78. See ibid.

79. See J. Braude, *Broadcasting Change: Arabic Media as a Catalyst for Liberalism*, Lanham: Rowman and Littlefield, 2017.

80. U. Lindsey, 'TV Versus Terrorism: Why This Year's Ramadan Shows Tackled One "Controversial" Subject, But Were Barred From Broaching Others', *Arab Media and Society*, 1 Sept. 2005, https://www.arabmediasociety.com/tv-versus-terrorism-why-this-years-ramadan-shows-tackled-one-controversial-subject-but-were-barred-from-broaching-others/

81. Braude, 2017, op. cit., p. 95.

4. LAUGHING TO THE BACK TEETH: HUMOUR AND ISLAMIC FUNDAMENTALISM

1. 'Adel Imam: How Khaled al-Jundi Says I am Bit of an Actor!', *Masress*, 2009, https://www.masress.com/alshaab/21403 (accessed 19 Sept. 2018).

2. 'Sheikh Wajdi Ghonaim and Adel Imam', 2017, https://www.youtube.com/watch?v=gfCJ1Bx1Xi8 (accessed 19 Sept. 2018).

3. The statement of the General Presidency of Scholarly Research and Ifta regarding the prohibition of series that are opposed to the holy Sharia including (Tash Ma Tash), 'Said al-Faua'id', 2000, http://www.saaid.net/fatwa/f9.htm (accessed 19 Sept. 2018).

4. 'The ruling of the Mufti of the Kingdom on Tash Ma Tash', 2011, https://www.youtube.com/watch?v=eiOSpLXL7d4 (accessed 19 Sept. 2018).

5. 'What Sheikh Muhammad al-Arefe Said on Series Tash Ma Tash', 2011, https://www.youtube.com/watch?v=7KoWnfVuDKc (accessed 19 Sept. 2018).

6. 'Excommunicating Nasser al-Qassabi by Sa'id bin Farwa', 2015, https://www.youtube.com/watch?v=WGqHwAiXKQ4 (accessed 19 Sept. 2018).

7. *Tafsir (explication) of Ibn-Katheer*, Volume 7 [Arabic], Giza: Qurtuba Institution, 2000, pp. 226–229. The traditional commentary on this

verse is that it concerns a remark by one of Muhammad's companions—the *Sahaba* (companion) who, after the Battle of Tabuk, made some disparaging comments concerning the personal moral conduct of reciters of the Quran. When this was reported to the prophet, the accused tried the 'only conversing and playing' defence, and it is to this that the divine revelation refers.

8. Morreall, 1999, op. cit., p. 147.
9. Berger, 2014, op. cit., chapter 3.
10. M. Screech, *Laughter at the Foot of the Cross*, Chicago: University of Chicago Press, 1997, p. 72.
11. Berger, 2014, op. cit.
12. Jalal al-Din Rumi, 'A Children's Game', in *Rumi: Selected Poems*, trans. C. Barks, London: Penguin Classics, 2004.
13. Cited in J. Smith, 'Karagöz and Hacivat: Projections of Subversion and Conformance', *Asian Theatre Journal*, vol. 21, no. 2, 2004, pp. 187–193.
14. J. Schielke, *The Perils of Joy: Contesting Mulid Festivals in Contemporary Egypt*, New York: Syracuse University Press, 2012.
15. M. Marty and R. Scott Appleby, 'The Fundamentalism Project: A User's Guide' in *Fundamentalisms Observed*, eds M. Marty and R. Scott Appleby, Chicago: University of Chicago Press, 1991, p. viii.
16. W. Davies, 'Fundamentalism in Japan: Religious and Political' in *Fundamentalisms Observed*, 1991, p. 784.
17. E. Gellner, 'Soviet Marxism and Islamic Fundamentalism' in *Fundamentalisms Comprehended*, eds M. Marty and R. Scott Appleby, Chicago: University of Chicago Press, 1995, p. 280.
18. See L. Hudson, 'Reading al-Sha'rani: The Sufi Genealogy of Islamic Modernism in Late Ottoman Damascus', *Journal of Islamic Studies*, vol. 15, no. 1, 2004, pp. 39–68.
19. M. Cook, *Commanding Right and Forbidding Wrong in Islamic Thought*, Cambridge: Cambridge University Press, 2000.
20. Another distinction that should be noted is the one Olivier Roy draws between political Islamists and those he calls 'neofundamentalists'. Since neofundamentalists' aim is not to capture the machinery of the state but rather 'to re-Islamize society on the grassroots level', the term often applies to groups that are described as Salafi, although it also encompasses others who do not share precisely the same theological premises as Salafists. See O. Roy, *The Failure of Political Islam*, trans. C. Volk, Cambridge, MA: Harvard University Press, 1996.
21. B. Haykel, 'On the Nature of Salafi Thought and Action' in *Global Salafism: Islam's New Religious Movement*, ed. R. Meijer, London: Hurst, 2009, p. 33.
22. Schielke, 2012, op. cit. p. 90.

23. G. Kepel, *Muslim Extremism in Egypt: The Prophet and the Pharaoh*, trans. J. Rothschild, London: Al-Saqi, 1985, p. 174.

24. For an overview see essays in B. Graaf and J. Skovgaard-Petersen, eds, *Global Mufti: The Phenomenon of Yusuf Al-Qaradawi*, London: Hurst, 2008.

25. M. Mir, 'Humor in the Quran', *The Muslim World*, vol. 81, no. 304, 1991, pp. 173–179.

26. G. Tamer, 'The Qur'ān and Humor' in *Humor in der Arabischen Kultur*, ed. G. Tamer, Berlin: De Gruyter, 2009.

27. Quran, *Al-Qisas*: 76.

28. *Sunan Abi Dawud* [Arabic], Volume 7, Hadith Number 5098, Damascus: Al-Risala Al-'Alamia, 2009, p. 427.

29. Wit and Comic Anecdotes in Arabic Literature, *Alnassabon*, no date, http://www.alnssabon.com/t52673.html (accessed 19 Sept. 2018).

30. Ibn al-Jawzī, *Virtues of the Commander of the Faithful Umar ibn Al-Khattāb* [Arabic], Beirut: Dar al-Kotob al-Ilmiyah, 1978, p. 187.

31. According to *Al-Mu'jam al-Wasit*, the word means 'molar: the most distant of the molars in the last part of the palate'. Delightfully, it illustrates this meaning with the usage example 'and the prophet, upon whom be prayer and peace, laughed until his *nawajidh* were visible', https://www.almaany.com/ar/dict/ar-ar/%D9%86%D9%88%D8%A7%D8%AC%D8%B0/ (accessed 19 Dec. 2018).

32. Al-Hafiz Ibn Adul Bir, *Biography of Companions*, Al-Isti'ab fi ma'rifat al-ashab [Arabic], Beirut: Dar al-Jeel, 1992, pp. 1529. For an example of how this story is used in contemporary context, see also 'The Joking of The Messenger of God May Peace Be Upon Him by Sheikh Muhammad al-Arefe', 2011, https://www.youtube.com/watch?v=IGBk3xfbTqw (accessed 19 Sept. 2018).

33. Ibid., p. 1528.

34. *Musnad Ishāq ibn Rāhwayh* [Arabic], volume 4, Medina: Dar al-Ayman, 1995, pp. 97–98. Al-Hafiz Ibn Adul Bir, *Biography of Companions*, Al-Isti'ab fi ma'rifat al-ashab [Arabic], Beirut: Dar al-Jeel, 1992, pp. 1526–1527. M. Zahid, 'The Prankster Sahaba—Wait, Whaaaaat?', *Musings of a Musafir*, 2014, https://musingsofamusafir.wordpress.com/2014/06/15/the-prankster-sahaba-wait-whaaaaat/ (accessed 19 Sept. 2018).

35. Al-Hafiz Ibn Adul Bir, *Biography of Companions*, Al-Isti'ab fi ma'rifat al-ashab [Arabic], Beirut: Dar al-Jeel, 1992, pp. 1528–1529.

36. Z. Maghen, 'The Merry Men of Medina: Comedy and Humanity in the Early Days of Islam', *Der Islam*, vol. 83, no. 2, 2008.

37. Fahed Bin Nasser al-Sulayman, ed., *Compilation of Fatwas and Letters of Sheikh Muhammad bin Salih al-'Uthaymeen*, volume 2, Riyadh: Dar al-Watan, 1986, p. 157.

38. *Quran* 49:11, *Quran.com*, no date, https://quran.com/49/11?translations= 20,22 (accessed 19 Sept. 2018).

39. *Al-Adab Al-Mufrad: Book of Dealings with People and Good Character, sunnah.com*, no date, https://sunnah.com/urn/2202650 (accessed 19 Sept. 2018).

40. *Bulugh al-Maram*, Book 16, Hadith 1559, available online from *Sunnah. com*, no date, https://sunnah.com/urn/2118300 (accessed 19 Sept. 2018).

41. Al-Arefe, 2011, op. cit.

42. Ibid.

43. 'Lying is Essence of Joking', https://www.youtube.com/watch?v= htHwUFoEjNI (accessed 19 Sept. 2018).

44. 'Ruling on Lying with the Intention of Laughter and Joking', *The Official Website of Imam Ibn Baz*, no date, http://www.binbaz.org.sa/ noor/794 (accessed 19 Sept. 2018).

45. Al-Maktaba al-Shamila, no date, http://shamela.ws/browse.php/book-10786/page-63475 (accessed 19 Sept. 2018). 'Sayings of Scholars on the Ruling of False Jokes and Anecdotes', *The Official Forum of Sheikh Muhammad al-Arefe*, 2011, http://www.3refe.com/vb/showthread. php?t=164887 (accessed 19 Sept. 2018).

46. Ibid.

47. Ibid.

48. *Warning of Sheikh Ibn al-'Uthaymeen on April Fool's Day*, 2012, https:// www.youtube.com/watch?v=OXSa8-BNflI (accessed 19 Sept. 2018).

49. In Islamic theology, the Unseen (*al-ghayb*) refers to those parts of the universe (such as Heaven, Hell and fate) that are viewed as inherently unknowable to human intellect. Intellectual interrogation of what these things may contain is traditionally considered sinful by many scholars (though, of course, scholars differ on the limits on what can be legitimately questioned). *Ruling on Lying When Joking and Speculation in the Unseen*, 2016, https://www.youtube.com/watch?v=AocXPtCLeZY (accessed 19 Sept. 2018). The Unseen is an Islamic term that refers to the realm of things that only God can know. 'Speculation in the Unseen' is a specific term for a sin in Islam. 'Light on the Path of Sheikh Muḥammad bin Ṣālih al-'Uthaymīn,' ahl-al-ḥadith wa al-athār, 2005, http://alathar.net/home/esound/index.php?op=tadevi&id=3791 (accessed 19 Sept. 2018).

50. Ibid.

51. 'The Companions' Stories, Episode 21, The Companion Nu'ayman Bin Amr', 2014, https://www.youtube.com/watch?v=B1pD0VyA2dc&in dex=4&list=WL (accessed 19 Sept. 2018).

52. Ibid.

53. Al-Qarni, 2012, op. cit.
54. Al-Arefe, 2011, op. cit.
55. Egyptian scholar Omar Abdelkafy, for example, compares Nu'ayman's pranks approvingly to the 'hidden camera' genre of modern television comedy. See 'A Story of Nu'ayman and an Amusing Prank he Played on Abu Bakr's Cook', 2017, https://www.youtube.com/watch?v=p4EJ YNZzCZI (accessed 19 Sept. 2018).
56. Qaradawi uses the word *komedi*—a direct loan from European languages, which is striking in a work of Islamic theology.
57. Y. al-Qaradawi, *The Fiqh of Entertainment and Leisure*, Cairo: Maktabat Wahba, 2006.
58. Ibid.
59. Ibid.
60. Ibid.
61. Ibid.
62. U. Marzolph, 'The Muslim Sense of Humour' in *Humour and Religion: Challenges and Ambiguities*, eds H. Geybels and W. Van Herck, London: Bloomsbury, 2012. See also Ibn al-Jawzī, 'Abd al-Rahman, Abu 'l Farash, ed. A. Muhannan, *Reports of Fools and Idiots* [Arabic], Beirut: Dar al-Fikr wal-Bayyanat, 1990, available online from http://www. islamicbook.ws/adab/akhbar-alhmqa-walmgflin.pdf (accessed 19 Dec. 2018); Ibn al-Jawzī, 'Abd al-Rahman, Abu 'l Farash, ed. B.A. Al-Jabi, *Reports of Wits and Wags* [Arabic], Limassol, Cyprus: Al-Jaffan & Al-Jabdi, 1983, available online from https://www.almeshkat.net/books/ archive/books/Dhiraaf.pdf (accessed 19 Dec. 2018).
63. Attardo, 2010, op. cit.
64. B. Lewis, *Hammer and Tickle: A History of Communism Told Through Communist Jokes*, London: W&N, 2009.
65. C. Davies, *Ethnic Humour Around the World: A Comparative Analysis*, Bloomington: University of Indiana Press, 1980, p. 141.
66. Hierocles, translated and edited by B. Baldwin, *The Philogelos, or Laughter Lover*: London Studies in Classical Philology, Amsterdam: JC Gieben, 1984.
67. For a critical discussion of this claim within humour studies, see M. Dynel, 'There is Method in the Humorous Speaker's Madness: Humour and Grice's Model', *Lodz Papers in Pragmatics*, vol. 4, no. 1, 2008.
68. al-Jawzī, 'akhbār al-ḥumaqā wa al-mughāfilīn' (*Accounts of Fools and Idiots*), http://www.islamicbook.ws/adab/akhbar-alhmqa-walmgflin. pdf.
69. Marzolph, 2010, op. cit.
70. Aristotle, *Poetics*, section 1: part five, available on: http://classics.mit. edu/Aristotle/poetics.1.1.html (accessed 27 Dec. 2018).

71. al-Jawzī, op. cit., 1983, p. 42.
72. Ibid.
73. See S. Kazarian, 'Humor in the Collectivist Arab Middle East: The Case of Lebanon', *Humor: International Journal of Humor Research*, vol. 24, no. 3, 2011.
74. A. Darwish, 'Obituary: Sheikh Mohamed Mutwali Sharawi', *Independent*, 19 June 1998, https://www.independent.co.uk/arts-entertainment/obituary-sheikh-mohamed-mutwali-sharawi-1165880.html (accessed 19 Dec. 2018).
75. Humorous Anecdotes of Sheikh Ibn al-'Uthaymeen, *Arab Forum for Human Resources Management*, 2010, https://hrdiscussion.com/hr13499.html (accessed 19 Sept. 2018).
76. Some humorous anecdotes of Imams Ibn al-'Uthaymeen, al-Albani, and al-Wadi'i, *Ahl al-Hadith*, 2005, https://www.ahlalhdeeth.com/vb/showthread.php?t=34962 (accessed 29 Sept. 2018). See also *The story of Sheikh Ibn al-'Uthaymeen with a taxi driver—Abu Abdullah*, 2016, https://www.youtube.com/watch?v=r5iHt1JELaM (accessed 29 Sept. 2018).
77. Wafa' al-Shami, 'The Humorous Anecdotes of Al-Sha'rawi's [encounter] with al-Sadat and the Shoes are Unforgettable', *Elbalad*, 2015, https://www.elbalad.news/1611098 (accessed 29 Sept. 2018).
78. 'Some Humorous Anecdotes of Imams Ibn al-'Uthaymeen, al-Albani, and al-Wadi'I', *Ahl al-Hadith*, 2005, op. cit.
79. 'I am a married man but I want to marry for a second time with the intention of saving a girl from wrongdoing', al-Ajurry, 2012, https://www.ajurry.com/vb/showthread.php?t=29054 (accessed 29 Sept. 2018).
80. 'Some Humorous Anecdotes of Imams Ibn al-'Uthaymeen, al-Albani, and al-Wadi'I', *Ahl al-Hadith*, 2005, op. cit.
81. Ibid.
82. Ibid.
83. Hussein Saleem Asad (verification), Musnad Abu Ya'la al-Musali, Vol. 7, Hadith Number 4476, 1st edition, Damascus: Dar al-Ma'mun lil-Turath, 1986, pp. 449–50, http://library.islamweb.net/hadith/display_hbook.php?bk_no=327&hid=4412&pid=155509 (accessed 19 Sept. 2018).
84. Al-Arefe, 2011, op. cit.
85. 'Al-Jubaylan and the Egyptian belly dancer', 2014, https://www.youtube.com/watch?v=MXOQlg9vkUQ (accessed 29 Sept. 2018).
86. 'A funny clip of Sheikh al-Arefe on the Bengali and paradise', 2010, https://www.youtube.com/watch?v=DOWu8cmlKCU (accessed 29 Sept. 2018).

87. Davies, 1987, op. cit.

88. 'The Imam and virgins in the paradise, very funny', Sheikh Abdulkafy, 2014, https://www.youtube.com/watch?v=7kCzGg2Fwyw (accessed 29 Sept. 2018).

89. A. Qourshah, 'EhsebhaSah' [YouTube Channel] Kharabeesh, 2011, https://www.youtube.com/channel/UCtJd1bzs3Y86MB4Ru2ioY3g (accessed 20 Dec. 2018).

90. Interview with Hazem Azmi, 1 May 2018, op. cit.

91. Y. Hussein, 'JoeTube' [YouTube Channel], no date, https://www.youtube.com/user/JoeTubeVid/featured (accessed 23 Aug. 2018; at the time of writing (20 Dec. 2018), it appears that Hussein has removed from his channel many of his earliest—and most religiously conservative—videos). The first episode can still be found on other accounts, for example https://www.youtube.com/watch?v=SqwPm2CcNl4 uploaded 12 Nov. 2013 (accessed 20 Dec. 2018).

92. *Rami Mohamed | sawf nabqa hona*, 2014, https://www.youtube.com/watch?v=E5Q1lD_rw3s (accessed 22 Sept. 2018).

93. 'Ḥawādīt Abū Jahl' (Tales of Abu Jahl), posted to forum discussion on c4arab.com, http://www.ce4arab.com/vb7/showthread.php?p=814 669 (accessed 20 Dec. 2018).

5. TERRORISM AT THE GATES: ARAB COMEDY AND THE ISLAMIC STATE

1. See D. Byman, 'After the Hope of the Arab Spring, the Chill of an Arab Winter', op. ed. Brookings, 4 Dec. 2011, https://www.brookings.edu/opinions/after-the-hope-of-the-arab-spring-the-chill-of-an-arab-winter/ (accessed 3 Oct. 2018).

2. The text of the letter itself can be accessed on the West Point military college website: https://ctc.usma.edu/harmony-program/zawahiris-letter-to-zarqawi-original-language-2/ (accessed 4 Oct. 2018).

3. Literally, The Islamic State of Iraq and al-Sham—Sham can mean greater Syria or the Levant—hence the alternative English acronym: ISIL.

4. 'ISIS Abu Bakr al-Baghdadi First Friday Sermon as So-Called "Caliph",' https://english.alarabiya.net/en/webtv/reports/2014/07/07/ISIS-Abu-Bakr-al-Baghdidi-first-Friday-sermon-as-so-called-Caliph-.html (accessed 4 Oct. 2018).

5. 'In video: sectarianism of garbage!' [Arabic], https://www.lebanese-forces.com/2016/03/04/waste-problem-61/ (accessed 4 Oct. 2018).

6. *Bas Mat Watan* Episode 21, "100 Khalifa'", 2015, https://www.youtube.com/watch?v=9PngGfkr2J8 (accessed 20 Sept. 2018).

7. The allegation that groups such as IS practiced 'sex jihad' (*jihad al-nikah*),

meaning the supposedly religiously justified trafficking and prostitu-tion of women in order to improve fighters' morale is controversial even among some of the group's ideological opponents (see below). See also A. Grami, 'Narrating Jihad al-Nikah in Post-Revolution Tunisia', b2o: The Online Community of the Boundary 2 Editorial Collective, 5 July 2018, https://www.boundary2.org/2018/07/amel-grami-narrating-jihad-al-nikah-in-post-revolution-tunisia-english/ (accessed 5 Oct. 2018).

8. 'Irbit Tinhal, Uncle Daesh', 2014, https://www.youtube.com/watch?v=2AxAIdT5ZDA&t=25s (accessed 20 Sept. 2018).

9. 'Irbit Tinhal, Daesh and 14 March', 2014, https://www.youtube.com/watch?v=yGCqWaBZpnM (accessed 20 Sept. 2018).

10. M. Sinkiewitz, 'Out of Control: Palestinian News Satire and Government Power in the Age of Social Media', *Popular Communication: The International Journal of Media and Culture*, vol. 10, nos 1–2, 2012, pp. 106–118.

11. M. Abbas, 'Has Al-Qaeda Found Zarqawi's Successor?', Al-Monitor, 15 Jan. 2014, https://www.al-monitor.com/pulse/originals/2014/01/iraq-isis-shaker-wahib-zarqawi.html (accessed 5 Oct. 2018).

12. '*Watan ala Watar* 2014, Daesh', 2014, https://www.youtube.com/watch?v=D-GtD3Ahv9I&t=3s (accessed 20 Sept. 2018).

13. F. Van Tets, 'Syrian Drama Industry Battles on Despite War', *Independent*, 27 July 2014, https://www.independent.co.uk/arts-enter-tainment/tv/news/syrian-drama-industry-battles-on-despite-war-9630865.html (accessed 5 Oct. 2018).

14. '*Spotlight* Season 10, "The Road of Safety"', 2014, https://www.you-tube.com/watch?v=KgN2-TAMDu0&t=679s (accessed 20 Sept. 2018).

15. '*Spotlight* Season 11, "Secret Hideouts"', 2016, https://www.youtube.com/watch?v=qqr4Pq1jiTc&t=131s (accessed 20 Sept. 2018).

16. '*Spotlight* Season 10, "Initiative"', 2014, https://www.youtube.com/watch?v=iCXOJRVQ5uc&t=6s (accessed 20 Sept. 2018).

17. '*Spotlight* Season 10, "Photograph"', 2014, https://www.youtube.com/watch?v=_NMMBvQSRG0 (accessed 20 Sept. 2018).

18. '*Spotlight* Season 12, "Religion Detector"', 2017, https://www.you-tube.com/watch?v=muqqJs1H5Ow (accessed 20 Sept. 2018).

19. '*Selfie*, "The Devil's Egg—Part 1"', 2015, https://www.youtube.com/watch?v=a9PeWPYBsyU&t=1147s (accessed 20 Sept. 2018). '*Selfie*, "The Devil's Egg—Part 2"', 2015, https://www.youtube.com/watch?v=V3NtuRqjCmM&t=12s (accessed 20 Sept. 2018).

20. '*Shabab al-Bomb 5*, "Preachers of Satan part 1"', 2016, https://www.youtube.com/watch?v=ENcEVZMAGMc (accessed 20 Sept. 2018); '*Shabab al-Bomb 5*, "Preachers of Satan part 2"', 2016, https://www.youtube.com/watch?v=UgO-AQ-UnPQ (accessed 20 Sept. 2018).

21. Interview with Egyptian comedian, 2 May 2018, op. cit.
22. Interview with Hazem Azmi, 1 May 2018, op. cit.
23. Interview with Egyptian comedian, 2 May 2018, op. cit.
24. A. Hashad, *Da'dush*, Elgozour Cinema Production, Cairo, 2017.
25. A. Al-Badry, *Al-Armouty Fe Ard El Nar [Al-Armouty in The Land of Fire]*, Giza, El Sobky Film Production, 2017.
26. S. Mandawir, *Ma'lish ihna bnatbahadal*, Egypt, Arabia Cinema, 2005.
27. https://www.youtube.com/watch?v=TYlfbXoA_aY (accessed 5 Oct. 2018).
28. https://www.youtube.com/watch?v=8CeRBwuDt88 (accessed 5 Oct. 2018).
29. Mustafa Bakri demands the cancellation of 'Ramez' and 'Mini Daesh', Al-Araby, 12 July 2016, https://www.alaraby.co.uk/miscellaneous/2016/6/12/ (accessed 18 Aug. 2018).
30. S. al-Saeed, 'Mini Daesh: Prank Show Depicting ISIS Hostage Situation and New Low for Egyptian Television', *Egyptian Streets*, 14 June 2018, https://egyptianstreets.com/2016/06/14/mini-daesh-prank-show-depicting-isis-hostage-situation-a-new-low-for-egyptian-television/ (accessed 5 Oct. 2018).
31. L. Morris & L. Sly, 'Insurgents in Northern Iraq Seize Key Cities, Advance Toward Baghdad', *The Washington Post*, 12 June 2014, https://www.washingtonpost.com/world/middle_east/insurgents-in-northern-iraq-push-toward-major-oil-installations/2014/06/11/3983dd22-f162–11e3–914c-1fbd0614e2d4_story.html?utm_term=.da4da972466f
32. Muhammad Tha'er Jayyad, interviewed by Gilbert Ramsay, 9 Sept. 2016, via Skype.
33. J. McLaughlin, 'The Case for Making Fun of ISIS', *Mother Jones*, 6 Mar. 2015 https://www.motherjones.com/politics/2015/03/snl-dakota-johnson-isis-middle-east-satirical-cartoons/ (accessed 5 Oct. 2018); 'Iraq's "State of Myths" TV Satire Takes Aim at ISIS Extremists', NBC News, https://www.nbcnews.com/storyline/isis-terror/iraqs-state-myths-tv-satire-takes-aim-isis-extremists-n240636 (accessed 5 Oct. 2018).
34. 'Mythical State': Television series on Iraqiyya satirises the thinking of the "Islamic State Organisation", https://www.france24.com/ar/2014 تنظيم-الدولة-الإسلامية-الخرافة-مسلسل-العراقية-علي-القاسم-0928
35. Interview with Tha'er Jayyad, 9 Sept. 2016, op. cit.
36. See M. Kraidy, 'Fun Against Fear in the Caliphate: Islamic State's Spectacle and Counter-Spectacle', *Critical Studies in Media Communication*, vol. 35, no. 1, pp. 40–56.
37. Interview with Tha'er Jayyad, 9 Sept. 2016, op. cit.
38. T. Cavanaugh, 'Iraq State TV's Anti ISIS Comedy is the Plan 9 from

Outer Space of Political Satire', *National Review*, 29 Sept. 2014, https://www.nationalreview.com/corner/iraq-state-tvs-anti-isis-comedy-plan-9-outer-space-political-satire-tim-cavanaugh/ (accessed 9 Oct. 2018).

39. See N. Bajekal, 'With Hearts, Mind and Humor: Combating ISIS by Making Fun of It', *Time*, 1 Oct. 2015, http://time.com/4056234/hearts-mind-and-humor-combating-isis-by-making-fun-of-it/

40. Interview with Tha'er Jayyad, 9 Sept. 2016, op. cit.

41. A.Qassem, *Dawlat al-Khurafa*, Iraq, Al Iraqiyya, 2014, episode 9 'The Daesh Olympics', https://www.youtube.com/watch?v=yogSXd6AHlU&t=1203s (accessed 9 Oct. 2018).

42. Interview with Tha'er Jayyad, 9 Sept. 2016, op. cit.

43. 'Dawlat al-Khurafa episode 20, "The Daeshi *Aku Fad*"', https://www.youtube.com/watch?v=ATLmCTVWfEo (accessed 9 Oct. 2018).

44. Interview with Tha'er Jayyad, 9 Sept. 2016, op. cit.

45. Ibid.

46. S.D. Leavitt and S.J. Dubner, *Freakonomics: A Rogue Economist Explores the Hidden Side of Everything*, New York: Penguin, 2005, p. 49.

47. S. Dubner, S. Levitt, 'Hoodwinked', *New York Times Magazine*, 8 Jan. 2006, https://www.nytimes.com/2006/01/08/magazine/hoodwinked.html

48. Interview with Tha'er Jayyad, 9 Sept. 2016, op. cit.

49. '*Dawlat al-Khurafa* "The Final Episode"', https://www.youtube.com/watch?v=FvVxqMA8oFY (accessed 9 Oct. 2018).

50. M. Kraidy and J. Khalil, *Arab Television Industries*, London: British Film Institute, 2009, pp. 47–49.

51. M. Simon, *The Axis of Evil Comedy Tour*, USA: PIAS Comedy, 2009.

52. G. Ramsay and S. Fatani, 'The New Saudi Nationalism of the New Saudi Media' in N. Mellor, ed., *Political Islam and Global Media*, London: Routledge, 2016.

53. Ibid.

54. Ibid.

55. According to Bassem Yousef's memoir (*Revolution for Dummies: Laughing Through the Arab Spring*, New York: HarperCollins, 2017, p. 55), when he set up his own prime-time TV show *Al-Bernameg* (The Programme), he 'wanted a simpler version of Jon Stewart's *The Daily Show*'.

56. Bajekal, 1 Oct. 2015, op. cit.

57. Maan Watfe and Yousef Hillali, interviewed by Gilbert Ramsay and Moutaz Alkheder, 12 June 2017, via Skype.

58. Ibid.

59. Ibid.

60. Ibid.

61. Ibid.
62. Ibid.
63. Ibid.
64. Ibid.
65. Ibid.
66. 'ISIS Series', 2015, https://www.youtube.com/watch?v=Ih_V45B 5uEo&t=28s&list=PLb_KzPFWvNb-uD4PIneuL2fcu1Pu_ AUX0&index=6 (accessed 20 Sept. 2018).
67. 'ISIS Series, Episode 01, The War', 2015, https://www.youtube.com/watch?v=rhG342VUlUw (accessed 20 Sept. 2018).
68. 'ISIS, Episode 05, Datrix', 2015, https://www.youtube.com/watch?v=f6URquOrl4Q (accessed 20 Sept. 2018).
69. 'ISIS Series, Episode 06, The Worrior', 2015, https://www.youtube.com/watch?v=BJXm7kyRAS0 (accessed 20 Sept. 2018).
70. 'ISIS Mario,' 2015, https://www.youtube.com/watch?v=Ih_V45B 5uEo (accessed 20 Sept. 2018). 'ISIS Mario 2', 2015, https://www.youtube.com/watch?v=K4Heno7MD1g (accessed 20 Sept. 2018).
71. 'We Are All Julani', Dayaaltaseh, 2016, https://www.youtube.com/watch?v=CuHYFvrCBv8 (accessed 20 Sept. 2018).
72. Joshua Walker, response to a question asked at the talk: 'Fighting ISIS and Building a New Middle East', talk given to the University of St. Andrews Socialist Society, 7 Mar. 2018.
73. M. Thomson, 'A Sarcastic Response to Syria's Militants', *BBC*, https://www.bbc.co.uk/news/magazine-38912958
74. For a development of this general point see F. Devji, *Landscapes of Jihad: Militancy, Morality, Modernity*, London: Hurst, 2005.
75. The work of Hassan Sabaileh, discussed below, is not exhaustive of Jordanian theatre relating to this subject. Another example would be the play *Kharbana* by comedian Hussein Tabishat. A clip of this can be seen here: https://www.youtube.com/watch?v=hJY3vM9r2nk (accessed 9 Oct. 2018).
76. 'UNHCR Jordan Factsheet—February 2018', UNHCR, 22 Feb. 2018, https://reliefweb.int/report/jordan/unhcr-jordan-factsheet-february-2018 (accessed 10 Oct. 2018).
77. Ramsay's personal observation, visit to Zaatari camp in January 2014.
78. See J. Wagemakers, *Salafism in Jordan: Political Islam in a Quietist Community*, Cambridge: Cambridge University Press, 2016; M. Abu Rumman, *I Am a Salafi: A Study of the Actual and Imagined Identities of Salafis*, Amman: Friedrich-Ebert-Stiftung, 2014.
79. J. Wagemakers, *A Quietist Jihadi: The Ideology and Influence of Abu Muhammad Al-Maqdisi*, Cambridge: Cambridge University Press, 2012.
80. For an account of Zarqawi's early life and background, see J. Brisard, *Al-Zarqawi: The New Face of Al-Qaeda*, Cambridge: Polity Press, 2005.

81. K. Sowell, 'Jordanian Salafism and the Jihad in Syria', *Current Trends in Islamist Ideology*, vol. 18, May, 2015, pp. 41–71.
82. 'Jordanian Authorities Arrest Controversial Islamic Preacher Amjad Qourshah', 14 June 2016, https://www.albawaba.com/news/jordanian-authorities-arrest-controversial-islamic-preacher-amjad-qourshah-851872 (accessed 10 Oct. 2018).
83. 'Policy Brief: From Jordan to Jihad: The Lure of Syria's Violent Extremist Groups', MercyCorps, 28 Sept. 2015, https://www.mercycorps.org/sites/default/files/From%20Jordan%20to%20Jihad_0.pdf (accessed 10 Oct. 2018).
84. N. Bondokji, K. Wilkinson and L.Aghabi, *Trapped Between Destructive Choices: Radicalisation Drivers Affecting Youth in Jordan*, Amman: WANA Institute, 2016.
85. A. Osborne, 'Ma'an: Dangerous or just Desperate', *WANA Institute*, 2 May 2017, http://wanainstitute.org/en/blog/maan-dangerous-or-just-desperate
86. Hassan Sabaileh, interviewed by Gilbert Ramsay, Amman, 16 Oct. 2016.
87. Jordan TV (YouTube Channel), https://www.youtube.com/channel/UC4Zl5EaAGG_JHKyxmMpzigw (accessed 10 Oct. 2018).
88. Interview with Hassan Sabaileh, 16 Oct. 2016, op. cit.
89. Ibid.
90. Ibid.
91. '"Dangerously High" rates of diabetes among Palestinian refugees', UNRWA Press Release, 11 Feb. 2014, https://www.unrwa.org/newsroom/press-releases/%E2%80%9Cdangerously-high%E2%80%9D-rates-diabetes-among-palestinian-refugees
92. 'Top Entertainers Perform at Jordan's Health Awareness Fair', Johns Hopkins Centre for Communication Programmes, 21 Oct. 2010, https://ccp.jhu.edu/2010/10/21/top-musicians-comedians-entertain-huge-crowd-at-jordans-health-awareness-fair/ (accessed 10 Oct. 2018).
93. One of these can be seen at https://www.youtube.com/watch?v=qsjgonS8Dg4 (accessed 10 Oct. 2018)
94. Interview with Hassan Sabaileh, 16 Oct. 2016, op. cit.
95. Ibid.
96. Interview with Hassan Sabaileh, 16 Oct. 2016, op. cit.
97. 'Awareness Session Held on Theatre's Role Against Extremism', *Jordan Times*, 18 Apr. 2017, http://jordantimes.com/news/local/awareness-session-held-theatre%E2%80%99s-role-against-extremism (accessed 10 Oct. 2018).
98. The performance took place on 20 Oct. 2016
99. Interview with Hassan Sabaileh, 16 Oct. 2016, op. cit.

100. Adam Hansen writes, for example (A. Hansen 'Writing, London and the Bishops' Ban of 1599', *The London Journal*, vol. 43, no. 2, 2018, pp. 102–119), that in 1597 the Privy Council ordered not only the banning of theatrical performances, but that all theatres be 'plucked down' (the order was never implemented).

101. A. Boal, *Theatre of the Oppressed*, London: Pluto Press, 2018.

6. 'WE'RE THE OTHERS!' THE JIHADI SENSE OF HUMOUR

1. J. Sasson, O. bin Laden & N. bin Laden, *Growing Up Bin Laden: Osama's Wife and Son Take Us Inside Their Secret World*, New York: OneWorld, 2001.

2. Technically, this should be written 'Ibn Laden', not 'bin Laden', but we use the latter to avoid confusion.

3. F. Miller, *The Audacious Ascetic: What Osama Bin Laden's Sound Archive Reveals About Al-Qa'ida*, New York: Hurst, 2015.

4. See J. Wagemakers, 'Defining the Enemy: Abu Muhammad al-Maqdisi's reading of Surat al-Mumtahana', *Die Welt Des Islams*, vol. 8, no. 3, 2008, pp. 348–371.

5. 'Full Transcript of Bin Laden's Speech', Al Jazeera, 1 Nov. 2004, http://www.aljazeera.com/archive/2004/11/200849163336457223. html (accessed 29 Dec. 2018).

6. *Fahrenheit 9/11*, USA, Dog Eat Dog Films, June 2004. The film was released a few months before bin Laden's speech, and the 'My Pet Goat' story had become highly popularised as a result.

7. Al-Zawahiri Obama's position concerning the hostilities against Gaza, Al-Bawaba, 4 Feb. 2009, https://www.albawaba.com/ar/%D8%A3% D8%AE%D8%A8%D8%A7%D8%B1/%D8%A7%D9%84%D8%B8% D9%88%D8%A7%D9%87%D8%B1%D9%8A-%D9%8A% D8%B3%D8%AE%D8%B1-%D9%85%D9%86-%D9%85% D9%88%D9%82%D9%81-%D8%A7%D9%88%D8%A8%D8%A7% D9%85%D8%A7-%D8%AD%D9%8A%D8%A7%D9%84-%D8%A7‾ %D9%84%D8%B9%D8%AF%D9%88%D8%A7%D9% 86-%D8%B9%D9%84%D9%89-%D8%BA%D8%B2%D8%A9.

8. 'Al-Zawahiri Criticizes Obama's Stance Towards Gaza', Al Jazeera News, 4 Feb. 2009, https://www.aljazeera.net/news/international/ 2009/2/4/ (accessed 20 Dec. 2018).

9. Abu Muhammad al-Adnani, 'Nonviolence is Whose Religion?', Al-Furqan Media, 30 Aug. 2013, https://archive.org/details/baqiah5 (accessed 20 Dec. 2018).

10. J. Bamford, 'Reading This Magazine Could Land You in Jail', *Foreign Policy*, 25 Mar. 2015, http://foreignpolicy.com/2015/03/25/reading-this-magazine-could-land-you-in-jail/

11. A. F. Lemieux, J.M. Brachman, J. Levitt & J. Wood, '*Inspire* Magazine: A Critical Analysis of its Significance and Potential Impact Through the Lens of the Information, Motivation and Behavioural Skills Model', *Terrorism and Political Violence*, vol. 26, no. 2, 2014, pp. 354–371.

12. 'Jihadist Memes Are a Real Thing', *Motherboard*, 2017, https://motherboard.vice.com/en_us/article/nzee4d/western-jihadis-memes-are-a-real-thing (accessed 15 Sept. 2017).

13. *Exclamation* [Facebook group], https://www.facebook.com/moslim11222/

14. 'Hey Band Head, Where Are You?', 2015, https://www.dailymotion.com/video/x2whpjh (accessed 20 Sept. 2018).

15. Ibid.

16. Khattab here refers to the Saudi militant Bin al-Khattab, who fought in the first and second Chechen wars.

17. 'Tunisian rapper Amino killed in Syria?', 2015, https://www.youtube.com/watch?v=JS-fWMOFVBc (accessed 20 Sept. 2018).

18. 'Aleppo, al-Sakhour, Da'wa Tent, Elderly Competition', 2013, https://www.youtube.com/watch?v=HqmcdfJcA0g (accessed 20 Sept. 2018).

19. The video of this event has been removed from YouTube, however, the authors retained a copy in their collection. In general, in this chapter we provide up-to-date (at the time of writing) online sources for jokes and humorous materials wherever possible. However, much material has (unsurprisingly) been removed since we originally downloaded it. Where the original link we used to access a particular joke (*turfa*) is no longer available, we provide instead the number assigned to the joke in our own collection and, where we have been able to find one, an alternative link.

20. *Ta'rif 'ala nukat al-da'shiyīn?* (Do you know the Daeshis' jokes?), Al-Sawsana, 4 Oct. 2014, https://www.assawsana.com/portal/pages.php?newsid=190906&fbclid=IwAR1y628z3t35vz7iHE9_Ugbbypw DQOdrOr2gWytbrO1ur8pw8rnDJzVrL1Q (accessed 27 Dec. 2018).

21. H. al-Qatari, *The Life and Stories of The Mujahedeen in Afghanistan and Bosnia*, no date, https://saaid.net/Doat/hamad/index.htm (accessed 9 December 2018).

22. H. al-Qatari, *The Stories of Arab Martyrs*, no date, https://saaid.net/Doat/hamad/1/index.htm (accessed 9 Dec. 2018).

23. 'Painful Images: Saudi-Afghan Fighter in Syria Publishes Pictures of Victims among the Supporters of the Assad's Army, Boasts about Massacring Them', *Al-Watan Voice*, 8 Oct. 2013, https://www.alwatanvoice.com/arabic/news/2013/08/10/423198.html (accessed 8 July 2019).

24. Najm al-Din Azad, 'Index of Links to the Stories and Letters of the

Mujahid Najm al-Din Azad', 2013, https://justpaste.it/2kej (accessed 9 Dec. 2018).

25. A. Sinjer, 'Stories of the Mujahideen and Martyrs in the Land of Jihad: Stories of al-Sham', 2014, https://justpaste.it/ibwx (accessed 9 Dec. 2018). Facebook Account: https://www.facebook.com/ALsultan. Sinjr/?hc_ref=SEARCH&fref=nf. Blog of al-Sultna Singer on Justpasteit: https://justpaste.it/AL_sultan_Sinjr

26. Interview with Gilbert Ramsay, Edinburgh, 23 Apr. 2017.

27. Razeez Kandahar, *Anecdotes of The Mujahideen*, 2014, https://archive.org/details/Razeez_1/21.mp3 (accessed 9 Dec. 2018).

28. 'The Army Rumour Service', https://www.arrse.co.uk/community/forums/ (accessed 8 Feb. 2018).

29. Joke # 70. Khalid Yasouf (2016),12 Apr. 2016. Available at: https://www.facebook.com/permalink.php?story_fbid=224763174553638&id=100010598701284 (accessed on 20 Dec. 2018).

30. T. Cook, '"I will meet the world with a smile and a joke": Canadian Soldiers' Humour in the Great War', *Canadian Military History*, vol. 22, no. 2, 2015, article 5.

31. Joke # 83 'Way to Allah' (2014), 27 Sept. 2014. Available at: https://www.facebook.com/PraytotheMessenger/posts/799760150081712?__tn__=-R (accessed on 20 Dec. 2018).

32. Najm al-Din Azad, *A Story: The Soviets Makes a Swimming Pool for the Afghani Mujahideen*, 2013, https://justpaste.it/2fyv (accessed 9 Dec. 2018).

33. Najm al-Din Azad (A. al-Utaybi), *Stories of the Mujahideen*, op. cit.

34. Joke # 16. Omar Muhammad (2014), 22 Sept. 2014. Available at: https://www.facebook.com/permalink.php?story_fbid=341435246038825&id=100005170569374 (accessed on 20 Dec. 2018).

35. Joke #24. Mu'az Ghanem al-Hassan (2014), 27 Sept. 2014. Available at: https://www.facebook.com/permalink.php?story_fbid=1502875349955107&id=100006979681031 (accessed on 20 Dec. 2018).

36. Al-'Hawara' al-'Aina', 'Some of the Mujahideen's Anecdotes Narrated by Abu 'Huzaifa al-Muhajer', *Twitmail*, 2013, http://www.twitmail.com/email/942524438/125/942524438 (accessed 19 Sept. 2018).

37. This episode seems to echo a point made in Slavoj Žižek's article 'The Christian-Hegelian comedy', *Cabinet Magazine*, 17, Spring 2005. Here, Žižek argues, drawing on the case of the Argentinian Minister of the Economy Domingo Cavallo, who escaped from rioting protestors by donning a mask of his own face, that 'the ultimate comical occurs when, after removing the mask, we confront exactly the same face as that of the mask'.

38. Joke # 10. The Best of Sheikh Khaled al-Rashid (2013), 28 Dec. 2013.

Available at: https://www.facebook.com/permalink.php?story_fbid=569549103124656&id=371446372934931&__tn__=-R (accessed 19 Sept. 2018).

39. Joke # 4. Khaled Abu a-Khulood (2013), 29 Aug. 2013. Available at: https://www.facebook.com/khalid.R.w.Barghoud/posts/580700 415325018 (accessed 20 Sept. 2018).

40. Joke # 23. The Finest of Incidents and the Best of Anecdotes, *al-Fitan wa al-Malahim*, 2009, http://alfetn.net/vb3/showthread.php?t=84663 (accessed 20 Sept. 2018).

41. Joke # 29. 'Suhaib al-Rumi (2017), 4 Mar. 2017. Available at: https://www.facebook.com/permalink.php?story_fbid=200268470455169 &id=100014160517169 (accessed 20 Sept. 2018).

42. Joke # 31. Alshehri Ahmed (2014), 25 Sept. 2014. Available at: https://www.facebook.com/ahmed.alshehri.140/posts/1020 3800420904834 (accessed 20 Sept. 2018). The play is Zi'ab al-Hibl available at: https://www.youtube.com/watch?v=QmRLNXlmuXc (accessed 20 Sept. 2018). The relevant clip is available at: https://www.youtube.com/watch?v=WGLzg4Iuv8A (accessed 20 Sept. 2018).

43. Joke #2. Ahmad Sha'ban Abu Arwa (2015), 4 Nov. 2015. Available at: https://www.facebook.com/permalink.php?story_fbid=1672565469 686116&id=100007980365006 (accessed 20 Sept. 2018).

44. Joke #8. Sheikh Mashari Rashid a-Affasi (2013), 7 Sept. 2013. Available at: https://www.facebook.com/trieeq.elgana/photos/a.2925160041 21126/585911714781552/?type=3&theater (accessed 20 Sept. 2018).

45. A. Sinjer 'The Beautiful Lady', 2014, https://justpaste.it/i4po (accessed 9 Dec. 2018).

46. Joke # 118. Fatayat al-Tawheed (2014), 25 Sept. 2014. Available at: https://www.facebook.com/permalink.php?story_fbid=6359273965 27598&id=342772905843050&__tn__=-R (accessed 20 Sept. 2018).

47. Joke # 1. Stories and Videos on the Jihad in the Path of God (2016), 15 Sept. 2016. Available at: https://www.facebook.com/permalink. php?story_fbid=1764343260504779&id=1755758454696593 (accessed 20 Sept. 2018).

48. Joke # 17.

49. Joke # 28. 'Suhaib al-Rumi (2017), 4 Mar. 2017. Available at: https://www.facebook.com/permalink.php?story_fbid=200268470455169 &id=100014160517169 (accessed 20 Sept. 2018).

50. Joke # 9. Sheikh Mashari Rashid a-Affasi (2013), 7 Sept. 2013. Available at: https://www.facebook.com/trieeq.elgana/photos/a.29251600 4121126/585911714781552/?type=3&theater (accessed 20 Sept. 2018).

51. A. Utaybi, *Anecdotes of Mujahideen No 49*, 2013, https://medadalmisk. wordpress.com/2013/04/20/49-%d8%b7%d8%b1%d8%a7%

d8%a6%d9%81-%d8%a7%d9%84%d9%85%d8%ac%d8%a7%d9%87
%d8%af%d9%8a%d9%86/ (accessed 9 Dec. 2018).

52. Miracles and Anecdotes of the Afghani Mujahideen, *Sawalif lil Jami'*, 2014, http://www.swalif.com/forum/showthread.php?t=191728 (accessed 20 Sept. 2018).
53. Abu Muhammad Al-Adnani, 'The scout doesn't lie to his people', *justpaste.it*, 2014, https://justpaste.it/e103 (accessed 20 Sept. 2018).
54. https://www.independent.co.uk/news/world/middle-east/syrian-civil-war-the-day-i-met-the-organ-eating-cannibal-rebel-abu-sakkars-fearsome-followers-8617828.html
55. Joke # 12. Muslim women's steadfastness at the time of tribulations (2014) 29 Sept. 2014. Available at: https://www.facebook.com/permalink.php?story_fbid=754612781287261&id=679382938810246&tn=-R, (accessed 20 Sept. 2018).
56. Joke # 3.
57. 'Laugh with the Chechen Mujahideen of the Islamic State', 2014, https://www.youtube.com/watch?v=HZbTJKKjkv4 (accessed 20 Sept. 2018).
58. S. Vucetic, 'Identity is a Joking Matter: Intergroup Humour in Bosnia', *Spaces of Identity: Tradition, Cultural Boundaries and Identity Formation in Central Europe and Beyond*, vol. 4, no. 1, 2004, https://soi.journals.yorku.ca/index.php/soi/article/view/8011 (accessed 20 Dec. 2018).
59. Credit goes to 'Dennis', a guitarist and Kurt Cobain fan, for this joke recounted to Gilbert Ramsay in the summer of 2000.
60. A. Dundes, *Cracking Jokes: Studies of Sick Humor Cycles and Stereotypes*, Quid Pro Quo: New Orleans, 1987, chapters 3 and 4.

7. THE GOD OF DAESH: POPULAR AND ONLINE JIHADI JOKES

1. B. McKernan and agencies, 'Alleged Killer Who Shot Jordanian Writer Identified', *Independent*, 25 Sept. 2016, https://www.independent.co.uk/news/world/middle-east/alleged-killer-who-shot-atheist-jordanian-writer-charged-with-offensive-facebook-post-identified-a7329391.html (accessed 24 Oct. 2018).
2. The original cartoon can be viewed on 'M80/'Musa's' page at https://www.facebook.com/M80Caricatures/ (accessed 24 Oct. 2018).
3. S. al-Ris, 'A Conversation with "Musa", author of the "paradise" cartoon which ended Hattar's life', *Raseef 22*, 28 Sept. 2016, https://raseef22.com/life/2016/09/28 (accessed 24 Oct. 2018).
4. Observed by G. Ramsay, 26 Sept. 2018.
5. R. Fiske, 'A year on from the Murder of Christian Writer Nahed Hattar in Jordan, Many Questions Remain Unanswered', *Independent*, 21 Sept.

2017, https://www.independent.co.uk/voices/middle-east-jordan-chris-
tians-nahed-hattar-murder-king-abdullah-government-a7959026.html

6. S. Narwani, 'Murder of Prominent Jordanian Writer Nahed Hattar:
who pulled the trigger?', *Russia Today*, 5 Oct. 2016, https://www.
rt.com/op-ed/361652-jordan-nahed-hattar-extremism-isis/ (accessed
24 Oct. 2018).

7. See A. Ramsay's interview with Moutaz Hattar, 'Lessons for Trumpland:
Adventures with Demagoguery in the Middle East', *openDemocracy*,
14 Nov. 2018 (accessed 24 Oct. 2018).

8. Isam Uraiqat, interviewed by Gilbert Ramsay, London, 19 Mar. 2018.

9. The original document, 'File in support of Prophet Muhammad, Prayer
and Peace Upon Him', is available from https://www.biblen.info/
Ressourcer/5679.pdf (accessed 24 Oct. 2018).

10. A. Al-Rawi, 'Facebook as a Virtual Mosque: The Online Protest Against
Innocence of Muslims', *Culture and Religion*, vol. 17, no. 1, 2016, pp. 19–34.

11. A. Al-Rawi, 'Online Reactions to the Muhammad Cartoons: YouTube
and the Virtual Ummah', *Journal for the Scientific Study of Religion*,
vol. 54, no. 1, May 2015, pp. 261–276.

12. Al-Rawi, 2016, op. cit.

13. J. Grimm, 'We are not Charlie: Muslims' Differentiated Reactions to
the Paris Attacks, and the Dangers of Indiscriminate Finger-Pointing',
German Institute for International and Security Affairs, Dec. 2015,
https://www.ssoar.info/ssoar/bitstream/handle/document/42448/
ssoar-2015-grimm-We_are_not_Charlie_Muslims.pdf?sequence=1
(accessed 24 Oct. 2018).

14. Gallup, 'Global Index of Religion and Atheism', 2012, https://sid-
mennt.is/wp-content/uploads/Gallup-International-um-tr%C3%BA-
og-tr%C3%BAleysi-2012.pdf (accessed 24 Oct. 2018).

15. 'Saudi Arabia' Freedom of Thought Report, https://freethoughtreport.
com/countries/asia-western-asia/saudi-arabia/#Atheism_asterrorism
(accessed 24 Oct. 2018).

16. Zogby Research Services, 'Muslim Millennial Attitudes on Religion
and Religious Leadership', 2015, available online https://static1.
squarespace.com/static/52750dd3e4b08c252c723404/t/569ee
bcccbced6e361dce467/1453255667316/Millennials+2015+FINAL.pdf
(accessed 24 Oct. 2018).

17. The regional average is 36.8 per cent as of 2016, according to the
Arab Development Portal, http://www.arabdevelopmentportal.com/
indicator/education (accessed 24 Oct. 2018).

18. The keywords used were '*nukat daesh*', '*tahshish daesh*' and '*mazah daesh*'
(Daesh jokes, Daesh funnies and Daesh humour). As in the preceding
chapter, these will be referenced to by the numbers they are assigned
in our collection.

19. These 'visual jokes' might be called 'memes', but we have avoided this designation in the interest of clarity, since all the items in our collection could potentially be considered to be memes in some sense.

20. 'Al Qaeda in Iraq Alienated by Cucumber Laws and Brutality', *Telegraph* 11 Aug. 2008, https://www.telegraph.co.uk/news/world-news/middleeast/iraq/2538545/Al-Al-Qaeda-in-Iraq-alienated-by-cucumber-laws-and-brutality.html (accessed 24 Oct. 2018).

21. 'Jokes from Sana'a' [Facebook page] https://www.facebook.com/Nakt.sana/posts/864086516935171 (accessed 3 May 2017).

22. Anti-IS joke # 23.

23. Anti-IS joke # 16.

24. This joke was provided by one of the respondents to our survey.

25. 'A Joke Every Day', https://www.facebook.com/permalink.php?story_fbid=976623269075789&id=239388419465948 (accessed 2 May 2017).

26. Anti-IS meme # 259.

27. Anti-IS meme # 142.

28. This joke, was passed on to us by Dr Haian Dukhan from the University of Leicester.

29. Anti-IS memes # 68, 122 and 170

30. Anti-IS joke # 24.

31. Anti-IS meme # 192.

32. Anti-IS meme # 82.

33. Anti-IS meme # 283.

34. Anti-IS meme # 91.

35. Anti-IS meme # 159.

36. Raskin, 1984, op. cit.

37. Anti-IS meme # 27.

38. See D. Awad, 'The Evolution of Arabic Writing Due to European Influence: The Case of Punctuation', *Journal of Arabic and Islamic Studies*, vol. 15, 2015, pp. 117–136.

39. Anti-IS meme # 157.

40. Anti-IS meme # 194.

41. U. Marzolph, 'The Qoran and Jocular Literature', op. cit.

42. We are indebted, once again, to Dr Haian Dukhan from the University of Leicester for sharing this joke.

8. INFIDELS OF IDEOLOGY: FINAL THOUGHTS AND FUTURE DIRECTIONS

1. J. Morreall, *Comic Relief: A Comprehensive Philosophy of Humor*, Oxford: Wiley-Blackwell, 2009, chapter 2.

2. A.R. Radcliffe-Brown, 'On Joking Relationships', *Africa: Journal of the International African Institute*, vol. 13, no. 3 1940, pp. 195–210.

3. E.J. Ziolkowski, 'The Laughter of Despair: Irony, Humor and Laughter in Kierkegaard and Carlyle' in *Play, Literature, Religion: Essays in Cultural Intertextuality*, eds V. Nemoianu and R. Royal, Albany: State University of New York Press, 1992.

4. See S. Kierkegaard, *The Concept of Dread*, trans. W. Lowrie, Princeton: Princeton University Press, 1967, p. 13.

5. Kraidy, 2017, op. cit.; Greenberg, 2017, op. cit.

6. Emad Hajjaj, interviewed by Gilbert Ramsay, Amman, Jordan, 5 Aug. 2016.

7. Emad Hajjaj, 5 Aug. 2016, op. cit.

8. 'Video of Celebrity Iraq Fighter Slicing Body Goes Viral', Al-Jazeera, 28 Aug. 2015, https://www.aljazeera.com/news/2015/08/video-celebrity-iraq-fighter-slicing-body-viral-150828145749447.html

9. Video from Moutaz's collection.

10. Melon City video.

11. M. Coker and F. Hassan, 'A Ten Minute Trial, A Death Sentence: Iraqi Justice for ISIS suspects', *New York Times*, 17 Apr. 2018, https://www.nytimes.com/2018/04/17/world/middleeast/iraq-isis-trials.html (accessed 27 Dec. 2018).

12. Emad Hajjaj, 5 Aug. 2016, op. cit.

13. See A. Nagle, *Kill All Normies: Online Culture Wars from 4Chan and Tumblr to Trump and the Alt-Right*, New York: Zero Books, 2017.

14. An example of this would be far right website The Daily Stormer, whose editor Andrew Anglin has had a specific policy of using satire as a means of blurring the distinction between serious and playful belief in Nazism. See A. Feinberg, 'This is the Daily Stormer's Playbook', *Huffington Post*, 14 Dec. 2017, https://www.huffington-post.co.uk/entry/daily-stormer-nazi-style-guide_us_5a2ece19e4b0ce3b344492f2 (accessed 27 Dec. 2018).

15. Interview with Isam Uraiqat, 19 Mar. 2018, op. cit. Urayqat also spoke about this during a seminar delivered as part of the MECASS programme (Middle East and Central Asian Security Studies), Department of International Relations. University of St Andrews, 22 Nov. 2018.

16. 'Meeting with Ahmad Massad on Joe Show', https://www.youtube.com/watch?v=tRsXnQhtJ3A (accessed 28 Dec. 2018).

17. See 'The most unbelievable story in history... The Arabic version of *Titanic*', 2018, https://www.youtube.com/watch?v=uV9yWAqa3z Q&t=2s, (accessed on 22 Dec. 2018); Beware of magicians of social media sites and selfie that causes cancer, 2017, https://www.youtube.com/watch?v=2_He6EiIxTU (accessed on 22 Dec. 2018); 'Beware of

the Jews, they are spying on… Subhanullah', 2016, https://www.youtube.com/watch?v=xS-cZasFv8g (accessed on 22 Dec. 2018). 'Apple causes cancer… but camel's urine heals… Subhanallah', 2017, https://www.youtube.com/watch?v=RkpUI_AT-N8 (accessed on 22 Dec. 2018). 'Watch these 3 ways that will let you enter the paradise easily', 2018, https://www.youtube.com/watch?v=niCCw35N 3qo, (accessed on 22 Dec. 2018); 'Chicken writing Allah', 2016, https://www.youtube.com/watch?v=uIoWYHi7RBc (accessed on 22 Dec. 2018), among others.

18. Salem, 2014, op. cit., p. 239.
19. *Joe Show, Season 3, Episode 20: He is innocent may God protect him*, 2018, https://www.youtube.com/watch?v=z0fKbYRNt88 (accessed on 22 Sept. 2018).
20. *Joe Show, Season 3, Episode 8: Red! Oh Opposition*, 2018, https://www.youtube.com/watch?v=NzKmXpldsuE (accessed on 22 Sept. 2018).
21. *Joe Show, Season 3, Episode 16, A fight with a saw*, 2018, https://www.youtube.com/watch?v=6rF_8eeRumQ (accessed on 22 Sept. 2018).
22. See S. Heritage, 'Who is America: Why Sacha Baron Cohen's comedy Failed to Land a Punch', *Guardian*, 28 Aug. 2018, https://www.theguardian.com/film/2018/aug/28/who-is-america-why-sacha-baron-cohens-comedy-failed-to-land-a-punch (accessed 27 Dec. 2018).

SELECT BIBLIOGRAPHY

Books, Journal Articles and Selected Reports

Abdulla, R.M., *The Internet in the Arab World: Egypt and Beyond*, Oxford: Peter Lang, 2007.

Abu Dawud, Suleiman al-Ash'ath al-Sijistani, *Sunan Abi Dawud* [Arabic], Volume 7, Hadith Number 5098, Damascus: Al-Risala Al-'Alamia, 2009.

Abu Lughod, L., 'Movie Stars and Islamic Morality in Egypt', *Social Text* no. 42, Spring 1995, pp. 53–67.

———, *Dramas of Nationhood: The Politics of Television in Egypt*, Chicago: University of Chicago Press, 2004.

Abu Rumman, M., *I Am a Salafi: A Study of the Actual and Imagined Identities of Salafis*, Amman: Friedrich-Ebert-Stiftung, 2014.

Aldis, O., *Play Fighting*, Cambridge, MA: Academic Press, 2013.

Allagui, I. and A. Najjar, 'Framing Political Islam in Popular Egyptian Cinema', *Middle East Journal of Culture and Communication*, vol. 4, no. 2, 2011.

Allen, R., ed., *Critical Perspectives on Yusuf Idris*, Washington, D.C.: Three Continents Press, 1992.

Alinsky, S., *Rules for Radicals: A Pragmatic Primer for Realistic Radicals*, New York: Vintage Books, 1989.

Amitai-Preiss, R., *Mongols and Mamluks: The Mamluk-Ilkhanid War*, Cambridge: Cambridge University Press, p. 47.

Armbrust, W., 'Islamists in Egyptian Cinema', *American Anthropologist*, vol. 104, no. 3, 2002, pp. 922–931.

Arquilla, J. and D. Ronfeldt, eds, *Networks and Netwars: The Future of Terrorism, Crime and Militancy*, Santa Monica: RAND, 1999.

Attardo, S., *Humorous Texts: A Semantic and Pragmatic Analysis*, Berlin: De Gruyter, 2001.

Awad, D., 'The Evolution of Arabic Writing Due to European Influence: The

Case of Punctuation', *Journal of Arabic and Islamic Studies*, vol. 15, 2015, pp. 117–136.

Badawi, M.M., 'Medieval Arabic Drama: Ibn Daniyal', *Journal of Arabic Literature*, vol. 13, pp. 83–107.

Baker, R., 'Combative Cultural Politics: Film Art and Political Spaces in Egypt', *Alif: Journal of Comparative Poetics*, no. 15, Arab Cinematics: Toward the New and the Alternative, 1995, pp. 6–38.

Bakhtin, M., *Rabelais and His World*, trans. Hélène Iswolsky, Bloomington: Indiana University Press, 1984.

Bamford, J., 'Reading This Magazine Could Land You in Jail', *Foreign Policy*, 25 Mar. 2015.

Bartlett, J. and A. Krasodomski-Jones, 'Counter-Speech on Facebook', *Demos*, September 2016.

Bateson, P. and P. Martin, *Play, Playfulness, Creativity and Innovation*, Cambridge: Cambridge University Press, 2013.

Berger, A.A., *An Anatomy of Humor*, New Brunswick, NJ: Transaction Publishers, 1993.

Berger, P., *Redeeming Laughter: The Comic Dimension of Human Experience*, second edition, Berlin: De Gruyter, 2014.

Billig, M., *Laughter and Ridicule: Towards a Social Critique of Humour*, Thousand Oaks: SAGE, 2005.

Boal, A., *Theatre of the Oppressed*, London: Pluto Press, 2018.

Bondokji, N., K. Wilkinson, and L. Aghabi, *Trapped Between Destructive Choices: Radicalisation Drivers Affecting Youth in Jordan*, Amman: WANA Institute, 2016.

Boyd, D., 'Egyptian Radio: Tool of Political and National Development', *Journalism Monographs*, no. 48, Association for Education in Journalism, February 1977.

Braude, J., *Broadcasting Change: Arabic Media as a Catalyst for Liberalism*, New York: Rowman and Littlefield.

Brisard, J., *Al-Zarqawi: The New Face of Al-Qaeda*, Cambridge: Polity Press, 2005.

Byman, D., *The Five Front War: The Better Way to Fight Global Jihad*, Hoboken: Wiley, 2008.

Campbell, J.L. and F. Collinson, *Hebridean Folksongs Volume 2: Waulking Songs from Barra, South Uist, Eriskay and Benbecula*, Oxford: Clarendon Press, 1977.

Carlson, M., 'The Arab Aristophanes', *Comparative Drama*, vol. 47, no. 2, 2013, pp. 151–66.

Cicero, *De Oratore*, ed. A.S Wilkins, [online] Perseus.tufts.edu

Cook, M., *Commanding Right and Forbidding Wrong in Islamic Thought*, Cambridge: Cambridge University Press, 2000.

Cook, T., '"I will meet the world with a smile and a joke": Canadian Soldiers'

Humour in the Great War', *Canadian Military History*, vol. 22, no. 2, 2015, article 5.

Critchley, S., *On Humour*, London: Routledge, 2002.

Darnton, R., *The Great Cat Massacre and Other Episodes in French Cultural History*, New York: Basic Books, 2009.

Darwish, H., 'Egyptian Cinema and Terrorism' [Arabic] in Rima al-Mismar and Ahmad Zu'bi, eds, *Terrorism and Cinema: Controversies of the Relationship and Possibilities for Employment* [Arabic], Beirut: Madarek, 2010, pp. 27–105.

Davies, C., *Ethnic Humour Around the World: A Comparative Analysis*, Bloomington: University of Indiana Press, 1980.

Davila Ross, M., J. Owren and E. Zimmerman, 'Reconstructing the Evolution of Laughter in Great Apes and Humans', *Current Biology*, vol. 19, no. 13, 2009, pp. 1106–1111.

Dundes, A., *Cracking Jokes: Studies of Sick Humor Cycles and Stereotypes*, Quid Pro Quo: New Orleans, 1987

Dynel, M., 'There is Method in the Humorous Speaker's Madness: Humour and Grice's Model', *Lodz Papers in Pragmatics*, vol. 4, no. 1, 2008.

Eisend, M., 'A Meta-Analysis of Humor in Advertising', *Journal of the Academy of Marketing Science*, vol. 37, no. 2, 2009, pp. 191–203.

Elias, N., *The Civilizing Process: The History of Manners, and State Formation, and Civilization*, trans. Edmund Jephcott, Oxford: Blackwell, 1994.

Elsayed, L. T. Faris and S. Zeiger, 'Undermining Violent Extremist Narratives in the Middle East and North Africa: A How-To Guide', Hedayah Institute, 2017.

Ewin, R.E., 'Hobbes on Laughter', *Philosophical Quarterly*, vol. 51, no. 202, 2001.

Fanon, F., *The Wretched of the Earth*, trans. R. Philcox, New York: Grove Press, 2004.

(Al)-Faruque, M., 'The Mongol Conquest of Baghdad: Medieval Accounts and their Modern Assessments', *Islamic Quarterly*, vol. 32, no. 4, pp. 194–206.

Farwell, J.P., 'Jihadi Video in the War of Ideas', *Survival: Global Politics and Strategy*, vol. 52, no. 6, 2010, pp. 127–150.

Freud, S., *The Joke and Its Relation to the Unconscious*, trans. J. Crick, London: Penguin, 2002.

Fu'ad, A., *Censorship: The Expressive Dilemma Between Writer and Producer* [Arabic], Cairo: Arab Press Agency, Nashiroon, 2018.

Geybels, H. and W. Van Herck, eds, *Humour and Religion: Challenges and Ambiguities*, London: Bloomsbury, 2012.

Goodall, H. P., Cheong, K. Fleischer and S. Corman, 'Rhetorical Charms: The Promises and Pitfalls of Humor and Ridicule as Strategies to Counter Extremist Narratives', *Perspectives on Terrorism*, vol. 6, no. 1, 2012.

Gourevitsh, P., *We Wish to Inform You That Tomorrow We Will Be Killed With Our Families*, London: Picador, 2000.

SELECT BIBLIOGRAPHY

Graaf, B. and J. Skovgaard-Petersen, eds, *Global Mufti: The Phenomenon of Yusuf Al-Qaradawi*, London: Hurst, 2008.

Greenberg, N., 'Mythical State: The Aesthetics and Counter-Aesthetics of the Islamic State in Iraq and Syria', *Middle East Journal of Culture and Communication*, vol. 10, nos. 2–3, 2017.

Greenhill, P., *Make the Night Hideous: Four English-Canadian Charivaris, 1881–1940*, Toronto: University of Toronto Press, 2010.

Grimm, J., 'We are not Charlie: Muslims' Differentiated Reactions to the Paris Attacks, and the Dangers of Indiscriminate Finger-Pointing', German Institute for International and Security Affairs, Dec. 2015.

Grossman, D., *On Killing: The Psychological Cost of Learning to Kill in War and Society*, revised edition, New York: E-Rights/E-Reads Ltd, 2009.

Gruner, C., 'Wit and Humor in Mass Communications' in *Humour and Laughter: Theory, Research and Applications*, ed. A. Chapman and H. Foot, New York: Transaction, 1995.

Guo, L., 'Paradise Lost: Ibn Daniyal's Response to Baybars' Campaign against Vice in Cairo', *Journal of the American Oriental Society*, vol. 121, no. 2, 2001, pp. 219–235.

———, 'The Devil's Advocate: Ibn Daniyal's Art of Parody in His Qasidah No. 71', *Mamluk Studies Review*, 2003.

(Al)-Hafiz Ibn Adul Bir, *Biography of Companions* [Arabic], Beirut: Dar al-Jeel, 1992.

Haidt, J., *The Righteous Mind: Why Good People are Divided by Politics and Religion*, New York: Penguin, 2012.

Hamam, I., 'Disarticulating Arab Popular Culture: The Case of Egyptian Comedies, *Arab Cultural Studies: Mapping the Field*, ed. T. Sabry, London: IB Tauris, 2012.

Hamdar, A. and L. Moore, eds, *Islamism and Cultural Expression in the Arab World*, London: Routledge, 2015.

Hammond, A., *Pop Culture in North Africa and the Middle East*, Santa Barbara, CA: ABC-Clio, 2017.

Hansen. A., 'Writing, London and the Bishops' Ban of 1599', *The London Journal*, vol. 43, no. 2, 2018, pp. 102–119.

Haugbolle, S., 'That Joke isn't Funny Anymore: Bass Mat Watan's Nasrallah Skit and the Limits of Laughter in Lebanon', *Arab Culture and Society*, 2008.

Hegghammer, T., ed., *Jihadi Culture: The Art and Social Practices of Militant Islamists*, Cambridge: Cambridge University Press, 2017.

———, *Jihad in Saudi Arabia: Violence and Pan-Islamism since 1979*, Cambridge: Cambridge University Press, 2011.

Heine, S., T. Proulx and K. Vohs, 'The Meaning Maintenance Model: On the Coherence of Social Motivations', *Personality and Social Psychology Review*, vol. 10, no. 2, 2006, pp. 88–110.

SELECT BIBLIOGRAPHY

Hierocles, translated and edited by B. Baldwin, *The Philogelos, or Laughter Lover* (London Studies in Classical Philology), Amsterdam: JC Gieben, 1984.

Hobbes, T. *Leviathan*, edited with and introduction and notes by J.C.A Gaskin, Oxford: Oxford University Press, 2008.

Hodgart, M., *Satire*, London: Weidenfeld and Nicolson, 1959.

Horowitz, D., *The Deadly Ethnic Riot*, Oakland: University of California Press, 2001.

Holland, N.N., 'Tickled Rats and Human Laughter', *Neuropsychanalysis*, vol. 9, no. 1, 2007, pp. 41–57.

Hudson, L., 'Reading al-Sha'rani: The Sufi Genealogy of Islamic Modernism in Late Ottoman Damascus', *Journal of Islamic Studies*, vol. 15, no. 1, 2004, pp. 39–68.

Hussein, G. and E.M. Saltman, 'Jihad Trending: A Comprehensive Analysis of Online Extremism, and How to Counter It', Quilliam Foundation, 13 May 2014.

Hussein, S.A. (verification), Musnad Abu Ya'la al-Musali, Vol. 7, Hadith Number 4476, 1st edition, Damascus: Dar al-Ma'mon lil-Turath, 1986.

Ibn al-Jawzī, 'Abd al-Rahman, Abu 'l Farash, *Virtues of the Commander of the Faithful Umar ibn Al-Khattāb* [Arabic], Beirut: Dar al-Kotob al-Ilmiyah, 1978.

———, 'Abd al-Rahman, Abu 'l Farash, ed. A. Muhannan, *Reports of Fools and Idiots* [Arabic], Beirut: Dar al-Fikr wal-Bayyanat, 1990.

———, 'Abd al-Rahman, Abu 'l Farash, ed. B.A. Al-Jabi, *Reports of Wits and Wags* [Arabic], Limassol, Cyprus: Al-Jaffan & Al-Jabdi, 1983.

Ibn Kathir, Abu'l Fida' Isma'il, *Tafsir* Volume 7 [Arabic], Giza: Qurtuba Institution, 2000.

Ibn Nasser al-Sulayman, Fahed, ed., *Compilation of Fatwas and Letters of Sheikh Muhammad bin Salih al-'Uthaymeen* [Arabic], volume 2, Riyadh: Dar al-Watan, 1986.

Ibn Rāhwayh, Isḥāq, *Musnad of Ibn Rāhwayh* [Arabic], vol. 4, Medina: Dar al-Ayman, 1995.

Innocenti, B. and E. Miller, 'The Persuasive Force of Political Humor', *Journal of Communication*, vol. 66, 2016, pp. 366–385.

Institute for Strategic Dialogue and Radicalisation Awareness Network Centre of Excellence, 'Counter Narratives and Alternative Narratives', RAN Issue Paper, 1 Oct. 2015.

Jenkins, R., *Subversive Laughter: The Liberating Power of Comedy*, New York: The Free Press, 1994.

Johansson, A., 'ISIS-Chan: The Meanings of the Manga Girl in Image Warfare against the Islamic State', *Critical Studies on Terrorism*, vol. 11, no. 1, 2018, pp. 1–25.

Kazarian, S., 'Humor in the Collectivist Arab Middle East: The Case of

Lebanon', *Humor: International Journal of Humor Research*, vol. 24, no. 3, 2011.

Kedourie, E. *Afghani and Abduh: An Essay on Religious Unbelief and Political Activism in Modern Islam*, London: Cass, 1966.

Kepel, G., *Muslim Extremism in Egypt: The Prophet and the Pharaoh*, trans. J. Rothschild, London: Al-Saqi, 1985.

Kierkegaard, S., trans. W. Lowrie, *The Concept of Dread*, Princeton: Princeton University Press, 1967.

Khatib, L., 'Arab Film and Islamic Fundamentalism' in *Media and Society*, ed. J.L. Curran, London: Bloomsbury, 2010.

Kishtainy, K., *Arab Political Humour*, London: Quartet Books, 1985.

Kozintsev, A. *The Mirror of Laughter*, trans. R.P. Martin, New York, New Brunswick, NJ and London: Transaction 2012.

Kraidy, M., 'Fun Against Fear in the Caliphate: Islamic State's Spectacle and Counter-Spectacle', *Critical Studies in Media Communication*, vol. 35, no. 1, 2017, pp. 40–56.

Kraidy, M. and J. Khalil, *Arab Television Industries*, London, British Film Institute, 2009.

Krikmann, A., 'Linguistic Theories of Humour', *Folklore*, vol. 33, 2014.

Kuiper, N., S. Kazarian, J. Sine and M. Bassil, 'The Impact of Humor in North American versus Middle Eastern Cultures', *Europe's Journal of Psychology*, vol. 6, no. 3, 2010.

Lacroix, S., *Awakening Islam: Religious Dissent in Contemporary Saudi Arabia*, Cambridge, MA: Harvard University Press, 2011.

Lance Holbert, R., J. Hmielowski and P. Jain, 'Adding Nuance to the Study of Political Humor Effects: Experimental Research on Juvenalian Satire Versus Horatian Satire', *American Behavioral Scientist*, vol. 55, no. 3, 2011.

Leaman, O., ed., *Companion Encyclopedia of Middle Eastern and North African Film*.

Lemieux, A.F., J.M. Brachman, J. Levitt & J. Wood, '*Inspire* Magazine: A Critical Analysis of its Significance and Potential Impact Through the Lens of the Information, Motivation and Behavioural Skills Model', *Terrorism and Political Violence*, vol. 26, no. 2, 2014, pp. 354–371.

Lewis, B., *Hammer and Tickle: A History of Communism Told Through Communist Jokes*, London: W&N, 2009.

Lockyer, S. and M. Pickering, *Beyond a Joke: the Limits of Humour*, New York: Palgrave Macmillan, 2005.

MacDonald, M.V., 'Orally Transmitted Poetry in Pre-Islamic Arabia and Other Pre-Literate Societies', *Journal of Arabic Literature*, vol. 9, 1978, pp. 14–31.

Maghen, Z., 'The Merry Men of Medina: Comedy and Humanity in the Early Days of Islam', *Der Islam*, vol. 83, no. 2, 2008.

SELECT BIBLIOGRAPHY

Mahfouz, S. and M. Carlson, *Theater from Medieval Cairo: The Ibn Daniyal Trilogy*, New York: Martin E. Segal Theatre Centre, 2013.

Martin, R. et al., 'Individual Differences in Uses of Humor and Their Relation to Psychological Well-Being: Development of the Humor Styles Questionnaire', *Journal of Research in Personality*, vol. 37, no. 1, 2003, pp. 48–75.

Marty, M. and R. Scott Appleby, eds., *Fundamentalisms Observed*, Chicago: University of Chicago Press, 1991.

————, eds, *Fundamentalisms Comprehended*, Chicago: University of Chicago Press, 1995.

Marzolph, U., 'The Qoran and Jocular Literature', *Arabica*, vol. 47, no. 3, pp. 478–487.

Matsusaka, T., 'When Does Play Panting Occur During Social Play in Wild Chimpanzees?' *Primates*, vol. 4 (October) no. 5, 2004, pp. 221–229.

McLaughlin, J., 'The Case for Making Fun of ISIS', *Mother Jones*, 6 Mar. 2015.

Meijer, R. ed., *Global Salafism: Islam's New Religious Movement*, London: Hurst, 2009.

Mellor, N. ed., *Political Islam and Global Media*, London: Routledge, 2016.

Miller, F., *The Audacious Ascetic: What Osama Bin Laden's Sound Archive Reveals About Al Qaeda*, New York: Hurst, 2015.

Mir, M., 'Humor in the Quran', *The Muslim World*, vol. 81, no. 304, 1991.

Morreall, J., *Comic Relief: A Comprehensive Philosophy of Humor*, Oxford: Wiley-Blackwell, 2009.

————, *Comedy, Tragedy and Religion*, Albany: State University of New York, 1999.

————, ed., *The Philosophy of Laughter and Humor*, Albany: State University of New York Press, 1985.

————, 'The Rejection of Humor in Western Thought', *Philosophy East and West*, vol. 39, no. 3, 1989, pp. 243–265.

Mulkay, M., *On Laughter: Its Nature and Place in Modern Society*, Cambridge: Polity, 1989.

Nagle, A., *Kill All Normies: Online Culture Wars from 4Chan and Tumblr to Trump and the Alt-Right*, New York: Zero Books, 2017.

Nasr, A., 'An Historical Perspective on Fundamentalist Media: The Case of Al Manar Television', *Global Media Journal*, vol. 6, no. 11, 2007.

Neitzel, S. and H. Welzer, *Soldaten—On Fighting, Killing and Dying: The Secret World War Tapes of German POWs*, London: Simon and Schuster UK, 2013.

Nemoianu, V. and R. Royal, eds, *Play, Literature, Religion: Essays in Cultural Intertextuality*, Albany: State University of New York Press, 1992.

Nye, J., *Soft Power: The Means to Success in World Politics*, New York: Public Affairs Press, 2005.

Panskepp, J., 'Neuroevolutionary Sources of Laughter and Social Joy: Modelling Primal Human Laughter in Laboratory Rats', *Behavioural Brain Research*, vol. 182, no. 2, 2007, pp. 231–244.

————, 'Beyond a Joke: From Animal Laughter to Human Joy', *Science*, vol. 308, no. 5718, 2005, pp. 62–63.

Perelman, C. and L. Olbrechts-Tyteca, *The New Rhetoric: A Treatise on Argumentation*, trans. J. Wilkinson, Notre Notre Dame, Indiana: University of Notre Dame Press, 1973.

Popovic, S., *Blueprint for Revolution: How to Use Rice Pudding, Lego Men and Other Non-Violent Techniques to Galvanise Communities, Overthrow Dictators or Simply Change the World*, Melbourne and London: Scribe, 2015.

Potegal, M. and D. Einon, 'Aggressive Behaviors in Adult Rats Deprived of Playfighting Experience as Juveniles', *Developmental Psychobiology*, vol. 22, pp. 159–172.

Proulx, T., S. Heine and K. Vohs, 'When is the Unfamiliar the Uncanny? Meaning Affirmation After Exposure to Absurdist Literature, Humor and Art', *Personality and Social Psychology Bulletin*, vol. 36, no. 6, 2010, pp. 817–829.

(Al)-Qatari, H., *Stories of the Arab Martyrs in Bosnia and Herzogovina*, 2002.

Radcliffe-Brown, A.R., 'On Joking Relationships', *Africa: Journal of the International African Institute*, vol. 13, no. 3 1940, pp. 195–210.

(El-)Ramly, L., 'The Comedy of the East, or, The Art of Cunning: A Testimony', trans. H. Azmy, *Ecumenica: Journal of Theater and Performance*, vol. 1.2. Autumn, 2008, pp. 75–86.

Rapp, A., *Origins of Wit and Humor*, New York: EP Dutton & Company, 1951.

Rasheed, R., *Kingdom Without Borders: Saudi Arabia's Political, Religious and Media Frontiers*, London: Hurst, 2008.

Raskin, V., *Semantic Mechanisms of Humour*, New York: Springer, 1984.

Al-Rawi, A., 'Anti-ISIS Humour: Cultural Resistance of Radical Ideology', *Politics, Religion and Ideology*, vol. 17, no. 1, 2016, pp. 52–68.

————, 'Facebook as a Virtual Mosque: The Online Protest Against *Innocence of Muslims*', *Culture and Religion*, vol. 17, no. 1, 2016, pp. 19–34.

————, 'Online Reactions to the Muhammad Cartoons: YouTube and the Virtual Ummah', *Journal for the Scientific Study of Religion*, vol. 54, no. 1, May 2015, pp. 261–276.

Rowell, A., *Vintage Humour: The Islamic Wine Poetry of Abu Nuwas*, London: Hurst, 2018.

Roy, O., *The Failure of Political Islam*, trans. C. Volk, Cambridge, MA: Harvard University Press, 1996.

Rumi, Jalal-al-Din, *Rumi: Selected Poems*, trans. C. Barks, London: Penguin Classics, 2004.

Sadgrove, P.C., *The Egyptian Theatre in the Nineteenth Century*, New York: Ithaca Press, 2007.

Sakr, N., *Satellite Realms: Globalisation, Transnational Television and the Middle East*, London: I.B. Tauris, 2002.

Salim, A., *The Image of Islamists on the Screen* [Arabic], Beirut: Nama Centre for Research, 2014.

Sasson, J., O. bin Laden and N. bin Laden, *Growing Up Bin Laden: Osama's Wife and Son Take Us Inside Their Secret World*, New York: OneWorld, 2001.

(Al)-Sayyid Marsot, L., *Egypt in the Reign of Muhammad Ali*, Cambridge: Cambridge University Press, 1984.

Schielke, J., *The Perils of Joy: Contesting Mulid Festivals in Contemporary Egypt*, New York: Syracuse University Press, 2012.

Screech, M., *Laughter at the Foot of the Cross*, Chicago: University of Chicago Press, 1997.

Shafik, V., *Popular Egyptian Cinema: Gender, Class and Nation*, Cairo: American University in Cairo Press, 2007.

Shapiro, J., *The Terrorist's Dilemma: Managing Violent Covert Organisations*, New Haven: Princeton University Press, 2015.

Simpson, P., *On The Discourse of Satire, Towards a Stylistic Model of Satirical Humour*, Amsterdam: John Benjamins, 2003.

Sinkiewitz, M., 'Out of Control: Palestinian News Satire and Government Power in the Age of Social Media', *Popular Communication: The International Journal of Media and Culture*, vol. 10, nos 1–2, 2012, pp. 106–118.

Sombatpoonsiri, J., *Humour and Nonviolent Struggle in Serbia*, New York: Syracuse University Press, 2015.

Sørensen, M., *Humorous Political Stunts: Speaking the Truth to Power*, Sparsnäs, Sweden: Irene Publishing, 2015.

Sowell, K., 'Jordanian Salafism and the Jihad in Syria', *Current Trends in Islamist Ideology*, vol. 18, May, 2015, pp. 41–71.

Smith, J., 'Karagöz and Hacivat: Projections of Subversion and Conformance', *Asian Theatre Journal*, vol. 21, no. 2, 2004, pp. 187–193.

Speckhard. A. and A. Shajkovci, 'Perspective: Debating the use of ISIS Counter-Narratives in the Heart of Europe', *Homeland Security Today*, 4 Apr. 2018.

Stroumsa, S., *Freethinkers of Medieval Islam*, Leiden: Brill, 2016.

Tamer, G., 'The Qur'ān and Humor' in *Humor in der Arabischen Kultur*, ed. G. Tamer, Berlin: De Gruyter, 2009.

Tilly, C., *From Mobilization to Revolution*, New York: Random House, 1973.

Trofimov, Y., *The Siege of Mecca: The Forgotten Uprising in Islam's Holiest Shrine*, London: Penguin, 2008.

Volpi, F., *Political Islam Observed*, London: Hurst, 2010.

Wagemakers, J., *Salafism in Jordan: Political Islam in a Quietist Community*, Cambridge: Cambridge University Press, 2016.

———, *A Quietist Jihadi: The Ideology and Influence of Abu Muhammad Al-Maqdisi*, Cambridge: Cambridge University Press, 2012.

———, 'Defining the Enemy: Abu Muhammad al-Maqdisi's Reading of Surat al-Mumtahana', *Die Welt Des Islams*, vol. 8, no. 3, 2008, pp. 348–371.

SELECT BIBLIOGRAPHY

Waller, J.M., *Fighting the War of Ideas like a Real War*, Washington: Institute of World Politics Press, 2007.

Wedeen, L., *Ambiguities of Domination: Politics, Rhetoric and Symbols in Contemporary Syria*, Chicago: University of Chicago Press, 2015.

Weinberger, M. and C. Sulas, 'The Impact of Humor in Advertising: A Review', *Journal of Advertising*, vol. 21, no. 4, 1992, pp. 35–59.

Whitlock, F.A., 'The Ganser Syndrome', *The British Journal of Psychiatry*, vol. 113, pp. 19–29.

Wickberg, D., *The Senses of Humor: Self and Laughter in Modern America*, Ithaca: Cornell University Press, 1998.

Yousef, B., *Revolution for Dummies: Laughing Through the Arab Spring*, New York: HarperCollins, 2017.

Yue, X., F. Jiang, S. Lu and N. Hiranandani, 'To Be or Not To Be Humorous? Cross Cultural Perspectives on Humor', *Frontiers in Psychology*, vol. 7 article. 1495, 2016.

Ziadeh, R., 'Revolution in Syria: The Struggle for Freedom in a Regional Battle' in *The Arab Spring and the Arab Thaw: Unfinished Revolutions and the Quest for Democracy*, ed. J. Davis, second edition, London: Routledge, 2016.

Žižek, S., 'The Christian-Hegelian Comedy', *Cabinet Magazine*, 17, Spring 2005.

Online Resources

Ancient Greek and Roman texts

Perseus Digital Library: http://www.perseus.tufts.edu/hopper/
The Internet Classics Archive: http://classics.mit.edu/

Islamic Scriptural Texts

The Quran: https://quran.com/?local=en
The Hadith: sunnah.com

Select Filmography

Abdelaziz, S., *Cabaret*, Cairo, El Sobky Film Production, 2008.

Ahmad Ali, M., *Mawlana [Our Master]*, iProductions and El Adl Group, 2016.

Al Eryan, T., *Al Khaliya [The Cell]*, Cairo, Raw Entertainment and Al Remas Film Production, 2017.

Al-Badry, A., *Al-Armouty Fe Ard El Nar [Al-Armouty in The Land of Fire]*, Giza, El Sobky Film Production, 2017.

————, *Anaa Mish Ma'ahum [I am not with them]*, Giza, Lord for Cinema Production, 2007.

Arafa, A., *Ibn el-Qunsul [Son of the Consul]*, Cairo, United Bros, 2010.

————, *Al Seefara Fil Eemara [The Embassy in the Building]*, Cairo, Essam-Imam Productions, 2005.

SELECT BIBLIOGRAPHY

Arafa, Sh., *Al-Irhab Wal Kabab [Terrorism and Kebab]*, Cairo, Essam-Imam Productions, 1992.

———, *Toyour Elzalam [Birds of Darkness]*, Cairo, Wahid Hamed Films, 1995.

Chahine, Y., *Al-Maseer [Destiny]*, Cairo, Misr International Films, 1997.

———, *Al-Akhar [The Other]*, Cairo, Misr International Films, 1999.

El-Tayeb, A., *Kashf El Mastour [Revealing All]*, Cairo, AL Ahram for Cinema and Video, 1994.

Galal, N., *Amn Dawla [State Security]*, Cairo, Muhammad Mukhtar Films, 1999

Galal, N. and Imam, R. *Elwad Mahrous Betaa Alwazir [Mahrous; The Minister's Guy]*, Cairo, Oscar for Distribution & Theater, 1999.

Galal, N., *Hello America*, Cairo, Al-Nasr Films, 2000.

———, *Al-Irahab [Terrorism]*, Cairo, Muhammad Mukhtar Films, 1989.

———, *Al-Irhabi [The Terrorist]*, Cairo, Pop Art Film, 1994.

Hamed, M., *'Imarat Ya'qubian [The Yacoubian Building]*, Cairo, Good News Group, 2006.

Hashad, A., *Da'dush*, Elgozour Cinema Production, Cairo, 2017.

Ibrahim, H., *El Bih El Bawab [His Highness, The Doorman]*, Cairo, Arab Egypt Films, 1987.

Idris, A., *Al Thalatha Yashtaghalonaha [Three Men Deceive Her]*, Cairo, Arabica Movies, 2010.

Imam, R., *Hassan and Marcus*, Cairo, Good News Group, 2008.

Marzouk, S.M., *Infijar [Explosion]*, [Unknown production], 1990.

Morris, C., *Four Lions*, UK, Film Four, 2010.

Salama, A., *Sheikh Jackson*, Cairo, iProductions, 2017.

Yassine, M., *Dam Al-Ghazal [The Gazelle's Blood]*, Cairo, El Arabia, 2005.

Youssef, Kh., *Hena Maysara [Until the Time of Ease]*, Cairo, Albatros for Film Production and Distribution, 2007.

———, *Dukkan Shehata [Shehata's Shop]*, Cairo, Misr for Cinema, 2009.

Zaki, A.L., *Al-Khatar [The danger]*, Cairo, Panorama, 1990.

Selected Series, Shows and Plays

Abdul Hafiz, I., *Al A'ela [The Family]*, Cairo, Egyptian TV, 1994.

Al-Qasabi, N., and A. Al-Sadhan, *Tash Ma Tash [You Get it Or You Don't]*, Riyadh, Al-Hadaf for Media Production, 1993–2011.

Al-Qasabi, N., *Selfie*, Riyadh, O3 Productions, 2015–17.

Al-Rantesi, H., *Gharabeeb Soud [Black Crows]*, Riyadh, O3 Productions and Beirut, Sabah Pictures, 2017.

Assaf, N., and J. Lahhoud, *Kteer Selbi, [Really Bad]*, Beirut, Lebanese Broadcasting Corporation (LBC), 2013–present.

El-Adl, J., *Al-Da'ia [The Preacher]*, Cairo, El Adl Group, 2013.

Farajin, I., *Watan ala Watar [Nation on a String]*, Ramallah, Palestine TV, and Amman, Roya TV, 2009–present.

SELECT BIBLIOGRAPHY

Feghali, E., *Irbit Tinhal [Almost Sorted Out]*, Beirut, al-Jadeed TV, 2004–present.

Hanoun, A., *Caricature*, Baghdad, Al-Sharqiya TV, 2004.

Hussien, Y., *Joe Show*, London, Al-Araby Channel, 2013-present.

Ismail Anzour, N., *Al-Hur al-'Ayn [The Maidens of Paradise]*, Damascus, Najdat Ismail Anzour Institution, 2005.

———, *Ma Malakat Aymanukum [What Your Right Hand Possesses]*, Damascus, Grand Production and Najdat Ismail Anzour Institution, 2010.

Khaled Musa, A., *Abo Omar El-Masry*, Cairo, Tarek Al Ganaini, TV Vision, 2018.

Khalil, Ch. *Bas Mat Watan*, (The Nation Just Died/Smiled) Beirut, Lebanese Broadcasting Corporation (LBC), 1995–present.

Masoud, M., *Khutuwat al-Shaytan [Satan's Steps]*, Dubai, MBC1 TV, 2017.

Reda, A. and Yakhour, B. *Buqa'at Daw' [Spotlight]*, Damascus, Syrian Art Production International, 2001–present.

Sabaileh, H., *Dababis [Needles], Amman*, The Jordanian TV, 2004–2015.

———, *Irhab Ala al-Bab [Terrorism at the Door]*, Amman, 2016.

Qassem, A. *Dawlat al-Khurafa [The Mythical State]*, Al Iraqiya TV, 2014.

Watfe, M. and Hillali, Y. *Dayaaltaseh [Lost the Cup]*, YouTube, 2015.

Yassin, M., *Al-Gama'a [The Group]*, Cairo, Albatros for Film Production and Distribution, 2010.

Yousef, B., *Elbernameg [The Show]*, Qsoft, Dubai, 2011–13.

INDEX

INDEX

INDEX

INDEX

INDEX

INDEX

INDEX

INDEX

INDEX